THE
NEOLIBERALS

Creating the New American Politics

Randall Rothenberg

SIMON AND SCHUSTER

NEW YORK

Published by Simon and Schuster
A Division of Simon & Schuster, Inc.
Simon & Schuster Building
Rockefeller Center
1230 Avenue of the Americas
New York, New York 10020
SIMON AND SCHUSTER and colophon are registered trademarks
of Simon & Schuster, Inc.
Designed by Eve Kirch
Manufactured in the United States of America

1   3   5   7   9   10   8   6   4   2

Library of Congress Cataloging in Publication Data
Rothenberg, Randall.
The neoliberals.
Includes bibliographical references and index.
1. Liberalism—United States.   2. United States—
Politics and government—1945-   . I. Title.
JA84.U5R68   1984   320.5'13'0973   84-5427
ISBN 0-671-45881-7

Acknowledgments

After months of apparent isolation, an author surfaces to discover that a book is a wonderfully collaborative experience. While the faults in this one are wholly mine, its existence I owe to others.

Chris Johnson was an indefatigable researcher; I still marvel at the obscure facts I requested that she unfailingly unearthed from the bowels of Princeton University's library. I also benefited from research done by other students, notably Betsy Kenny at Princeton, Frederick Nathan, Jr., at Williams, and Alan Khazei at Harvard.

My cross-country interviewing jaunts were aided by friends and acquaintances who opened their homes to me. These included Larry Simon in San Francisco; Kath Reitman and Fred Branfman in Sacramento; Hardy Price in Phoenix; Anne M. Leibeskind and George Noble in Boulder, Colorado; Jonathan Blake in Chicago; Kate Heston in Madison, Wisconsin; in Washington, Emily and Peter Morgenstern, Kent Redford (and the entire Redford clan), Peter and Alison Fenn, and Paul J. Fishman; and in Cambridge, Massachusetts, Dirk Giseburt. All this traveling would not have been possible without the wizardry of Lynn Charter.

Many press secretaries and administrative aides in state capitals and in Washington helped me with scheduling. Alison Thomas and the tireless Dick Lerner went above and beyond the call of their positions to assist me generally with interviews and research. Phillip Longman, Michael Barker, and Ross Baker harangued me and harassed me after reading versions of the manuscript, forcing me to refine my ideas until they became coherent. I. Mark Sandler's political commentary also proved invaluable. And the wisdom and debating skills of Professor Eric Goldman more than once prevented me from embarrassing myself with a hasty conclusion. To him, especially, my gratitude is great.

If it were not for the support of Jerry Goodman, this book would never have been a reality. Jerry saw the article on which this work is based through to publication in *Esquire* magazine, and was a rock throughout the book's nascent stages. His and Sally's home served as a haven several times during its composition. At *Esquire*, Phillip Moffitt and Priscilla Flood also dispensed valued advice. I've been lucky in my association with them and their magazine.

To the editors who helped me along the way—Dozier Hasty, Victor Navasky, and Michael Aron—goes my appreciation. To the friends who put up with my plaints—Judy Prouty, Janet Bukovinski, Steven Levy, Teresa Carpenter, Jonathan Bumas, Sarah Henry, Ross Brown, and (late in the game, but so important nonetheless) Susan Roy—goes my love. And to my agent, Gail Hochman, and my editor, Bob Bender, go my thanks; that I am still sane at this late date is a tribute to their calming voices.

Many others have helped me during this process, and to those I have inadvertently failed to mention, my apologies and thanks. But I would particularly like to single out those individuals who took time to submit to interviews. This book in large part reflects their thoughts. They include:

Gar Alperovitz, Marsha Aronoff, Bruce Babbitt, Michael Barker, Craig Barnes, Bob Beyers, David Birch, Barry Bluestone, Sid Blumenthal, Bill Bradley, Ray Bramucci, Taylor Branch, Sam Brown, Jerry Brown, John Bryson, Kathy Bushkin, Chuck Buxton, Becky Cantwell, Roger Carrick, Bill Chandler, Pat Choate, B. T. Collins, Richard Danzig, Sheldon Danziger, Gina DesPres, Christopher Dodd, George Eads, Mary Eccles, Robert Edgar, James Fallows, Ava Feiner, James Florio, Robert Friedman, Martin Frost, Ed Furtek, James Galbraith, Nathan Gardels, Richard Gephardt, Rita Goldman, Peter Golenbock, Albert Gore, Jr., Josh Gotbaum, Otis Graham, Mark Green, Phil Greenberg, Joe Grimsley, Ferrel Guillory, Lew Haas, Robert Hamrin, Gary Hart, Robert Haveman, Roland Hayden, Roger Hickey, Mark Hogan, Kent Hughes, James Hunt, Jr., Jim Jaffe, Paul Jensen, Chalmers Johnson, Huey Johnson, Bob Judd, Alfred E. Kahn, Marshall Kaplan, Ted Kaufman, Robert M. Kaus, Eugene Keilin, Steve Kellman, Michael Kieschnick, Morton Kondracke, Richard Lamm, Larry Landry, Doug Lea, Cindy Lebow, Nicholas Lemann, Suzannah

Lessard, Jim Lyons, Ira Magaziner, Robert Maher, Charles Moskos, Pat Murphy, John Naisbitt, Richard Nathan, Robert Nicholas, Leslie E. Nulty, Betty Owen, Leon Panetta, John Parr, Jane Patterson, Duane Pearsall, Michael Pertschuk, Charles Peters, Perry Quick, Robert Reich, Felix Rohatyn, Marla Romash, Leon Shull, Rusty Schweickert, Albert Shapero, Bill Shore, Larry Smith, G. M. Sollenberger, Kevin Sullivan, Bill Taylor, Susan Thomases, Lester Thurow, Paul Tsongas, Roger Vaughan, Phil Wallace, Lee Webb, Doug Wilson, Timothy Wirth, R. James Woolsey, and Dan Yergin.

Finally, to my parents, Marvin and Janet Rothenberg—who taught me what liberalism really means, who nurtured this project from the beginning, whose emotional (and financial) largesse allowed one scribe to write—this book is dedicated.

Contents

11

**Part Four. The Beginning of Neoliberalism . . .
or the End of Liberalism?**

PART ONE

Reflections

CHAPTER 1

The Day After

NOVEMBER 5, 1980. The Day After. The day after Jimmy Carter's landslide defeat by Ronald Reagan, only the third time in this century an incumbent President has been turned away by the voters. The day after the Democratic Party lost effective, if not nominal, control of the House of Representatives. The day after twelve Democratic senators were turned out of the nation's capital by the folks back home, who saw fit to hand jurisdiction over the United States Senate to the Republicans for the first time in twenty-six years. The great liberals of the day—Frank Church of Idaho, John Culver of Iowa, Birch Bayh of Indiana, and the man who carried the banner against Richard Nixon in 1972, George McGovern—all were soundly rejected. There was no ambiguity in the message: The American electorate loudly declared, "We don't like your kind."

Appearing that night on the PBS "MacNeil–Lehrer Report" to analyze the results of the day the Democratic Party died were *New York Times* columnist Anthony Lewis, conservative writer and former Nixon speechwriter Patrick J. Buchanan, and Morton Kondracke, executive editor of *The New Republic,* a magazine identified with Democratic liberalism since its founding in 1914, but which in 1980 had endorsed an independent candidate, former Republican Congressman John Anderson.

Lewis, a Pulitzer Prize winner whose articles and columns in the *Times* had mirrored much of liberalism's trends over the past two decades, assessed the Democratic Party's position gloomily. It had been "swept away," he said; it was a "party without an idea." Its likeliest leader, Senator Edward M. Kennedy, was a man whose ideology, whose New Deal/Fair Deal–era intellectual history, had been "decisively rejected as a pattern for today's America." Lewis spoke of the Democratic Party in terms usually reserved for old racehorses being led out to pasture. The once glorious contender was now only a pale, dying reflection of its former self. The Democrats, he said, were "a lost party."

Buchanan eagerly shared Lewis's assessment. "Twelve Democratic senators went down the tubes," he gloated. "I think the entire dean's list of Americans for Democratic Action went down. So in that sense, I think it's a repudiation of the liberal philosophy. . . ."

Yes, answered Lewis, somewhat glumly, "I think we're seeing a conservative revolution not principally directed at the person of Jimmy Carter."

Kondracke, a former reporter for the *Chicago Sun-Times,* a youthful, guileless Midwesterner with a dozen years in Washington and one at Harvard as a prestigious Nieman Fellow, gently disagreed with his colleagues. He presented something that must have seemed odd to the viewers: a *positive* view from a liberal. He was very specific about who and what the voters had rejected. "It was," he said, "a repudiation of Jimmy Carter as well as a repudiation of Great Society liberalism." The Democrats had done well on the state and local level, he added; it was not a rout. Instead, the election results should be interpreted as an "opportunity."

"It seems to me," said Kondracke, "that what the Democratic Party has to do is adopt some sort of a—what might be called a *neoliberal* ideology."

"What in the world is *that,* Mort?" asked co-host Jim Lehrer.

Kondracke had already given serious thought to liberalism's need to redefine itself. His magazine, which had only reluctantly endorsed Carter four years before, had been in the forefront of those questioning the President's slippage back into the traditional and worn-out dogma. That very week, assuming the worst for the Democrats, Kondracke had been refining an editorial about the subject, so he was ready for Lehrer's question. "Well," he replied, "[it is] an attempt to combine the traditional Democratic compassion for the downtrodden and outcast elements of society with different vehicles than categorical aid programs or quota systems or new federal bureaucracies." When he completed his editorial a week later, he added interest-group pandering to the list of Democratic problems, warning, "The danger is that Democrats will be as reflexive in shielding outworn and expen-

sive Great Society programs in the 1980s as Republicans were in opposing them in the 1960s."

But on The Day After, unflappable Jim Lehrer was merely curious. Who, he wanted to know, would provide the leadership for this
new philosophical approach? Kondracke answered quickly, "Well,
Gary Hart is one good example. Gary Hart's survival was a very important event in the Democratic Party. He is somebody who has tried
to realize that the Soviet Union does represent a threat to the United
States, and has tried to adapt a pro-defense policy to liberalism. And
similarly Paul Tsongas—"

Lehrer had caught on. "Tsongas falls into that same thing. Would
he fall into that 'neoliberal' category?" he asked.

Kondracke replied, "I think so."

Morton Kondracke's viewpoint was not generally shared. Instead,
the conventional wisdom in November 1980 was easily summarized
in two phrases: "The Democratic Party has died!" and "The Democrats have no ideas!" These cries rang through Washington and across
the editorial pages of America late in 1980 as pundit after pundit in-
toned the last rites for the world's oldest political party.

But new ideas were there, even in 1980. The establishment press's
obsession with well-known political leaders blinded it to the ferment
within the Democratic Party. To those like Kondracke who had taken
the time to seek out the party's fresher members in Washington, who
had bothered to visit the statehouses in which the newer Democratic
governors sat, it was clear that the Democrats indeed had new ideas.
Some were simply reaffirmations of classic tenets of the liberal creed
that had been forgotten during the domestic and international turmoil
of the 1960s and 1970s. Others would be considered heretical by liberals. Taken together, they provided a framework for a new liberal
future.

The most striking aspect of this new liberalism was its cursory
attitude toward the social programs of the Democratic Party's recent
past, the programs that, in the eyes of the public, defined liberalism
itself. It was not that the new liberals opposed the policies; it was just
that they had relegated them to a lesser position in their order of priorities. Replying to the question "Are social issues secondary?" Senator
Bill Bradley, in September 1980, said, "They are not secondary to the
structure of the economy. But social issues *are* secondary, I think, to
the health of the economy." A year later Paul Tsongas, the junior

senator from Massachusetts, replied to the same question unhesitat-
ingly: "Yes. Absolutely."

Something unsettling had happened to the Democratic Party. Its
great issues of the past—school busing, national health insurance,
welfare, equal employment, labor law reform, consumer protection,
environmentalism, and the First Amendment—had receded. The new
issue, the only issue, it seemed, was economics.

For mainstream liberals who had spent the previous twenty years
fighting these battles, the transition would be difficult, if not impossible. Their style had been reactive: The bigots segregated the schools?
Let's desegregate! Industry is polluting our rivers? Make 'em clean it
up! The CIA is breaking into people's homes? Open the files!

The new economic era was more complicated, harder to respond
to. It required new ideas. And new ideas meant growth, meant making government work. Both growth and government effectiveness had
disappeared from the liberal agenda during the preceding two decades.
It would be tough for the older Democrats to accept the changed realities *and* minority status at the same time. For the younger ones, the
vanguard of a revitalized Democratic Party, the intellectual reposi-
tioning, at least, would be easy. They'd been preparing for it for years.

At some juncture during the 1970s, subtle shifts began to take
place in the public statements of some elected officials, business leaders, and intellectuals. The deviations were generally so minor, and so
unrelated to each other, that few people detected anything significant
in them. The evidence was simply linguistic at first. People became
"human capital"; potholes were now "infrastructure decay." Economic
development turned into "managing the transition." Planning was
transformed as "industrial policy." The democratic experiment became "the zero-sum society."

But the new terminology arose from new concepts that soon became apparent. In the social arena, redistribution gave way to investment. In economics, macroeconomic policy was accompanied by a
fascination with microeconomic matters. In defense, "more is better"
and "less is better" were superseded by "better is better." It was all
part of a massive transformation taking place in America: the industrial age had given way to the information era.

And with it, liberalism was overtaken by neoliberalism.

Forget about Walter Mondale, ignore John Glenn, put Tip O'Neill
out of your mind. Disregard the Democratic Party as you've known

it. Whatever its fortunes in 1984, the old liberalism has already begun a slow, inexorable fade. The future belongs to the neoliberals.

Since 1981, the curiosity we now call neoliberalism has been one of the most controversial matters in American politics. To the true believers of traditional liberalism, the noises emanating from the Democratic Party's younger quarters have seemed like little more than a bugle-blaring retreat from the progressive values of the past.

As she departed the presidency of the liberal Americans for Democratic Action in 1981, former Hawaii Congresswoman Patsy Mink blasted away at unnamed revisionists. "There are too many knee-jerk nay-sayers who call themselves liberals but who now enjoy debunking the liberal programs of the past thirty years," declared Ms. Mink. "These are the folks who were quick to suggest the agenda for liberals is to find 'new' solutions to the problems of social injustice, of poverty, and of the other unmet human needs."

Historian Arthur Schlesinger, Jr., has put himself forward as the last stalwart defender of the great liberal tradition, hammering away, in the *Wall Street Journal* and *Playboy* magazine, among other publications, at a doctrine he considers "empty" and at people he calls fellow travelers in the Reagan revolution." Neoliberalism, he wrote, "is a politically futile course for the Democratic Party." He charged the neoliberals with having "more or less accepted [the Reagan] frameworks.

> They have joined in the clamor against "big government," found great merit in the unregulated marketplace, opposed structural change in the economy and gone along with swollen military budgets and the nuclear arms race. Far from rejecting the Reagan frameworks, they would at most rejigger priorities here and there.

If Schlesinger and Mink represent the antagonism felt by traditional liberals, certainly the political right thinks no more highly of the neoliberals. Michael Scully, editor of *Public Opinion,* the journal of the conservative and influential American Enterprise Institute, quipped that "if neoconservatives are liberals who got mugged by reality, then neoliberals are liberals who got mugged by reality but refused to press charges."

So what *is* neoliberalism? As is so often the case when analyzing politics, it is easier to define neoliberalism by what it is not than by what it is. Unlike neoconservatism, the much-heralded cause célèbre of the seventies, it is not an intellectual movement. The neoconservatives are the grown-up survivors of the ideological struggles that rent the left and center-left in the years following World War II. Their horror over what they perceived to be the cultural breakdown of the American nation as it entered the seventies impelled them to invent a philosophy grounded in anti-communism and national cultural unity. They nurtured their philosophy in the academy and vented it in the pages of journals with highbrow pretensions, if also with ill-concealed political intentions, and then attempted to ply their wares first within the Democratic Party and then, failing that, in the Republican Party.

Neoliberals are not intellectuals or theorists. When they stand in the front of university classrooms, it is to teach economics. Their public pronouncements are simple, measured, and pragmatic, rarely analytical. Time and again, politicians and advisers who have been popularly associated with the new liberalism assert that, unlike the neoconservatives, they are not interested in changing the goals of their party, but only the means of achieving certain goals. "We in Washington have gotten so inured to identifying a commitment to methods—in the case of Democrats, bureaus, agencies, programs, and taxes—that one's ideological commitment and integrity are linked to that," reflected Colorado Senator Gary Hart in 1981. "What is changing are not principles, goals, aspirations, or ideals, but methods. *Very* important that the distinction be made." "The purpose," the *New Republic*'s Morton Kondracke has written, "is to make good intentions marketable again." "Realism—some of it Republican in its origins—combined with a value system of the Democratic liberal tradition is the objective," wrote Massachusetts Senator Paul Tsongas in his 1981 book, *The Road from Here,* adding, "Reality does not bend to fit political theory." *Washington Monthly* editor Charles Peters is even more specific. "Neoliberalism recognizes that there were a lot of things wrong with a lot of the Big Government solutions we tried," he stated in 1981, "but there was never anything wrong with the ends we were seeking—justice, fair play, and liberal ideals."

But neoliberalism is not wholly a political movement, of the sort that occasionally arises to tear apart the fabric of an established party and sew it back together in a new pattern. Members of neoliberalism's policy subculture, economists mostly, are remarkably naïve about the realities of partisan politics and campaign rhetoric, and have felt blissfully free to propound grandiose schemes for industrial policy and human capital policy that, pragmatic as they may seem, present serious challenges to vested interests that control American politics. In fact, as the new terminology indicates, neoliberals *are* trying to change the ideas that underlie Democratic politics. They are insurgents, and they are opposed by representatives of the established constituencies, who always scrupulously avoid new ideas, recognizing the threat ideas present to the fragile balance of relationships that comprise a political party.

It would be easy to dismiss neoliberalism's adherents simply as "moderate" Democrats. But is it true that their philosophy is nothing more than (as the *New Republic* entitled a review of Paul Tsongas' book) "Reaganism with a Human Face"? Or was journalist Sidney Blumenthal correct to call neoliberalism (in *Working Papers* magazine) "Carterism Without Carter"? In May 1982 the *National Journal* studied the Senate in an attempt "to establish an objective method of analyzing congressional voting patterns that avoids the value judgments characteristic of interest-group rating systems." This survey provides a convenient method for testing the critical hypothesis that neoliberals are more conservative than their traditionally liberal colleagues.

The *National Journal* categorized a selection of votes taken in 1981 as either economic votes or social votes. By totaling them, the magazine arrived at a profile of the "average" senator, and then, on an individual basis, was able to quantify how each legislator deviated from the mean. A senator more liberal than the average is denoted by a plus sign, and one more conservative than the average by a minus sign. A comparison of certain senators customarily referred to as liberals with those who have achieved recognition as neoliberals is shown in the chart on page 22. The numbers in parentheses indicate relative rank in each category.

Clearly, there is no statistically significant difference between traditional liberals and neoliberals. On both economic and social issues, their voting records indicate that the two groups are far more liberal than the "average" Democrat.

If we cannot tell a neoliberal from a liberal, even with a scorecard, how then are we to make the distinction? We can do little but pay attention, not to how they have voted or what they have done, but to what they have said; and not only to what they have said, but how they have said it. Voting records indicate little because on traditional issues, neoliberals tend to vote traditionally. But while the traditional issues are the ones that tend to come to a vote in the Senate, these issues for the most part are absent from the neoliberals' rhetoric. It is to the rhetoric that we will have to turn to try to define neoliberalism. Congressman Richard A. Gephardt of St. Louis, who has objected to the label in several interviews, admitted that something certainly does

SENATOR	ECONOMIC VOTES	SOCIAL VOTES	COMBINED SCORE
Traditional Liberals			
Eagleton	+193 (2)	+ 95 (14)	+288 (10)
Inouye	+112 (17)	+151 (4)	+263 (13)
Kennedy	+196 (1)	+136 (8)	+332 (2)
Leahy	+191 (3)	+140 (7)	+331 (1)
Levin	+187 (4)	+152 (3)	+339 (1)
Metzenbaum	+162 (8)	+153 (2)	+315 (5)
Neoliberals			
Bradley	+177 (6)	+147 (6)	+324 (4)
Hart	+150 (11)	+123 (10)	+273 (12)
Tsongas	+145 (12)	+147 (6)	+292 (8)
Bumpers	+131 (15)	+121 (11)	+252 (15)
Dodd	+196 (1)	+119 (12)	+315 (5)
Average Republican	− 68	− 32	−100
Average Democrat	+ 79	+ 39	+118
Average Neoliberal	+159.8	+131.4	+291.2
Average Traditional Liberal	+161.8	+137.8	+299.6

SOURCE: *National Journal,* May 8, 1982, compiled by Frederick Nathan, Jr.

exist beneath the posturing. "It's a group without a charter, without even a self-identification," Gephardt said in June 1982. "There are no meetings, no dues, no constitution. It is a group in general name only."

The group goes by many names; that so many young Democrats have felt compelled to assign some sort of label to their thinking is evidence that, despite the similarities in voting patterns, neoliberals consider themselves in some way different and apart from traditional liberals. In his much-discussed 1981 book, Paul Tsongas calls his politics "compassionate realism." Bill Bradley prefers "democratic pluralism." Gary Hart likes "Prairie Populist Jeffersonian democracy," a clear misnomer to those who follow Hart's politics. Congressman Albert Gore, Jr., of Tennessee favors "neopopulism." Others invoke "'neocapitalism" and "structuralism."

But by whatever name neoliberalism travels, who constitutes this congregation?

The core group, whose names were most frequently cited in the more than one hundred interviews I conducted and in the published reports I read, includes:

Gary Hart, the senior senator from Colorado, the popularizer of military reform, and a candidate for the 1984 Democratic presidential nomination.

Paul Tsongas, Massachusetts' junior senator, retiring in 1984 after one term; his 1981 book, *The Road from Here,* was one of the first attempts to define the party's new path.

Bill Bradley, the former basketball star and now a major player in Democratic economic thinking.

Timothy Wirth, congressman from Colorado, chairman of the House Telecommunications Subcommittee, and co-author of an economic strategy platform for the party with

Richard Gephardt, a fourth-term congressman from Missouri, a member of the Budget Committee and Ways and Means Committee, and co-author with Bradley of a comprehensive tax restructuring plan.

Albert Gore, Jr., congressman from Tennessee who is likely to follow in his father's path and run for the Senate in 1984, bringing with him an enviable grasp of military affairs and science policy.

Among the present and former statehouse residents prominent in redefining the Democratic role are:

Edmund G. (Jerry) Brown, Jr., whose spartan life style and visionary language sparked controversy throughout his two terms as California's governor.

Bruce Babbitt, governor of Arizona, a former civil rights lawyer, and vocal exponent of liberalism within limits.

Richard Lamm, a leader of the environmental movement of the early seventies, serving his third term as governor of Colorado.

James B. Hunt, Jr., governor of North Carolina, who has helped to place education and training policy in the forefront of Democratic concerns.

Other politicians who were frequently cited as representing the new liberalism include Congressmen James Florio of New Jersey and Leon Panetta of California, Governors Michael Dukakis of Massachusetts and Reubin Askew of Florida, and Senator Christopher Dodd of Connecticut.

Among journalists, economists, and academics, those who stand out for their contributions to the developing creed are:

Lester Thurow, professor of economics at the Massachusetts Institute of Technology and author of *The Zero-Sum Society*.

Charles Peters, editor of the *Washington Monthly*, the guru of a powerful, tight network of neoliberal journalists that includes

James Fallows, Washington editor of *The Atlantic*, whose 1981 book, *National Defense*, introduced certain neoliberal concepts to the public.

Michael Barker, former aide to Massachusetts Governor Dukakis, currently the director of the Gallatin Institute, a public-policy think tank, one of whose fellows is

Roger Vaughan, economic adviser to former New York Governor Hugh Carey and the formulator of a comprehensive national training and education strategy.

Pat Choate, senior economic adviser at TRW, Inc., and the Business Roundtable, who introduced the "infrastructure decay" problem to America.

Sam Brown, former antiwar activist and head of ACTION under Jimmy Carter.

Robert Reich, a lecturer at Harvard's John F. Kennedy School of Government and author of *The Next American Frontier*, the 1983 tract on industrial policy.

David Birch, director of MIT's Program on Neighborhood and Regional Change and the man behind the new-found prominence of small business in economic policy.

But again the persistent question, What *is* neoliberalism? "There is," said Congressman Gephardt in 1982, "a core of ideas, threads that *do* bind the people together." These threads constitute what author Peter Steinfels refers to as a "political tendency," a shared predisposition to interpret public events through a series of assumptions based on intuition, acculturation, education, and experience. These premises help to outline a world view encompassing both a diagnosis of the past and preferred paths to the future.

"I'm talking about a movement!" declared the voluble Charles Peters in late 1981. "And I think the movement has begun. . . . I think this is a movement that will turn this country around." But no, neoliberalism is not a movement. There is no necessary collusion between supposed members. Two early neoliberals, Gary Hart and Reubin Askew, contested each other for their party's nomination for the presidency; a third, Senator Dale Bumpers of Arkansas, considered entering the race. Early in the campaign season, Senator Tsongas endorsed John Glenn, who represents no consistent strain in his thinking. "Neoliberalism," explained economist Pat Choate, whose warnings on infrastructure decay and recommendations for industrial and human-capital policies have been extremely influential in neoliberal Democratic circles, "is really a study in pragmatism, of breaking past ideological boundaries to determine how to restore long-term economic growth, and to do it in a socially responsible and equitable manner."

Breaking past ideological boundaries—this is the first step in the development of any new political tendency. To understand why boundaries are being broken, we must first take a step backward.

CHAPTER 2

Roosevelt's World

BILL BRADLEY SLAMMED his big fist on the desk. The vibrations seemed likely to topple the pillars of papers, books, and *Congressional Records* precariously balanced upon it. "There is no new club!" shouted the senator from New Jersey.

Bradley had reason to be edgy. He was a most junior member of the Democratic Party. In April 1980, when he made his declaration of bona fides, he was barely through his first year in the U.S. Senate. The senior members of that august body, fully aware of Bradley's star status—a basketball hero at Princeton in the early sixties, he attended Oxford as a Rhodes scholar, then returned to the U.S. for a decade of professional ball with the New York Knicks, playing on two championship teams—had wondered whether the new arrival would be a "showhorse" or a "workhorse."

The senators had every reason to expect a showhorse; Bradley, after all, had never held public office before, and he had had the temerity to challenge the designated candidate of the New Jersey Democratic Party in the primary. Nobody was fooled for a minute into believing that his victory then, or his landslide in the general election, was the result of anything other than his sports fame.

But Bill Bradley understood that the stakes were high, and he was determined to prove himself a workhorse. He was now thirty-eight years old, and a bit paunchy. No, he answered, he did *not* practice hook shots in the Senate gym; there's no basket there. Yes, he agreed, perhaps he *did* need additional exercise. But always there remained more paperwork, more briefings, more hearings. The clutter in his office contrasted sharply with the somber, oak-grained serenity of most senators' inner sanctums. Edging off a cabinet was a plaque on which were engraved the words "Sen. Bill Bradley, former New York Knick," a joking reference to *The New York Times'* habitual identification of him. Taped to the bathroom door were a series of finger paintings by his four-year-old daughter. And behind the desk was a senator who absolutely did not wish to be categorized in any way apart from the mainstream of his party.

But by the spring of 1980 rumbles of discontent were clearly audible within the Democratic Party. Jimmy Carter's failure was apparent, but Teddy Kennedy's challenge to him provided little solace. Bradley was part of a surprisingly large group who declined to endorse either candidate. He portrayed his decision as a pragmatic political move, but it was hard to interpret it as anything other than dissatisfaction with the two sides of the status quo. And although he refused to be baited into even an implied criticism of either the President or his challenger, the tone—if not the substance—of much of what he was saying differed from the recommendations of the two candidates, and seemed to ally him with an increasingly vocal clique of junior party members. What about this so-called new realism, Senator? Do you and Gary Hart mean the same thing when you talk about "the end of the New Deal"? Is there a common ideology, beyond an allegiance to standard Democratic Party principles, that binds you and Paul Tsongas together? How is it that you and Tim Wirth are always hammering away at *investing* in the technological future? "There is no new club!" exploded a frustrated Bradley.

Less than a year later, freed from caution by the downfall of Jimmy Carter and the Senate's liberal leadership, Bill Bradley was more forthcoming. "You *do* find a group here trying to think through the problems of the eighties," said Bradley, "who see that the traditional Democratic responses really had their origins in the thirties and are not going to meet those problems."

The solutions of the thirties will not solve the problems of the eighties. Variations on this theme weave their way through neoliberal dialogue. What does it mean? Simply this: while the neoliberals adhere to traditional Democratic values, they are prepared to leave the mechanism of the New Deal behind. "The cutting edge of the Democratic Party," Colorado Governor Richard Lamm stated in 1982, "is to recognize that the world of the 1930s has changed and that a new set of public policy responses is appropriate. . . . A blind adherence to yesterday's solutions in trying to solve today's problems will doom the Democratic Party to second place in perpetuity."

All politics is reaction. At its most basic level, campaigning, it usually consists of little more than attacking or defending the records of those who have passed before. At its most advanced stage, ideology, it is an intellectual response to the prevailing difficulties of the time, be they economic, social, or moral. More often than not, what passes for political ideology is actually a rationalized answer to immediate problems. Occasionally it is the result of long intuited but unarticulated systemic needs. Rarely is it a combination of the two.

March 4, 1933. The nation Franklin Roosevelt inherited on this day bears scant resemblance to the one in which we live today. Yet Roosevelt's response to the dire conditions he faced upon uttering the oath of office hardened into a rigid ideology that has manacled the Democratic Party to a set of hidebound solutions increasingly untenable in today's world.

The Democratic campaign of 1932 was waged with the knowledge that Roosevelt's victory was virtually certain. There was no need for him to assure the public of any specific actions save that, yes, Prohibition would be repealed. Generalities, primarily salvos against the policies of the hapless Herbert Hoover, a lapsed progressive and an internationalist hero during and after World War I, would suffice. Although Roosevelt, in accepting his party's nomination, had pledged "to break foolish traditions," one ageless political custom remained unchallenged: Say as little as possible, and you shall rarely be on the defensive. The Democratic platform was notable for its lack of innovative proposals.

But a sharp hint of what was to follow had come in May 1932 when Roosevelt stated, "The country needs and, unless I mistake its temper, the country demands bold, persistent experimentation. It is common sense to take a method and try it. If it fails, admit it frankly and try another. But above all, try something."

That dictum would guide Roosevelt throughout his tenure as "Dr. New Deal." He was, as economist John Kenneth Galbraith would remark on the occasion of FDR's centenary, "unencumbered by ideological constraint." The crises he faced required radical experimentation, of a sort no President is ever again likely to be permitted. During his administration's earliest days, he would flirt with monetarism. He would listen to his budget director's pleas for fiscal orthodoxy, importunings remarkably similar to the recent calls for drastically reduced government spending and a lowered tax burden made by today's supply-side conservatives. But eventually, during the famed "Hundred Days" and thereafter, the New Deal took shape. It was a program rationally based on the urgent needs of the day, shaped by the interrelationships within the vast American economy.

By 1932 five thousand banks had failed, wiping out nine million savings accounts. To restore confidence in the system, the New Dealers passed the Emergency Banking Act, which gave the Federal Reserve the power to issue currency against bank assets, and put the banks under the government's direct supervision. They subsequently put through the Glass-Steagall Act, which separated commercial banking from investment banking activities. The second priority was to halt the disaster that had befallen American agriculture, in which 20 percent of the work force was employed. Government planning of agriculture was introduced through the Agricultural Adjustment Act, which established a method for subsidizing farm staples. Next, the mass-production economy and its workers, the basis of American prosperity, needed to be restored. The National Industrial Recovery Act established a system for government–business cooperation, centralizing government control over the planning of the economy, which was now regarded as a collection of national economic units needing direct supervision. And legislatively the New Deal enhanced the power of labor to organize and to bargain collectively, transforming the trade union movement into a "countervailing force" against the concentration of private capital. The National Recovery Administration helped enforce minimum wages and maximum hour limitations. The NIRA also channeled $3.3 billion into public works programs; some New Dealers saw this as a rational economic stimulus, others as a humanitarian necessity. Whatever its basis, the efficacy of public works was unchallenged. And the 1935 Social Security Act established a pension for the elderly through a system of mandatory contributions via a payroll tax. It was a regressive method of financing, but it made Social Security an entitlement, granting contributors, in FDR's words, "a legal, moral, and political right to collect their pensions and their unemployment benefits." The Tennessee Valley Authority, the Civilian Conservation Corps, the National Labor Relations Board, the Works Projects Administration were other ingredients in an alphabet soup of agencies that forever changed the government's role in the daily lives of its citizenry.

In 1935–36 the New Deal itself underwent a transformation, shifting from a conglomeration of programs having a purely national economic perspective to a Wilsonian program that emphasized competition, something that had been neglected, if not forgotten, in the administration's early years. World War II supplanted the experimentation of the thirties; Dr. New Deal joked that he had now become "Dr. Win-The-War." The massive war effort that began in 1942 seemed to guarantee endless economic recovery and vitality.

During the 1932 campaign, the Hundred Days, even into Roosevelt's second term, there existed no such beast as "the New Deal ideology." But during the course of the thirties and the forties the compulsion to experiment, the "by all means try something" credo that drove the young lawyers and social workers to Washington in the spring of 1933, took on a form. And the form gradually became an ideology, a body of political concepts—"New Deal liberalism."

The most important social change wrought by the New Deal was general public acceptance of affirmative government. Although the Reagan Administration successfully rolled back a host of government programs, it encountered insurmountable opposition from across a wide swath of social strata in its attempts to dismantle the interventionist progressivism introduced to government by President Roosevelt and expanded by his successors. But beyond the innovation of affirmative government, New Deal liberalism, as it evolved over the fifty years following FDR's inauguration, has come to be defined by three themes. Although the terminology may vary from analysis to analysis, they are: economic centralization, macroeconomics, and interest-group politics.

The centralization of authority within the federal government over economic decisions previously left to the private sector was the perhaps inevitable reaction to the perceived abdication of social and economic responsibility by business that brought on the Depression.

Loss of faith in the private sector allowed the New Dealers freedom to indulge in solutions requiring absolute federal authority. Many of the Brain Trust's early members, and even Roosevelt himself, to a degree, were old Bull Moose Republicans, adherents to the Teddy Roosevelt–Progressive Party platform of 1912 which advocated national planning of the economy. The Bull Moose dictum was "Concentration, cooperation, and control." The NRA and AAA developed out of this philosophy and represented a repudiation of free enterprise.

There were significant differences within the administration over the degree to which control ought to be exercised, but in the end centralization became an established canon. Even after the shift from the nationalist orientation of the early New Deal to the Wilsonian, pro-competition trend of the later New Deal, broad federal authority was still the rule. Federal power would smash monopolies, curtail big business's abuses, raise the competitive abilities of organized labor. "The central idea common to both principal reform traditions, the [Wilsonian] New Freedom and the New Nationalism," wrote historian Eric Goldman, "[was] the belief that the best solution for economic and social ills was action by the federal government under strong executive leadership." Indeed, during the following decades this would become the most significant element of liberalism.

The increasingly strict adherence to centralization of authority over the years, the belief in the unassailable benefits of the mass-production economy, and the idea that prosperity depended upon the functioning of large economic units drove liberals to the acceptance of a second key element, macroeconomics. In a system where government control was presumed to be the only way to guarantee vitality to the economy, it was a natural consequence to accept the theory that government intervention in the economy solely determined the conditions under which continuing growth and success could be assured.

Although the New Deal was fashioned as an ad hoc package with remarkably little theoretical backing, the writings of British economist John Maynard Keynes provided justification for the government's actions. Roosevelt had entered office a student of the day's conventional wisdom that government deficits were bad and balanced budgets good. But the relief programs of the New Deal required an enormous expenditure of government money and much deficit financing. Keynes's argument—that deficit spending, by reinflating the economy, would increase demand, then supply, and end depression and unemployment—provided a fine rationale for the New Deal. The success of its programs—particularly as the postwar economic boom solidified an unprecedented liberal political consensus in the United States—in turn lent Keynesian theory such weight that it was virtually beyond challenge. To Keynes, the economy was essentially a closed system, and maintenance of economic equilibrium was the fundamental problem faced by the doctors of the political economy. The determinant of proper equilibrium was the balance between demand and supply. The slackening of demand had created the Great Depression. It was government's duty, therefore, to assure proper levels of demand.

Not only was it government's responsibility, but *only* government had the capability to control demand. It could do this through the manipulation of fiscal and monetary policies—government spending, particularly in the absence of private spending, creation of deficits, control of the money supply, and the establishment of interest rates. The acceptance of the macroeconomic view of the national economy presupposed that individual and business activity was almost wholly determined by whatever economic maneuvering the federal government opted for—in other words, that the microeconomy was totally dependent on the macroeconomy.

After World War II, leading analysts of the day simply accepted without question the theoretical basis for the nation's current success. "Keynes, not Marx, is the prophet of the new radicalism," wrote Arthur Schlesinger, Jr., in 1949. Five years later Arthur Burns, chairman of Eisenhower's Council of Economic Advisers, declared, "It is no longer a matter of serious controversy whether the government shall play a positive role in helping to maintain a high level of economic activity." By the 1970s even conservative economist Milton Friedman of the University of Chicago and President Richard Nixon were declaring themselves Keynesians.

Government assumed another task in New Deal liberalism. It created for itself the role of broker between interest groups. In a 1936 commencement address at Rollins College, President Roosevelt articulated his interpretation of government's duty:

> There are . . . groups to which almost every man and woman is tied, connected in some way. They are connected with some form of association—the church, the social circle, the club, the lodge, the labor organization, the neighborhood farmers, the political party. Even business and commerce are wholly made up of groups. It is the problem of government to harmonize the interests of these groups, which are often divergent and opposing. The science of politics, indeed, may properly be said to be in large part the science of the adjustment of conflicting group interests.

Roosevelt properly understood that the coordination of group interests was a necessary step toward solving the two crises he faced as President, ending the Depression and winning the war. But as political writer Phillip Longman has noted, in the period of serenity and prosperity that followed World War II there was a consistent "effort by liberals to make interest-group politics an intellectually respectable idea."

By the 1970s the atomization of U.S. society had become a staple of American political thought. While it provided an excellent basis for helping those whose ethnic, cultural, or sexual minority status had rendered them underdogs in the game of economic advancement, it was also used to promote the demands of groups no longer necessarily suffering *as groups* from economic hardship. Yet the liberal Democratic politicians, whose careers were staked on the continued existence of the "New Deal coalition" first established by Franklin Roosevelt, found themselves loath to challenge that coalition's composition, even if, as was frequently charged in the early 1980s, the interests of some groups within the coalition no longer coincided with the national interest—the justification for the alliance in the first place. But to many stalwarts of New Deal liberalism, a challenge to interest-group politics was a challenge to liberalism itself.

Centralization, macroeconomics, interest-group politics—these were and are the chief elements of modern liberal ideology. A reaction to industrialism, liberalism was the legacy of Roosevelt's world to two generations of politicians. In its time, it was wildly successful. But too many public officials failed to notice that, as they became more committed to the ideology, the industrial paradigm was changing.

CHAPTER 3

Carter's World

JIMMY CARTER SENSED the change, although he never successfully figured out how to govern in response to it. And so he has become a pariah, the scapegoat for liberals. They conveniently blame him for all the ills that have beset the Democratic Party.

That his tenure and leadership were disenchanting cannot be argued. Carter was cursed with a personality too weak for the pressures of the presidency. But whether the public's rejection of him was caused by his abandonment of traditional liberal principles is far from clear. Rather, it can be argued that the Jimmy Carter elected in 1976 represented the first halting steps toward a post–New Deal liberalism, and that his defeat of Gerald Ford that year was occasioned by the electorate's innate awareness and approval of this shift. In this interpretation, the rejection of Jimmy Carter four years later was an expression of grave disappointment over his failure to justify his promise. "He recognized, as a candidate, out on the horizon, many of the issues we're talking about," said Arizona Governor Bruce Babbitt in 1982. "But the Democratic Party that elected him was not prepared to hear that message, so he finally threw in the towel."

"Carter," concluded Babbitt, "was a little too early."

Carter pledged during the 1976 campaign to lead "a government as good as its people." The phrase was shorthand for something people had been seeking—the vision of a unified America to replace the splintered public interest that was the residue of Vietnam. The Vietnam conflict had added a confrontational hue to the interest-group polity of the nation. The country was divided, so it seemed, into

34

young against old, students against labor, moralists against pragmatists. And these groups as well as others were internally divided as well. As the war wound down, antagonism remained an accepted part of political discourse. The issues of the day were increasingly couched in terms of opposition: environment vs. industry, minority groups vs. whites, women vs. men. As group interests dominated the political arena, the ethos of the "Me Generation" spread through every portion of the public domain.

By 1976 it was clear that the American public was fatigued by the polarization that imbued politics at all levels. The Public Agenda Foundation, a not-for-profit research organization, concluded on the basis of polling that:

> American fear that the country has been trending toward a psychology of self-interest so all-embracing that no room is left for commitment to national and community interests. They sense that we risk losing something precious to the meaning of the American experience. They fear that in the pursuit of their organizational goals, the politicians and the businessmen and the professions have lost sight of any larger obligation to the public and are indifferent or worse to anything that does not benefit—immediately and directly—themselves or their institutions. They fear that the very meaning of the public good is disappearing, drowned in a sea of self-seeking.

Pollster Daniel Yankelovich enlarged on the foundation's conclusions. Survey results revealed to him a public frustration bred by the institutional selfishness. Nevertheless, that frustration had not led to a turning inward, or to a desire, out of disgust, to gloss over the day's pressing problems. To the contrary, he concluded, people *wanted* government. But they required of it a realism and pragmatism they felt had slipped away. "What people are demanding," wrote Yankelovich, "is not less government but better government."

By preaching love, unity, trust, and moral guidance, Jimmy Carter provided a direction that, however vague its details, captured the Democratic primary voter and then the national electorate. Journalist James Fallows, who joined the Carter campaign in the summer of 1976 and later became chief White House speechwriter, best summarized the yearnings of a body politic sick of the partisan posturings of more traditional Democratic aspirants. "I felt that [Carter], alone among the candidates, might look past the tired formulas of left and right and offer something new," wrote Fallows retrospectively in mid-1979. "I was led on myself by the hope that Carter might make sense of the swirl of liberal and conservative sentiment then muddying the political orthodoxy.

> I told my friends that summer that Carter had at least the same potential [as Franklin Roosevelt] to leave the government forever changed by his presence: not by expanding federal responsibilities, as Roosevelt had done, or by continuing the trend of the Great Society, but by transforming the government, as in the 1930s, to reflect the needs of a different time.

Fallows was twenty-eight years old when he began crafting phrases for Jimmy Carter. Although young he was not a political neophyte; he had previously worked closely with consumer advocate Ralph Nader and as a political journalist for the *Washington Monthly*. Older and presumably wiser observers were equally entranced by the Carter presence. Charles Peters, founder and editor of the iconoclastic *Washington Monthly*, was among the first members of the capital's press establishment to suggest publicly that Carter was eminently fit for the Oval Office. In the May 1976 issue of his magazine, Peters published back-to-back articles, one of which he wrote, lambasting the media for failing to credit Carter's expertise.

Even a pair of left-leaning journalists jaded with the politics of the seventies—*Rolling Stone*'s Hunter S. Thompson, who had ridiculed the presidential process only four years before in *Fear and Loathing on the Campaign Trail,* and Norman Mailer, writing in *The New York Times*—found themselves enchanted by the Carter phenomenon. Mailer labeled him the "oddest politician" he had ever met, but nonetheless a "political genius." Thompson came away with the same impression, calling him "one of the most intelligent politicians I've ever met." "There is no question in my mind," wrote Thompson, ". . . that I was dealing with a candidate who had already done a massive amount of research on things like tax reform, national defense and the structure of the American political system."

Mailer was most impressed with Carter's grasp of and fascination with government, reporting the ex-governor's belief that "there were limits to what government could do, yet in those limits more could be done than was now being done," and that "his function was . . . to bring the human factor back to economics." "Quiet in his charisma," concluded Mailer of Carter. "Happiness came off him."

The American people wanted a President who could provide a sense of the national interest, who would restore fairness to society's institutions, who required of his government efficiency while recognizing its finite capacity, but who nevertheless believed in government as firmly as they did. And, according to commentators like Fallows, Peters, Thompson, and Mailer, Jimmy Carter was the one: the candidate of unity, pragmatism, the changed era. *He understood that liberalism must operate within limits.* On the strength of that perception, Jimmy Carter was elected President of the United States.

Carter's inability to follow that perception with a coherent plan for governing was the principal reason for his failure. If his vision emerged from his Christian side, it was overwhelmed upon his election by another part of his character. "Mr. Carter's at least as much of an engineer as he is a mystic," observed Mailer during the campaign. Yet the Christian and the engineer that both existed within him had no point of coincidence. Jimmy Carter's political schizophrenia was evident from the start of his campaign. The moral vision was ever-present; it was a dream of a city on the hill for America's third century, and it captured the imaginations of even cynics from the sixties. At the same time, Carter was quick to stress, that he knew the facts, that he had the programs. "I have gone to the people with my positions on every basic issue facing the nation—tax reform, health, welfare reform, the environment, jobs, government reorganization, honesty in government," he told an Ohio AFL-CIO convention on May 27, 1976, "and in state after state the people have endorsed my positions with their votes."

What escaped notice was the lack of a connection between the vision and the laundry list. Stumping in West Virginia, he could rail against "the impact of inadequate leadership on our families"—a charge all parents could certainly understand—but insist on validating the point with an endless, almost comical, array of statistics: "Forty percent of all marriages today end in divorce. . . . In 1960, children born of unwed mothers comprised one out of 20. Last year, one out of eight. . . . Among those in our society today, black and white, rich and poor, between 15 and 19 years old, the second most frequent cause of death is suicide. . . . In the last 10 years, the gonorrhea rate has tripled among our children less than 14 years old . . ." This was the Jimmy Carter who upon his election had his staff produce a 111-page memo listing every promise he had made during the race.

Jimmy Carter, in short, was a Christian technocrat: otherworldly, highly moralistic, yet devoted to tedious detail. The division between his two selves was his undoing. The anecdotes are legion: Carter in Vienna, carefully annotating the score to a Mozart opera while Soviet Premier Leonid Brezhnev chatted and dozed in an adjoining box; Car-

ter personally overseeing the use of the White House tennis courts;
Carter proudly telling a visitor that he had read every single page of
the Air Force budget. "He seemed to believe that if he could grasp all
the facts and figures of a problem, he would understand its dynam-
ics," observed veteran journalist Theodore H. White. Jim Fallows,
after leaving his White House job, confirmed White's impression. "I
came to think that Jimmy Carter believes fifty things, but no one
thing," wrote Fallows. "He holds explicit, thorough positions on every
issue under the sun, but he has no large view of the relations between
them, no line indicating which goals . . . will take precedence over
which . . . when the goals conflict."

Conflicting goals are, of course, the essence of politics, and his
unwillingness to choose between them illustrated Jimmy Carter's dual-
ity: he loved government, yet hated politics. His refusal to twist arms
in Congress and engage in horse-trading with the special-interest
groups that swarmed over his bills damaged his ability to pass any
substantive domestic legislation. One of Carter's first initiatives, the
now-forgotten Economic Stimulus Package designed to halt the rise
to 7.5 percent unemployment that had occurred under Gerald Ford,
was scuttled when blacks, then shoemakers, then westerners, sugar interests, machinists, dairy farmers, and bankers—none of whom had
been consulted in the package's formulation—all came out in opposition to it.

And yet Carter ended up playing to these interest groups. More
than any President who preceded him, he made appointments to top
administrative and judicial positions based openly on ethnicity, and
as his presidency faltered he engaged increasingly in a game of group
appeasement, but with no attempt to wring concessions from the various groups toward the effectuation of a larger national goal, the way
Roosevelt had. He had no taste for the quid pro quo; he was, according to Michael Blumenthal, his first Secretary of the Treasury, "completely non-confrontational." That quality manifested itself in two
ways: the drafting of important legislation in complete isolation from
the political interests that the laws would inevitably affect, and the consequent pandering to those interests when all else was lost.

What happened? Why did the candidate who preached unity,
pragmatism, and limits in 1976 become the President who delivered
fragmentation, inefficiency, and excess in his four years in office? Personality aside, Jimmy Carter simply fell prey to the nostrums of traditional liberal ideology.

Carter's problems had precedents within the liberalism that matured during the sixties and seventies. Even Carter's squeamishness with politics can be found writ large across the liberal dogma of the past two decades. It was the dislike of politics that saw liberals couch more and more issues in terms of rights—not part of the bargaining, the give-and-take of representative government, but entitlements owed as a matter of citizenship and administered by executive agencies. Yet if those "rights" conflict, as inevitably many do, there is no way of mediating the disputes that arise. Once legislation is enacted, once these group concerns become entitlements, they have effectively been removed from political negotiation. Carter did not like politics; neither did many of the liberals who preceded him, who passed along the eventual collision of rights to a future generation. He was a hapless participant in the game of interest-group politics with no idea how to resolve the conflict in the national interest. He allowed his administration to become dominated by apolitical experts.

In his election campaign, Carter discoursed on limits, but with a hopefulness that belied the impression that limits mean lowered expectations. By the end, he helped to create new, centralized institutions while at the same time promoting—against the grain of the American character—lowered expectations. He took several steps beyond the industrial paradigm and liberal ideology, only to fall back.

Carter's defeat in 1980, coupled with the defeat of so many staunchly liberal senators, was a purging of tradition, a message sent to the Democrats by the voters. The Republicans, under Ronald Reagan, had succeeded, in author Jeff Greenfield's words, in painting the Democrats as "the party of no-growth, pessimism, and fear." If the promise of the Jimmy Carter of 1976 and the fulfillment of what people seemed to want was to be realized by the Democrats, it would have to be done by a party out of power.

CHAPTER 4

The Neoliberal World

By the middle of 1980, it was clear that the American public desired a change. Jimmy Carter had promised one four years earlier, but the evening news now brought only Iranian taunts and increasingly dismal economic indicators, confirming President Carter's haplessness. Ronald Reagan, his supply-side boosters, and the New Right army promised a real transition. The electorate would turn to them.

But not all Democrats felt trapped by the old dogma and Carter's failure. Sensing the impending disaster, some of the party's newer figures felt the time had come to look forward.

The public debut of neoliberalism occurred on June 14, 1980, two months after Bill Bradley's staunch assertion that there was "no new club," and at the end of the bitter internecine struggle between President Carter and Senator Kennedy. The man responsible for the event was an unlikely leader, Massachusetts' junior senator, Paul Tsongas.

Tsongas entered the Senate in January 1979 with a varied—some might even say checkered—political career. His parents were Republicans; his father, Efthemios George Tsongas, was an especially conservative Republican. Emigrating to the United States from Greece at the age of four with his parents, the elder Tsongas epitomized the self-made man, growing up in Lowell, Massachusetts, one of America's oldest and grittiest industrial centers, excelling in school and work, attending Harvard, and returning to Lowell to open a successful dry-cleaning business. It was only natural, then, that his son would follow his example and adopt the father's political philosophy, given

40

the sheltered, middle-class life to which he had been exposed. By the time he was graduated from Dartmouth in 1962, Paul Tsongas had yet to travel farther from home than Annapolis, Maryland.

John Kennedy's presidential campaign, which took place when Tsongas was a college sophomore, was a turning point for him. He would later recall it as "a glorious time," and it remained a strong enough influence to convince him upon graduation from college to join the Peace Corps—"the last person you'd think of to do something like *that*," he recalled in the summer of 1981. While the Peace Corps years (he spent them in a small village in Ethiopia) liberalized Tsongas, they did not "Democratize" him. He returned to the United States, to Yale Law School, and served two summer internships on Capitol Hill with his liberal Republican congressman, then found his way to New York in 1965 to work on Republican John Lindsay's mayoral campaign. By 1968, shaken by Robert Kennedy's tragically abbreviated presidential race, Tsongas had switched parties. Moving back to Lowell, he was elected to the City Council, served later on the County Commission, and in 1974 joined the Watergate Babies entering Congress in the anti-Nixon backlash of that year.

The Class of '74 was one of the largest freshman classes in congressional history. Scholars and professionals, they were well-educated men and women who had been fired up by John and Robert Kennedy, who had entered the battles of the civil rights or antiwar or environmental movement because their liberal values, and their middle-class guilt, had been touched. What counted for them was values. They drew a strict line between values and programs. The '74 freshmen held classes and seminars in an attempt to differentiate between the two. Looking back on his first term in the House Tsongas recalled, "Whether it was economics or defense posture or what have you, we'd sit around, bring in the experts, and say, 'What the hell is going on?' and try to address it from that perspective. That was very different from the traditional Democrat, who would say, 'All right, what do the unions want? What does constituency X want?' As opposed to, 'Okay, what works? How do you solve a problem like this?' We were emotionally removed—which is a net plus in some cases, a minus in others—and much more analytical."

After two terms in the House, Tsongas challenged veteran Republican Senator Edward Brooke, a liberal, the only black in the upper body, but a vulnerable target in 1978. Tsongas won by more than 200,000 votes. But he did not enjoy his new position. Far from it; six months into his senatorial stint he admitted to a reporter that he was "floundering," and even considered resigning. His voting record marked him as one of the most liberal, if not *the* most liberal, member of the Senate.

For this reason Leon Shull, executive director of the Americans for Democratic Action, invited Tsongas to deliver the keynote address to the ADA's national convention on June 14, 1980, shortly after Senator Kennedy was to speak to the organization's members. The theory was to present liberalism's stalwart and vibrant past and its dynamic future, with Massachusetts' two senators bracketing the creed like bookends. The speech Tsongas' staff prepared, "a typical litany of liberal Democratic values and programs," as he would later write, did not satisfy him. So the day prior to his scheduled appearance, he scrapped the speech and substituted another—against the advice of some senior advisers—written by himself and a young aide named Douglas Pike.

Tsongas' short talk was not meant to be stirring, and he certainly didn't think of it as path-breaking. But it turned out to be one of those rare events that, through some ineluctable process, succeeds in changing the character of political debate. It was styled not as a prescription, but as a warning. "The fact is," declared Tsongas to the traditional liberals who made up his audience, "liberalism is at a crossroads. It will either evolve to meet the issues of the 1980s, or it will be reduced to an interesting topic for Ph.D.–writing historians."

Tsongas invoked a number of concerns about which he and his colleagues were worried, but which few had voiced publicly. Why was it the young were flocking to John Anderson in the 1980 presidential race, he wanted to know. How were liberal Democrats to mobilize a generation that never knew the abuses and injustices a previous generation of liberals had experienced? "This is a different generation," he said. "And if we do not speak to this generation in its terms, liberalism will decline, and if we do not meet these needs, liberalism *should* decline." He enumerated the problems of the eighties left unaddressed by the solutions of the thirties: consumption, productivity, long-term economic viability versus short-term relief, resource limitations, Soviet adventurism. He concluded his address by saying, "I call upon the people who will be at the [Democratic] convention to work for a new liberalism—rooted in sound values of the past but relevant to the all-too-real problems of the present and future."

The assemblage received Tsongas politely; few, if any, felt their doctrine had been sullied. But if the ADA conventioneers were the senator's intended audience, they were not to be his final audience.

Tsongas' call for "a new liberalism" was widely reported. The op-ed page of *The New York Times* carried a précis of Tsongas' remarks the day after their delivery. The following week, David Broder, who had been researching many of the themes touched upon by the senator for his book *Changing of the Guard* (a chronicle of the generational shift taking place in American politics), wrote a column about Tsongas' ideas for the *Washington Post*. Syndicated in forty-four newspapers, the Broder piece created a stir that never really subsided. The most influential newspaper in Tsongas' home state, the *Boston Globe,* headlined Broder's report "End of Kennedy-Style Liberalism?"

Ironically the press chose Tsongas as the representative of this new liberalism even though Tsongas' and Kennedy's voting records were nearly identical and Tsongas had endorsed Kennedy's bid for the presidency. (Tsongas had even shown Kennedy a copy of his ADA address before delivering it.)

It was further ironic because Tsongas, beyond asserting that liberalism needed to redefine itself, had very little to add to the discussion. His 1981 book, *The Road from Here,* an attempt to capitalize on the publicity he had gained as the spokesman for the new liberalism, showed that many of his "new ideas" were not new at all; in some cases he proved himself unacquainted with the truly original formulations his colleagues had begun to espouse.

Tsongas said at the time (and would repeat in his book) that the 1979–80 controversy over the Carter Administration's proposal to aid the ailing Chrysler Corporation was the seminal event in his rethinking. Opposed to the loan guarantees because of a long-standing and legitimate animus against the poor management practices of Detroit's executives, Tsongas rethought his position after a political journey to Detroit. He saw Detroit experiencing the wracking pain he remembered in Lowell at the time of the textile industry's contraction during his youth in the 1940s and 50s, and realized that allowing Chrysler to die would produce similar misery. Returning to Washington, he was appalled by the knee-jerk support and automatic opposition the Carter proposal spawned, and the hypocrisy to which it led. Republicans who had voted to save Lockheed during its near-failure in 1970 had to explain away their disapproval with aiding Chrysler, and Democrats who had faulted the Lockheed "national security" bail-out now easily defended their impending "aye" vote on Chrysler. It was all a question of constituencies—business for the Republicans, labor for the Democrats.

Tsongas, however, did not experience the hypocrisy firsthand until he entered the battle, co-sponsoring with conservative Indiana Republican Richard Lugar a bill calling for guarantees totaling $1 billion more than the Carter Administration was offering, but coupling them with a wage freeze and stock issuance plan for employees. The bill was opposed by most Democratic factions, and particularly by the United Auto Workers, for whom the wage-freeze concept was anathema. Tsongas, in fact, caught holy hell. Union members in Massachusetts contacted his office, wondering why a liberal had turned "anti-labor," and staffers in Ted Kennedy's employ indelicately inquired whether Tsongas knew what he was up to. Although the UAW would, more than a year later, endorse a wage freeze, Tsongas had learned a startling lesson after only one year in the Senate: "The workers' dilemma was ignored in the name of ideology, to wit: Thou shalt not endorse a wage freeze . . . I began thinking about matters that hadn't occupied my mind for a long time, such as whether liberals weren't trapped in rigid dogmas."

That was the point of the ADA address, and that was the message—perhaps it was Tsongas' only important message—picked up by the columnists, the editorial writers, and the others at the top of what journalist James Fallows had labeled "the hierarchy of information and attitudes." Although Tsongas would retire from the Senate in 1984, ill with lymphoma, the impact of his call for a new liberalism would long be felt.

Paul Tsongas' story epitomizes that of many neoliberals. Like Bradley, Hart, and Congressman Leon Panetta of California, he was the child of Republican parents; some neoliberals even began their political lives as Republicans themselves. All had their political sensibilities altered by the campaigns of John Kennedy in 1960 and Robert Kennedy in 1968. All were youthful activists; some (Tsongas, New York City Council President Carol Bellamy, Connecticut Senator Christopher Dodd) as members of the Peace Corps, others as participants in other programs of the Kennedy–Johnson years. Children of postwar prosperity, they came from secure, if not affluent backgrounds. They shared in the "can do" atmosphere of the Kennedy White House, then in a feeling of powerlessness during Vietnam, and in disappointment over the limitations of the Great Society.

Tsongas' tale not only signals who the neoliberals are, but discloses what they believe. We can begin by identifying a skepticism about interest-group politics. There is also the implicit declaration that affirmative government need not mean big government. And there are continual invocations of pragmatism. Without publicly saying so, the neoliberals seem to accuse their liberal forebears of falling prey to tenets that are no longer viable. "There very clearly is a group of us who are reacting against some common perceptions about the Democratic Party and its traditions," Arizona's Governor Babbitt said in May 1982. At the time, he entertained no illusions about what this meant. "There's a kind of struggle on for the heart and soul of the Democratic Party," he said. "I don't think it's clear what the outcome will be."

Realism, pragmatism, "workability"—all constitute a recurrent theme in neoliberal discourse. But this shouldn't be mistaken as a rejection of ideology and acceptance of the dubious concept of "the end of ideology" prevalent in the early sixties. Rather, neoliberal pragmatism signifies a return to economic growth as the first principle of liberalism. John F. Kennedy's maxim "A rising tide lifts all boats" has been modified by the neoliberals: "You can't slice a shrinking pie."

"In the old liberalism, there was the assumption that not only was government intervention positive and necessary, but there was no limit to what government could do to solve a problem," explained Susan Thomases, a New Jersey lawyer and sixties activist who managed Bill Bradley's first campaign for the Senate. "There was a sense that government resources could be harnessed to solve any problem and that there was a limitlessness to those resources."

The notion that government was the *best* problem solver originated with Franklin Roosevelt's New Deal. The conventional wisdom of the sixties was that Lyndon Johnson's Great Society was an extension of the New Deal. In fundamental respects, it was. But as the Great Society became layered with coat after coat of administration and bureaucracy in order to deal with problems that were being defined increasingly as "social," with no relationship to economics, some young Democrats (as well as Republicans) began to view the Great Society as a *perversion* of the New Deal.

"What Roosevelt was talking about was economic liberalism," said Susan Thomases. "What Johnson added to it was social liberalism, and that had a very high price tag. If anything, I think the neoliberals are returning to Roosevelt liberalism, or even more to classical liberalism, where there is a heavier emphasis on economic rather

than on social issues." Or, as Bill Bradley said to *Baltimore Sun* reporter Fred Barnes, "The key is how to get the economy moving
again, not how to get new government delivery systems."

This primary concern for economic growth has given rise to most
of the suggested programs that have come to be associated with the
new liberalism—for example, tax policy. Recommendations for a consumption tax to replace the loophole-ridden income tax system have
come from Gary Hart and Lester Thurow, as a way of bolstering the
nation's low savings rate; in 1982, Bill Bradley and Dick Gephardt
came in with a different plan, a radically simplified income tax, that
has wound its way into the Democratic mainstream. Both ideas seek
to promote investment—the only way, say the neoliberals, of meeting
the new economic challenge of growth within natural limits. The neoliberals advocate an energy policy that promotes conservation and the
use of renewable resources but confound their liberal predecessors by
arguing that a greater reliance on market forces, rather than on top-
down price controls, will aid the conservation-and-renewables drive.
It was the energy crises of the 1970s that convinced the neoliberals
that the world is now an interdependent economic unit, to which they
responded by ardently supporting free trade, in the face of increasing
pressure to protect American markets from foreign goods.

But tax, energy, and trade policies, as well as the larger, comprehensive subjects that form the bulk of neoliberal concerns—human
capital, military reform, and industrial policies—are not ends in themselves. Rather, they are manifestations of neoliberalism's three underlying themes—themes that contravene, in many ways, traditional liberalism's foundations in centralization, macroeconomics, and interest-
group politics:

> *Investment:* The method by which the economic pie that graces
> every neoliberal's favorite metaphor is made to grow larger, and
> which is used as a foil for the "redistribution" that characterized
> the liberal past.
> *Appropriate technology:* The belief that no one rigid system
> will serve to meet all goals, and that programmatic flexibility is
> the key to efficiency. Decentralization, microeconomic measure-
> ment, and use of market forces are significant manifestations—
> they might even be called appropriate political technologies.
> *Cooperation:* A sense of community—between nations, be-
> tween sectors (labor, management, government), and even in the
> workplace—is the most effective means of achieving growth and

equity. It replaces the antagonism and interest-group methodology of traditional liberalism.

But will it play? The overt pragmatism of the neoliberals will undoubtedly be crucial. Children of the fifties, under the political and stylistic thrall of John F. Kennedy, their first *real* President, the new liberals are cool. "All of us," Gary Hart, who managed George McGovern's disastrous 1972 presidential campaign, said in 1981, "are of a generation that, even though it is passionately involved, is not overly passionate. I worked for George McGovern because I was against the war. I never walked in a parade, never carried a sign, never broke a window. To end the war, you go out and organize the precincts and elect the President who'll end it. You don't demonstrate."

Hart's comment underscores the neoliberal style even as it ignores the role of passionate public action in ending the war and accomplishing social change in general. There are no bleeding hearts among the neoliberals. Coming from society's upper reaches, they believe that negotiation, cooperation, and organization can solve our problems. Hence the neoliberals' decidedly national perspective. They firmly believe that there exists such a creature as the national interest, something that, like a Platonic form, has a structure and a coherence unto itself and is separate from smaller group interests. "We have to start with a vision of where we want the country to be and then try to articulate that to people in broad terms and not fall back on interest-group politics," said Missouri's Dick Gephardt, voicing a perceived failure of the Carter presidency. "The last election showed that most people are not in a group, or if they are, they have a sense of the nation as a whole that is more important to them than their allegiance to that group."

In pragmatic terms, the neoliberals can justifiably state that interest-group politics has been disastrous for the Democrats and for the nation. Yet on this vision the neoliberals could well founder. Although many of them are skillful politicians, they will be in serious trouble if they fail to recognize the growing power of blacks in the political process, the rise of an influential Hispanic electorate, the demands of women, and the fears of organized labor—just four of the interest groups whose concerns do not, in some instances, mesh with the neoliberal viewpoint.

And yet, political necessity has a way of integrating political tendencies. Just two years after cynics questioned whether the new liberals comprised anything other than a minor debating society within the

Democratic Party, international trade burst forth as a major issue. The early front-runner for the party's 1984 presidential nomination, former Vice President Walter Mondale, was forced to vacillate between support for protectionism and advocacy of free trade, to protect both his vulnerable labor flank *and* his political tradition, before finally revealing himself as an ardent protectionist. Japan's industrial policy, which few outside the neoliberal ranks had heard of prior to 1980, was by 1982 front-page news and the subject of several best-sellers. Entrepreneurs, never a concern of politicians, flexed their political muscles in Massachusetts and California. High technology, not a mainstream issue when the crises of Lockheed and Chrysler engulfed us, emerged as *the* issue in economic growth. Education, which had virtually disappeared as a policy issue, reappeared with vigor in 1983, crowding our newspapers as various public and private bodies predicted dire economic consequences unless we reform our schools. Teddy Kennedy, the epitome of traditional liberalism, in a 1982 speech at the Democrats' midterm convention declared his support for "a new industrial policy," "a new and simpler tax system," "investment in basic industry, high technology, and microchips," and "invest[ment] in people, in human capital." Out of the dissension of 1980 emerged the Democrats' partial consensus in 1984. And soon, perhaps, official government policy.

So if neoliberalism causes strife within the Democratic Party, perhaps there's value to it. It was, after all, Franklin Roosevelt—a saint for *all* Democrats—who, when asked why liberals often fought bitterly among themselves while conservatives sat in serene agreement, said, "There are many ways of going forward, but only one way of standing still."

PART TWO

Realities

"NEW REALITIES" is the latest platitude in American politics. Paul Tsongas, in *The Road from Here,* labels his chapters "Reality Number One," "Reality Number Two," and so on; the first chapter of James Fallows' *National Defense* is "Realities." Although overused, the term "new realities" nevertheless indicates a remarkable consensus on the part of neoliberal politicians and pundits on the shape of the American economy and the look of contemporary society. By implication, they accuse traditional liberals of ministering to an America that no longer exists, a high-volume, mass-production economy. The neoliberals define *their* new world in four ways: a world in which growth is a necessary precondition to social justice; a world in which small economic units constitute the locus of growth; a world in which information and new technologies drive economic growth; and a world become an interconnected economic unit through the influence of the new technologies. If all politics is a reaction, then the neoliberals are reacting specifically to this postindustrial paradigm.

The concept of "paradigm shifts" occurs throughout the neoliberals' discourses on the new reality of postindustrialism. The notion of paradigm shifts, first formulated by historian James Bryant Conant, the president of Harvard, in the 1940s, was adapted and popularized by Thomas S. Kuhn in *The Structure of Scientific Revolutions.* Kuhn taught under Conant, and his book, published in 1962, became the seminal text in the relatively new field of philosophy of science. From Kuhn's interpretation of change in the scientific understanding of the world, neoliberal thinkers have extrapolated a theory of political transition. So pervasive was Kuhn's influence on social thought that his book was cited no less than seven times in the *Harvard Law Review* in the academic year 1981–82.

Kuhn defined paradigms as "universally recognized scientific achievements that for a time provide model problems and solutions to a community of practitioners." Accepted paradigms are first challenged, then thrown into turmoil, by anomalous discoveries. When the weight of the new evidence becomes so burdensome, when "external conditions . . . help to transform a mere anomaly into a source of acute crisis," in Kuhn's words, a new, emerging paradigm is accepted, replacing the old. Often as not, a social upheaval attends the process.

Whether or not Kuhn ever intended his theory of paradigm shifts to be applied to politics, the neoliberals embrace it; they believe that the pace of scientific progress has so changed the way the world works that the old industrial model must now be discarded, and with it the politics of both New Deal liberalism and traditional conservatism. Their challenge to the left and the right is predicated on acceptance of a new postindustrial paradigm. They see a transition from the high-volume mass-production economy of the industrial era to an economy based on information and high technology. This shift has transformed the world from independent national economic units to an interdependent global economy.

From this new paradigm emerges the key concept of the new liberalism. "One of the great realities of the 1980s," Colorado's Governor Lamm stated in 1982, "is that the economic pie is not growing." This revival of the doctrine that economic growth is a necessary condition for social justice—a reversal of the tenet that for the past generation held that the continuation of growth was secure—is a turning point in the history of American liberalism.

CHAPTER 5

Growth in an Era of Limits

ON JANUARY 19, 1977, the "era of limits" ended. It happened in California—always a bellwether of national trends—where the same era had started less than a decade before. Ironically, this sea change in American social and political thought was all but ignored outside the state, for the next day, across the continent, an apparently much more significant event took place: the inauguration of Jimmy Carter as the thirty-seventh President of the United States, the first Chief Executive to profess an intuitive understanding of limits. Four years later, Carter would leave office in political disgrace, because he could not comprehend the shift in thinking that had taken place that winter day in California. Limits—to natural resources, to government effectiveness, to American mastery of the world—were indeed still a problem, perhaps the nation's most severe. But suddenly on January 19, 1977, the context began to change and growth within limits became the great American dilemma.

On that day the Dow Chemical Company announced that it was shelving plans to construct a petrochemical refinery in the Sacramento–San Joaquin delta. On the surface, there would seem to be nothing extraordinary about Dow's withdrawal; in all fifty states industrial development schemes are proposed and abandoned by both corporations and governments nearly every day, with little public comment. The Dow decision was different. It threw the administration of Governor Edmund G. Brown, Jr., into a political and ethical turmoil from which it would finally emerge only three years later. It eventually called into question some of the most cherished beliefs held by Jerry Brown and his staff of intellectuals. It resulted in immediate changes in the way the Zen governor managed the political process in his state.

Windmills, grazing sheep, and ducks dot the landscape of the corner of Solano County that sits along the upper San Francisco Bay. An hour's drive northeast of San Francisco, fifty miles southeast of Sacramento, Collinsville is a quiet little town lying at the foot of the dry, rolling Montezuma Hills, on the banks of the Sacramento River. It was here in 1975 that Dow Chemical Company thought to take advantage of the oil bounty expected upon completion of the Alaska Pipeline by constructing a superfactory, one of thirteen individual units it hoped to build on an 834-acre site it already owned, to process the Arctic crude into a variety of industrial and commercial products. Dow, which at the time had one plant operating across the river from Collinsville, in Pittsburg, planned to spend $500 million on the facility, which would be the only major petrochemical refinery west of the Mississippi. The blueprint from Dow was the first of many expected to reach the governor's office, in anticipation of the two million barrels of oil it was presumed would be flowing each day, by 1978, through the pipeline from Alaska's North Slope.

Jerry Brown came to the statehouse on the strength of two factors: his name, which also belonged to his father, a renowned liberal and one of the state's most popular governors; and his advocacy of environmental causes. It was through Brown, and particularly his ill-advised 1976 presidential campaign (launched only sixteen months after he took office), that E. F. Schumacher's phrase "era of limits" reached the popular consciousness. In a series of essays, published in book form as *Small Is Beautiful* in 1973, the British economist expounded in lucid, nontechnical language on the failure of the mass-consumption society to satisfy all of man's needs; he argued for a new system, a "Buddhist economics," that would factor quality-of-life concerns into its theories. And, inasmuch as mass consumption meant ever-increasing growth and a concomitant permanent expansion in the use of resources, he recommended that Western society apply brakes to its fetish for growth and bigness, lest the limits be reached inadvertently and tragically.

Jerry Brown was a pure disciple of Schumacher's. When, early in his first term, his approval rating coasting above 80 percent in the polls, he would oppose a national "image of self-indulgence that is becoming increasingly inappropriate and ultimately inconsistent with the survival of this country," both liberal intellectuals and bedrock

conservatives could applaud, just as they would assent to his assertion, "I see a need for a more austere and leaner life style." Although
few were able to classify the then thirty-seven-year-old governor
within traditional political lines, his ability to seem all things to all
people allowed him a freedom from criticism rare for a high-profile
public official.

His popularity gave Brown the opportunity to circumvent issues
that normally are of paramount concern to politicians. Among his
first revisions in governmental structure was the elimination of the
state's department of commerce, one of whose tasks was to recruit
companies from out of state and induce them to relocate in California. For a man who posited the need for "some new political and
economic forms" to replace the corporation, the move was not out of
character. Although Brown was never a card-carrying member of the
zero-economic-growth school, his tacit belief that, at the least, a
proper amount of growth would occur naturally (making the progressive politician's job one of controlling it, not promoting it) marked
him as a fellow traveler of the ZEGs. His assumptions about the inevitability of growth also allowed him the luxury of speaking almost
exclusively about environmental and energy concerns and resource
problems "in a certain way," conceded one of his advisers, "that may
have been construed as anti-growth."

Dow Chemical launched itself headlong into the licensing process
for its petrochemical refinery in the midst of this political climate.
Organized environmentalists, more potent politically in California
than anywhere else in the nation, geared up early to prevent the creation of what they referred to as "Jersey City West" and "a new Ruhr
Valley." The company countered by citing the 1,000 permanent jobs
it expected to create in an economically depressed county (12 percent
unemployment in 1975, when Dow conceived the project) at a time
when the state's unemployment of 9.1 percent exceeded the national
average. Hearings dragged on. At one session, Dennis Banks, the
leader of the American Indian Movement, who had earlier testified
before a joint session of five permit-granting agencies that construction of the plant would be "passing a death sentence on animal life in
the area," sat in the back of the committee room and with his followers slowly beat a dirge for wildlife on tom-toms. If California politics
is theater, the Dow episode was high drama.

Members of the governor's inner circle began to sense the need
for a shift in the administration's posture on the Dow issue. A memorandum written in the late summer of 1976 by Bill Press, Brown's

director of planning and research, urged the governor to take immediate steps to soften what many in the media and business communities were now publicly interpreting as Sacramento's anti-business attitude. Press, ironically, had joined Brown's staff after leaving the executive directorship of the Planning and Conservation League, an environmental group that opposed the project. That fall, sensing Dow's impatience—it had received only four of the sixty-five permits needed before construction could begin—and understanding that negative sentiments were welling up in public, Brown followed part of Press's advice and introduced a proposal to streamline—somewhat—the licensing process. For even this small concession, Brown—who throughout had remained officially "neutral" on the Dow plan—was excoriated by professional environmentalists. "Proposals for streamlining the bureaucracy and reviving a favorable business climate are attempts by industry to restore control over the process that no longer provides them with assured approval," proclaimed an official of Friends of the Earth.

To be sure, whether or not Dow should be allowed to construct its facility was by no means clear. The operation's purpose, to convert a petrochemical derivative into styrene, vinyl chloride, and other substances used to make such products as Styrofoam cups and latex paint, could easily pollute an area that was environmentally sensitive (the proposed site was adjacent to the 55,000-acre Suisun Marsh, the largest marsh of its kind in the forty-eight contiguous states). Dow was not entirely cooperative with the local, federal, and state agencies, arguing (with some justification) that many of the questions for which answers were required of it would force the company to tip its hand to competitors. As a result of its reticence, Dow was accused of stonewalling.

But Dow's impatience with the licensing process was also valid. A 1975 report by an independent consulting firm had cited California's tangled regulatory procedures as a prime factor in what it called the state's poor business climate. The criticisms, however, were scattered and relatively muted. So, despite the nagging feeling in Sacramento that things were not proceeding as smoothly as they might, no air of crisis set in. Dow was even approached by members of Brown's staff and asked to donate $1,000 to a Save the Whales Day extravaganza the governor's office was sponsoring. (The request, of which Brown had no knowledge, was withdrawn when it hit the press.)

It was the calm that had prevailed over the entire matter that made the shock so severe when, on January 19, 1977, Dow withdrew.

The company's statement was measured and simple: Two years and $4 million for four of sixty-five permits was too much for too little. "While our studies indicate that west coast demand for our projects remains strong, our supply of capital has its limits," said Ray Brubaker, general manager of Dow's western division. "Dow has to act now to properly locate and develop the facilities necessary to meet those demands in the future." He refused to criticize the governor and, in fact, delivered what might even be considered slight praise. "We recognize that many efforts have been made by Governor Edmund G. Brown, Jr., and others to streamline California licensing procedures," said Brubaker. "However, the permitting process for new facilities has proved to be so involved and expensive that, for the time being at least, it is impractical to continue with this project."

Environmental activists reacted with approval. "It was a victory for environmentalists in the sense that Dow wasn't able to snow the state," said a representative of the Planning and Conservation League. But Dow's decision, which meant the loss of an expected 1,000 construction jobs as well as 1,000 full-time positions, tossed the Brown administration into a maelstrom, for the reaction of the public, the media, and the business community was immediate and severe. The president of the California Association of Manufacturers said he hoped the Dow situation would serve notice to the governor and the legislature "that they've got to do something about the regulatory process." A local newspaper editorialized against the "environmentalists vs. others" contest the conservation groups promoted; the paper accused the Sierra Club of engaging in the technique of the Big Lie and fomenting a "them vs. us syndrome, with 'profit' the prevailing dirty word." Jerry Brown, charged the paper, was the environmentalists' "foremost champion." The assemblyman from Concord, like the governor a Democrat, whose district would have included the Dow facility, declared that "red tape and bureaucracy are killing business . . . I just hope [Brown has] got the message now." Criticism grew as the weeks passed. At a California Labor Federation–sponsored conference, union leaders, one after another, accused Brown to his face of being a "no-growther."

Coming so shortly after his unsuccessful presidential fling and only a year before the start of his gubernatorial reelection campaign, the no-growth accusations scared Brown. Although he had personally interceded on Dow's behalf, and despite the fact that California's purportedly bad business climate was largely the result of problems that had arisen during the administration of the previous governor, Ronald

Reagan, Brown changed his public posture virtually overnight. He continued the legislative process of simplifying the procedure for obtaining development permits, although with public flourishes heretofore uncharacteristic of him. At his urging, the state assembly passed, 68 to 1, a bill setting an eighteen-month deadline for approval of licenses by state agencies. He created an Office of Business Development in the Business and Transportation Agency. He authorized, for the first and only time during his tenure, the printing of a button at state expense. He wore the button, which read "California Means Business," at virtually every public appearance through his 1978 reelection drive. "When that button came out, you knew a nerve had been touched," a close adviser recalled. "Jerry Brown hadn't done anything that brazenly public-relations conscious since he'd come into office."

But it was not entirely a public relations effort. Through the Dow problem, Brown recognized that public policy could be fragmented by inefficient management. The composition of the agencies with jurisdiction over industrial development projects guaranteed conflict and delay; one was made up of gubernatorial appointees with fixed terms, another's members served at the governor's pleasure, still another even contained *Republican* officials.

Most important, Jerry Brown began to understand that contemporary liberal values, such as those which sought to protect land, animals, and people from the ravages of pollution, needed to mesh with other, traditional liberal value. It mattered little that Brown may have been more of a hero than a goat in the Dow situation, or that Dow may actually have been an environmentally unsound project. Dow's withdrawal instigated a shift in one man's—one prominent young progressive Democrat's—public demeanor and private thinking. When, barely three months after the Dow debacle, Brown told reporters that his anti-red-tape bill "recognizes that the environment is the essential bottom line to economic growth," and followed up by saying that the "objectives of both economic growth and environmental protection *could* be met," he was making what was, for him, a revolutionary statement. Jerry Brown had never explicitly spoken about economic growth before.

What did it mean? It represented the end of the environmentalists' domination of Calfornia politics. And it indicated a turning point in Brown's attitude toward business and in his relation with the business community. From that time forward, it was possible to hear him begin listing pro-business stands he had taken by saying, "Since Dow, I . . ."

But above all, it signified the end of the era of limits. In the aftermath of Dow, Jerry Brown saw that the term had been twisted into defining an unpalatable strategy of no-growth in an age of decline. That was politically unwise. Moreover, the concept was faulty: no-growth meant no jobs, and with Gerald Ford leaving a legacy of 7.5 percent unemployment as he departed the presidency, neither growth nor jobs could be taken for granted anymore.

This turning point in Jerry Brown's career coincided roughly with a rethinking process in which other young Democrats were also engaged. At the top of their agenda was a pressing question: How to resolve the political implications, the ethical significance, and the technical difficulties of economic growth in an age of resource limitations?

In the three decades following the end of World War II, growth all but vanished from the liberal agenda. Its disappearance was a three-stage process. In the immediate aftermath of the war, with peacetime prosperity returning to America, liberals worshiped the great god Growth. In the fifties, as growth began to seem inevitable, liberals grew complacent. Finally, in the late sixties, with the Vietnam War spreading antagonism through the liberal left, growth was deemed the root of the country's problems and was directly opposed.

Liberal journalist Jack Newfield, writing at the height of the decade-long domestic turmoil over Vietnam and civil rights that had already toppled one President and would shortly depose another, dated the breakdown of liberalism to the 1950s, when the Democratic Party was captured by intellectuals who sought to shift the focus of progressivism from its classic emphasis. "Since only 'pockets of poverty' remained, the next great question facing liberals was the 'quality of civilization,' " wrote Newfield in 1971, with thinly veiled contempt for the "false premises" of the ideology. He continued:

> They argued that the new issue confronting liberalism was identity and fulfillment in an affluent mass society. . . . Liberals have become absolute geniuses at inventing fads and fashions to evade [the] fundamental question of wealth and poverty. They have made ecology, the abolition of the House Un-American Activities Committee, the admission of mainland China to the United Nations, busing to achieve school

integration, better TV programming—almost *anything* else—their central concern in their efforts to avoid facing up to a question the Populists had put first on the agenda of justice.

The seeds of the attitude Newfield identified were planted in 1947, when a group of 250 prominent liberals, primarily academics and intellectuals, founded Americans for Democratic Action. The initial impetus behind the ADA's formation was the impending third-party presidential candidacy of former Vice President Henry A. Wallace, who claimed to be flying the true liberal flag, but whose Progressive Party was riddled with Communists. Gradually, the ADA became the leading organization of liberalism.

One of the ADA's most distinguished spokesmen was Arthur M. Schlesinger, Jr. The recipient of the 1946 Pulitzer Prize in history, Schlesinger firmly divided the liberal creed into two distinct categories, qualitative liberalism and quantitative liberalism. Writing in 1956 in *The Reporter* magazine, the prominent center-left journal, he posited the need for "a new liberalism, addressed to the miseries of an age of abundance." In unequivocal language, he counted the riddle of economic growth as solved. "The central problems of our time are no longer problems of want and privation," he proclaimed in his essay "The Challenge of Abundance," "and the central sources of discontent are no longer, as they were in the 1930s, economic in character."

Schlesinger outlined the recently resolved problems of quantitative liberalism as the provision of food for the hungry, shelter for the homeless, and employment for the jobless. Qualitative liberalism was comprised not of solutions to poverty, want, and unemployment, but of responses to inadequacies in education, medical care, opportunities for minorities, civil liberties, and a host of other concerns to which attention could be paid now that the other fight had been won. Schlesinger's distinctions among liberal interests revealed a firm disjunction between progressive economic and social policies. The cleavage was most visibly manifest in the liberals' disdain toward business and their adoration of government.

The Schlesinger viewpoint was rather elegantly echoed shortly afterward when Professor John Kenneth Galbraith of Harvard, who came to personify the liberal "New Economics," published *The Affluent Society* (1958). Galbraith labeled the urgency of production a "myth." He argued that the belief that growth was a fundamental, necessary part of a free society, something to which attention need always be paid, was simply mistaken. America had inadvertently become a society of abundance, he declared, and the emphasis on ever more growth and production gave rise to more problems than it solved. The incessant increase in production created more demand, which in turn was the engine of inflation and instability in society. *This* was public enemy number one. Perhaps, mused Galbraith, a little unemployment—cushioned with better benefits, of course—mightn't be a bad thing if it curbed these excesses. Work, in his opinion, had little to recommend itself per se, especially in a society where abundance was assured.

Ironically, Galbraith and Schlesinger were two of the bona fide intellectuals who gave early support to the presidential candidacy of John Kennedy. Of the ADA, Kennedy had said in a 1953 interview, shortly after taking his seat in the U.S. Senate, that he was "not comfortable with those people." Most of "those people" reciprocated in 1960, supporting Adlai Stevenson's third, half-hearted stab at the nomination. But with Schlesinger drafting speeches and Galbraith acting as one of his floor managers at the 1960 Democratic Convention, JFK won the nomination. He eventually charmed the intellectual wing of the party, drawing more than three dozen ADA members into his administration.

Economic growth was very much a part of John Kennedy's thinking. The young President had to contend with a recession that had begun in the late fifties, and to this end he initiated a series of expansion-oriented measures, notably the tax cut passed in 1962. It wasn't until the Johnson years that the assumption set in that the growth problem had really been licked. This new complacency about the inevitability of economic growth could be gleaned from the Great Society's kickoff statement, delivered by Lyndon Johnson to a crowd of 90,000 attending the commencement exercises at the University of Michigan on May 22, 1964:

> Your imagination, your initiative, and your indignation will determine whether we build a society where progress is a servant of our needs, or a society where old values and new visions are buried under unbridled growth. [The Great Society] is a place where leisure is a welcome chance to build and reflect, not a feared cause of boredom and restlessness. It is a place where the city of man serves not only the needs of the body and the demands of commerce, but the desire for beauty and the hunger for community.

And then, raising the issue that would be at the center of liberalism from the mid-sixties on, Johnson proclaimed the Great Society as "a place where men are more concerned with the quality of their goals than the quantity of their goods."

By LBJ's presidency, Keynesian economics, introduced from England during Franklin Roosevelt's administration and crystallized in the 1950s by economists Paul Samuelson, Arthur Okun, and Walter Heller, held not only the high ground, but the only ground. Even the Republican administrations that would guide America until 1977 refused to confront the possibility that Keynesian economic policy was no longer sufficient to guarantee growth. Far from it, they locked into place a system that virtually assured a period of stagnation for the American economy. Despite the intermittent recessions that began in late 1969, Keynesian macroeconomic manipulation remained fundamentally unquestioned.

During the Nixon years, a tactical change was instituted in the way liberal goals were met, based on the belief that expansion, if temporarily at a halt, would nevertheless resume. Gradually, and with few noticing, the Nixon Administration, still caught up in the theory of abundance, dropped education (one of the Great Society's predominant concerns) as the means to achieve equality and substituted transfer payments. Payments to individuals exploded under the presidencies of Richard Nixon and Gerald Ford. In 1966 they totaled 28.1 percent of the federal budget, and by 1971 had mounted to 38.8 percent, having more than doubled during the five-year period to $82.1 billion. During the succeeding five years under Nixon and Ford, the figure more than doubled again, to $183.9 billion. In 1976, for the first time, transfers took up more than half the federal budget. Meanwhile, during the twenty years 1956–76, all other grants to states and localities, including educational grants, grew only from 2.8 percent to 10.4 percent of the budget. The reason for the transfer boom was the indexing of entitlements to the cost of living. Only sparingly used in the 1960s, indexing began to be institutionalized during Richard Nixon's tenure. The federal outlay in constant 1980 dollars for indexed entitlements jumped from $4.8 billion in 1968, the last year of Lyndon Johnson's term of office, to $119.5 billion in 1977, the first year of Jimmy Carter's presidency.

Since Roosevelt's day, transfers had stood as an adjunct to the liberal agenda. In Roosevelt's mind, all groups were considered interest groups and included in the grand coalition, ranging from Pullman porters to corporate chieftains, as long as they were willing to cooperate with the New Deal. To FDR, the groups were cogs in the great machine that produced economic prosperity; in other words, the group interests were subsumed into the national interest, the plight of the national economy (and then of world stability) allowing for a happy marriage of the two. Under Nixon and Ford, the forty-year-old group imperative still existed—something *had* to be done about blacks, something *had* to be done about the elderly—but since prosperity was no longer a serious issue, the buying off of the various groups became an end in itself, rather than the means it had been. The appeasement of group interests could be accomplished most efficiently via transfer payments. By the mid-1970s, qualitative issues and entitlements were the ruling liberal concerns. But as more slices were cut from the economic pie, few noticed that the pie itself was shrinking.

Even the young activists of the New Left failed to discern the economic contraction. This was the sixties' other cast, which grew in opposition to the dominant liberalism of the day. They found great fault with the Johnson/Nixon guns-and-butter mentality. Children of affluence, they did not doubt that the country could afford both guns and butter, but they were obsessed with the morality of the issue. The war exploited people, but many businesses—the "war machine"— profited. These same businesses exploited our natural resources. Therefore, said the left, business is to blame for America's problems. The movement countered with its own ethic, one of no-growth.

As America entered the 1970s an anti-science attitude flourished on the left. The same technology that was used to defoliate and destroy was driving the gross national product ever upward. Science and technology were components of the Vietnam War; they were also components of productivity growth, and growth irreparably harmed the environment. On all counts, then, science itself, and research and development, were bad. As the first Earth Day dawned on April 14, 1970, heretical thoughts began to form in the minds of the movement's followers and their liberal confederates. Perhaps economic growth, as well as its elements, ought to be stopped. Former *Harper's* editor John Fischer, an adviser to Adlai Stevenson during the latter's presidential forays, typified the rapidly coalescing view of the day. "Our prime national goal, I am now convinced," he wrote in 1970, "should be to reach Zero Growth Rate as soon as possible. Zero growth in people, in GNP, and in our consumption of everything. That is our only hope of attaining a stable ecology: that is, of halting the deterioration of the environment on which our lives depend." He added a swipe at science. "Every time you look at one of the marvels of modern technology," he declared, "you find a by-product—unintended, unpredictable, and often lethal. . . . Moreover, technology works best on things nobody really needs, such as collecting moon rocks or building supersonic transport planes."

The peak of no-growthism occurred with the publication of *The Limits to Growth* in February 1972. This thin report, funded by a consortium of businessmen and intellectuals known as the Club of Rome, and prepared at the Massachusetts Institute of Technology using the innovative techniques of computer modeling and systems analysis, received front-page coverage in America's leading newspapers and generated thousands of column inches of commentary. The reason for the attention paid it was the perceived scientific proof for its dire assertion that all economic growth must stop immediately. Its conclusions were three:

(1) If the present growth trends in world population, industrialization, pollution, food production and resource depletion continue unchanged, the limits to growth on this planet will be reached sometime within the next one hundred years. The most probable result will be a rather sudden and uncontrollable decline in both population and industrial capacity.

(2) It is possible to alter these growth trends and to establish a condition of ecological and economic stability that is sustainable far into the future. The state of global equilibrium could be designed so that the basic material needs of each person on earth are satisfied and each person has an equal opportunity to realize his individual human potential.

(3) If the world's people decide to strive for this second outcome rather than the first, the sooner they begin working to attain it, the greater will be their chances of success.

Although the Club of Rome report was merely the latest in a series of products from what had become a sort of cottage industry of futurology, none of the others had employed computers and sophisticated analytical methodology to "prove" their predictions. What's more, *The Limits to Growth* used these techniques to assess two problems, pollution and resource depletion, that were accorded nary a mention in the two best-known "futurology" treatises of the 1960s, Herman Kahn and Anthony J. Wiener's *The Year 2000* (1967) and Dennis Gabor's *Inventing the Future* (1964).

Much of the commentary occasioned by the Club of Rome's report was critical, faulting the limitations of its analytical mechanics. In addition, there was little that was new in the study—it could be interpreted as yet another in a long series of scientific doomsday scenarios that dated back to Thomas Malthus and David Ricardo. Nevertheless, the alarm sounded in this and other reports that appeared at the time perplexed and worried many influential members of the intelligentsia. The liberal community reacted with proper gravity. At a symposium at the Smithsonian Institution on March 2, 1972, Secretary of Health, Education and Welfare Elliot Richardson, a liberal Republican, declared *The Limits to Growth* "too thoughtful and significant" to ignore. Senator Claiborne Pell of Rhode Island, a Democrat, wanted more. "You presume man is rational, but man is an emotional creature," he told the report's authors. "How do you convert this into an action program?"

In short, *The Limits to Growth* was the culmination of the split between quantitative and qualitative liberalism. The quality of life was now so severely threatened that, many liberals concluded, growth must not only be deemphasized in order to save the planet, but halted entirely.

But even as the no-growth dogma took hold, there were signs that some observers were unhappy with it. Taylor Branch, a graduate student at Princeton's Woodrow Wilson School for Public and International Affairs, kept a diary during a summer spent as a voting-rights worker in the Deep South. He turned his diary into a policy recommendation, required as part of his course work, which was subsequently published in the *Washington Monthly,* an early seedbed of neoliberalism. Branch told of meeting an old, poor, black dirt farmer named John Saddler in rural Georgia, and of being repelled by the poverty in which he lived:

> The environmentalists would have us slow down, be wary of new products, and shun the compulsive need for growth and progress. . . . I I tell the story of John Saddler as a caution to those who would sacrifice economic growth for other values—such as a clean environment and a less cut-throat attitude toward other people. These values are good and must be affirmed, but there must also be a better economic life for people like John Saddler.

Branch's recommendation, ignored at the time, but quickly to become a staple of the *Washington Monthly,* was a reaffirmation of a long-standing American tradition. "The challenge—to have economic growth without environmental or ethical damage—is a personal one," wrote Branch. "We could each absorb the message of the new agrarians, and perhaps even *discover a new entrepreneurship, creating enterprises that give people enriching work without making the world ugly or dangerous*" [italics added].

Out of such mild proposals there slowly arose a new economic vision. Such traditional liberal concerns as income distribution and education were fused with the new issues of resource conservation and pollution control and such non-liberal notions as using social and economic incentives and disincentives to promote different kinds of expansion. All this was combined into an emerging theory of *qualitative growth,* a union of the two previously antithetical positions that some neoliberal thinkers would label "holistic economics."

But the no-growth doctrine had left its mark on the Democratic Party. By the mid-seventies the Democrats were the party of no-growth. Their reawakening was slow. Even as more progressive liberals began to disavow no-growthism, the general public was just catching on to it. This would leave an impression difficult for liberals in general and Democratic liberals in particular to shake, and damaging to their political goals. As Jerry Brown would discover in 1977, people are slow to forget the implications of fads that intellectuals replace with such alacrity.

But, ultimately, as Jimmy Carter took office in January 1977, new ideas had already begun to take hold in the minds of younger members of the liberal fraternity. The ideas were integrally connected to each other and arose from the new America of the post-Vietnam years. Politically, this new set of progressives now understood, growth had to remain part of the liberal program, but the natural limits to resources, and the limits to the ability of the ecosystem to absorb the products of economic expansion, had to be taken into account. As the seventies eased into the eighties, statements that would have been considered counterrevolutionary seven years before were pronounced by progressive politicians and by the thinkers from whom they received their ideas. Jerry Brown labeled the belief that environmental values are opposed to economic values "an archaic myth," less than a decade after the myth had first been propounded. Younger liberals, like Brown, who had inherited from their ideological elders an anti-business bias, began to shed this attitude, recognizing the intimate and necessary connection between business and growth. Colorado Senator Gary Hart would assert in a policy paper, "We must redefine the traditional economic questions"—which he said were posed as a series of "false choices" between inflation and recession, government control and the free market, and technological progress and jobs—"if we are to solve the problem of growth." And in one of the most widely read economics texts of the new era, Lester Thurow of MIT would declare, " 'Small is beautiful' sounds beautiful, but it does not exist because it does not jibe with human nature. Man is an acquisitive animal whose wants cannot be satisfied." Liberals who ten years before would have scoffed at such statements had by 1980 adopted Thurow as a mentor.

This new growth ethic would become the foundation of neoliberalism.

CHAPTER 6

The Business of America

CHARLES PETERS TOOK the new reality of growth in an era of limits to its next logical step: if growth was necessary to liberal values, then liberals must learn to esteem those who provide growth. In 1969 Peters founded a magazine in part to propound this principle and subsequently trained a cadre of journalists who shared his beliefs. His protégés have gone on to staff the top editorial positions at several important national magazines. As a result, neoliberalism looks very much like a political movement generated by the press. And, in fact, it was Peters who, in February 1979, at the tenth anniversary celebration for the *Washington Monthly,* invented for his colleagues and their guests the word that now defines them and their views. Late that evening, Peters marched up to the podium and gleefully announced to the crowd, "We're the neoliberals! We're the neoliberals!"

Peters felt the need to characterize his philosophy himself at least in part as a defense against inaccurate representations. Some people were calling him a conservative, a label he found repellent. Bureaucracy was his special nemesis; it was bureaucracy, in both the public and private sector, that stood in the way of progress. Because of his attacks on bureaucracy, which took the form primarily of salvos against big government, inefficient government, and wasteful government, he had come to be identified as *anti*-government. Peters took umbrage with the description. "A neoconservative is someone who took a long hard look at where liberalism went wrong, and became a conservative," he would quip. "A neoliberal is someone who took that same hard look at what was wrong with liberalism, and decided to

68

correct it, but still retain his liberal values." The main thing Peters wanted to correct was the liberal ardor for government *to the exclusion* of business, the businessman, the investor, and the investment.

"We think," he said in 1981, "that you have to have values that encourage the entrepreneur, values that make the entrepreneur more important than the kid who goes to *law school.*" He pronounced the final two words with contempt. "Because the horrible thing that's happened with ninety percent of our bright young kids of the 1970s is they've gone to law school. This is outrageous! This is frivolous! Compared to something that would create the new enterprise that would make the country move again.

"You've got to emphasize the importance of encouraging the *value* of the guy who starts the business, of the enterprise that creates jobs, that creates better ways of doing things," Peters continued. "Now today, a guy gets out of law school, or he goes to the high-class business school"—more contempt—"and what happens? What does he want to do? He wants to be a manager of one of those big companies. Or he wants to join one of those *management consultant firms!*

"That's whoring!" shouted Peters. "There's no better word for it. Lawyers and business school graduates today—and they are the best America has to offer—they are going into whoring."

Charlie Peters is one of the most easily caricatured figures in the nation's capital. He personifies the word "curmudgeon." In conversation, Peters is alternately a salesman, an ad man, and a theatrical producer—occupations which, at one time or another during his fifty-seven years, he has tried. With his West Virginia accent, Peters might sound like a country lawyer or down-home politician; he has held both those jobs as well. A state senator in Charleston in the late 1950s, he considered running for governor but instead chose to use his energies to help organize John F. Kennedy's crucial 1960 primary drive in West Virginia. Kennedy won that primary, and upon his election to the presidency he rewarded Peters with the job of director of evaluation in the newly formed Peace Corps, a post he held until 1968, when he left to start his magazine.

At times Charlie Peters resembles a tent-meeting preacher, something he has never been . . . officially. Yet the philosophy he espouses is tantamount to a religion with him. He and his disciples have long called it the Gospel.

Peters' Gospel began developing during his student days at Columbia University in the mid-1940s. The place, and the time, were important not only to his own intellectual development, but to the development of liberal ideology in the years following World War II. A hotbed of radicalism, socialism, every "ism" America housed at the time, Columbia, the most open of the country's elite colleges, was a maternity ward for young intellectuals. The hick from West Virginia was part of that group of firebrands influenced by Lionel Trilling and his critique of liberalism. Some of Peters' classmates, such as future *Commentary* editor Norman Podhoretz, would disavow their radicalism and become known more than a decade later as the "liberal anti-Communists"; still later, they would emerge as the neoconservatives. Forced by Trilling to scrutinize the foibles of American liberalism, Peters and Podhoretz would arrive at many similar conclusions. Both, for instance, decided that leaving policy decision-making to an elite group of professionals trained in the techniques of technocracy had contributed to the downfall of the liberal creed. But at the same time, the neoconservatives would be repelled by the countercultural movement of the 1960s, which threatened both their intellectual primacy and their role in the dominant liberal politics of the day. Peters, himself a member of the Johnson Administration, was, to the contrary, attracted by the romanticism of the counterculture. The neoconservatives' attacks on "big government" stemmed from their abhorrence of activism, born of their own professional success. But Peters' salvos were delivered with the same anti-technocratic bias that drove the movement.

"What went wrong with liberalism?" After John Kennedy's death, the subject became Charlie Peters' consuming passion. He had one of Washington's unique jobs; his position as the Peace Corps' director of evaluation not only afforded him the opportunity to witness the genesis of a bureaucracy, but also to cut through that bureaucracy to discover what was actually happening "beyond the Beltway," in Washington parlance. Some of the Corps' young volunteers, who would go on to become neoliberalism's elected vanguard, had the same first hand experience, but Peters was one of the few individuals who could return to Washington from stations throughout the world and relate what he had *seen* in the field to what was being *said* in the offices and boardrooms at 806 Connecticut Avenue, N.W. He realized then that a centralized bureaucracy was not always the best watchdog of liberal values.

Watching the transformation of government subsequent to Kennedy's assassination—he would call the President's death "the main event in my career"—he saw what he considered a "vulgarized New Deal" put into operation. Peters was not starry-eyed about JFK;

much older than the high school and college kids who first believed in the power of public service from listening to Kennedy's inaugural address, he knew from personal experience how cold and calculating the President could be, and how cynical were many of the men surrounding him. But Peters admired JFK's respect for businessmen. Kennedy understood businessmen, believed they had a role to play, but—thought Peters—he could be realistic, in a way Republicans were not, about *bad* business people, and about the natural tendency of too many business types to ignore the social effects of their activities. Over at Peace Corps headquarters, Charlie Peters knew that you couldn't keep spitting on the people who created the wealth to pay for social programs.

As the LBJ years drew to a close, Peters felt that Roosevelt's New Deal, the programs and philosophy on which he had been weaned, the experiment-upon-experiment platform that effected a liberalism that saved capitalism, had evolved into an insulated and entrenched government bureaucracy that only mouthed the sentiments of the liberalism he cherished. Peters, who looks, acts, and sounds as if he stepped out of a Frank Capra movie, took a decidedly Capra-esque step. He quit his job, mortgaged his home, and started a magazine.

The original *Washington Monthly* depended heavily upon big names; its initial contributors included such Washington veterans as Hugh Sidey, Bill Moyers, Richard Rovere, and Russell Baker (Rovere and Baker were the first two people Peters asked to serve on his magazine's board). But Peters soon saw the tack would not work. For the money he could pay, the stars of journalism would never turn their best material over to him. A year into his journal's existence, Peters made a decision that would have a profound effect on American journalism in the eighties: he decided to hire young people, kids with no experience, to put together his magazine.

Although the *Washington Monthly*'s circulation has never topped 40,000, and its staff size has never exceeded a handful, today's print media are awash with its alumni. Michael Kinsley cut his teeth writing for the *Monthly* while still a student at Harvard, and became the youngest editor in the history of *The New Republic*. He later succeeded Lewis Lapham as editor of *Harper's,* where he guided a stable that included political writers Tom Bethell and Taylor Branch, both former *Monthly* editors. Soon, Robert M. Kaus, also late of Peters' staff, would join *Harper's* as political editor. In 1983 Kinsley returned to *The New Republic* to take over the "TRB" column from the venerable Richard Strout. Meanwhile at *Texas Monthly,* the Austin-based journal that helped to stimulate the regional-magazine trend of the 1970s, executive editor Nicholas Lemann and senior editor Joseph Nocera claimed *Washington Monthly* roots. Lemann later went to *The Atlantic*. William Broyles, who founded the Texas magazine in 1972, thought of himself as a disciple of Peters; in 1982 Broyles took over the helm at *Newsweek,* bringing onto his staff former *Monthly* editors Walter Shapiro and Jonathan Alter. (Broyles resigned his position in early 1984.) Suzannah Lessard of *The New Yorker* was another of Peters' first generation of youthful slaves (for twelve years Peters did not raise the salary of his editors beyond $800 a month). And the man who brought the military reform movement before the public in his book *National Defense,* James Fallows, is yet another *Washington Monthly* graduate. By 1980, the hierarchy of opinion-shapers was mightily staffed with individuals who had daily listened to the Gospel according to Charlie Peters.

It was Peters' desire to make the *Monthly* the de facto department of evaluation for the entire U.S. government. Although much of the doctrine, in Michael Kinsley's words, "has become the conventional wisdom," it cannot successfully withstand point-by-point scrutiny without seeming petty: Trident submarines are not as effective as small subs; the unions are killing the public schools; the Peace Corps is wonderful; the whistle blower should be honored; bring back the draft. It is an odd mixture of hometown homilies, economics, political science, and management philosophy, which James Fallows describes as "like a big ball of wax with an arm sticking out here, a boot sticking out at another end, a lead pipe coming out another angle." The importance of the Gospel, according to Fallows, is greater than the sum of its parts. "Charlie thinks that pragmatic solutions are great, as far as they'll go," he said, "but when they fail, you have to look toward something deeper."

Peters' Gospel, in other words, is rooted in values. While many of today's neoliberal politicians have used a form of economic analysis to arrive at their picture of the world, Charlie Peters' analysis is strictly moralistic. Yet his conclusions match the other neoliberals'. Peters' fundamental tenet—if you start with a world of basically decent people, you must place great emphasis on the organizations in which they work and the circumstances of their daily lives that shape the way they think and act—translates into a harsh critique of both public and private organizations, inasmuch as they serve to distort essential liberal values. Boiled down, the *Washington Monthly* philosophy extols cooperation over confrontation. It blames artificial class distinctions, created by our society's esteem for credentials, for fomenting institutionalized confrontation, and thus argues in favor of a stronger educational system and compulsory national service as a way of breaking down credentialism. Peters attacks labor unions' rigidity and their antipathy toward benefits that are tied to productivity as a reason for the nation's economic decline. And he faults a business class rife with lawyers and MBAs—more credentials—for focusing on short-term profits rather than on long-term growth.

The policies Peters saw developing in the 1960s discouraged individual initiative, public and private, and encouraged the individual to subsume himself within the protective confines of the group. All the scorn heaped upon businessmen in the sixties and seventies caused an exodus from entrepreneurialism, a subject that has become a cause célèbre of the *Washington Monthly*. "What always got to me," reflected Peters at a dinner for neoliberals hosted by *Esquire* magazine in mid-1981, "was the snotty attitude of our liberal friends about anybody who was in business."

Not only have liberals been cavalier in their treatment of business, say the neoliberals, but both they and the conservatives have ministered to the wrong kind of business. Taylor Branch's and Charlie Peters' insistence on a "new entrepreneurialism" presaged the neoliberals' embrace of small business.

The liberal economists of the post–World War II era saw prosperity emanating strictly from the large corporation. "The methodological promise of the second half of the twentieth century is the management of organized complexity," predicted Harvard sociologist Daniel Bell in *The Coming of Post-Industrial Society*. It was a conclusion readily accepted by the preeminent "New Economist" of the sixties, John Kenneth Galbraith. Galbraith's 1967 book, *The New Industrial State* (originally begun a decade earlier as a companion piece to *The Affluent Society*), is a paean to the organization, a ringing annunciation of the final triumph of the hero of the fifties, the Organization Man, over that wheezing relic of the American past, the entrepreneur. Galbraith's message was simple: Big is beautiful. ". . . [T]he large business organization . . . alone," he wrote, "can mobilize the requisite skills" to run the American economy.

Galbraith's esteem for the organization was the logical extension of liberal ideology. The near-religious certainty that Keynesian macroeconomic manipulation—the mere "fine tuning" of fiscal and monetary policy by the federal government in a centrally planned economy—could cure depressions, ease unemployment, check inflation, and override the business cycle rested, in the end, on the acceptance of an economy comprised solely of large units. "To have, in pursuit of truth, to assert the superiority of the organization over the individual for important social tasks is a taxing prospect," wrote Galbraith. "Yet it is a necessary task." The notion that individual effort is superior to group effort Galbraith called "a cliché." Business decisions were now the province of the group, not the individual. The entrepreneur—"individualistic, ruthless, with vision, guile, and courage"—was a flickering image from the romantic past. "With the rise of the modern corporation," Galbraith wrote, "the emergence of the organization required by modern technology and planning and the divorce of the owner of the capital from control of the enterprise, the entrepreneur no longer exists as an individual person in the mature industrial enterprise." Planning of the economy in the postindustrial state would be the province instead of the government–industry "technostructure." The 1960s liberal view of business was a logical extension of the New Deal's image of an economy in which "bigness," in Arthur Schlesinger's words, "had been rendered inevitable."

Mutatis mutandis. A decade and a half after *The New Industrial State,* Senator Gary Hart would write in *A New Democracy,* "The most active, innovative, and diverse sector of the economy . . . is small business. . . . We should put our money where we can use it—within the reach of American entrepreneurs." A massive shift in thinking has occurred, one that has guided the neoliberals away from the traditional liberal acceptance of an economy comprised of large components and susceptible to simple "fine-tuning." The neoliberals acknowledge instead an economy composed of small, competing entrepreneurial entities.

The neoliberal economic reaction actually originated with E. F. Schumacher in the early seventies. His famous essay "Buddhist Economics" was styled, in part, as a rejection of Galbraith's assumptions. According to Schumacher, Galbraith and the other New Economists of the sixties failed to consider that man might be unwilling, even in an increasingly technological and complex society, to bury himself within the confines of the large industrial unit. And these economists, argued Schumacher, failed to realize that the competitive desires of the individual might render the large organization—at least the large organization with no entrepreneurial input—inefficient, unproductive, and unable to contribute to economic growth. The New

Economists, in Schumacher's words, "suffer from a metaphysical blindness, assuming that theirs is a science of absolute and invariable truths." In their attempts to alter their discipline from a social science to a pure science, they managed to eliminate all social considerations from what is, after all, a study of man, not particles.

Schumacher's criticism of the New Economics has become a principle of neoliberalism. The neoliberals believe that there are serious limitations to the standards employed by their predecessors to measure the economy's actual performance. The GNPs, GDPs, prime rates, and aggregates are a context, to be sure, but they are not the only economic measurements.

"Basically, what I think the neoliberals are doing—again, to dote on what was happening in the economics profession in the seventies—is to recognize that the 'macro' perspective was not sufficient, that we really needed to get a more 'micro' understanding of the economy," stated Robert Hamrin in 1982. Hamrin had just become Gary Hart's chief economic adviser. Earlier he had served on the staff of the Joint Economic Committee of Congress, and had written a book, *Managing Growth in the 1980s.* "Growth comes from the health of our basic industries, from the institutional entities in our society. It's not just something that flows from the Fed and the Treasury Building.

"That's also the Reagan approach," Hamrin continued. "If we just manipulate these aggregate levers, then we'll have a hunky-dory world. I thought that as economists we had left that naïve, all-sufficient macro perspective behind. And yet it comes back with a vengeance with Reagan. We have a number of realities that will challenge us in the eighties that require a more micro look at what's going on."

By taking that "micro" look, neoliberals have embraced the cause of the entrepreneur; this is the future of the economy as they see it, yet another of the new realities comprising the postindustrial paradigm. The entrepreneur has become a neoliberal icon; the high-technology entrepreneur especially has been deified.

In 1979 MITs Program on Neighborhood and Regional Change, of which David Birch is the director, published "The Job Generation Process." The paper's conclusions had an electrifying impact in top policy circles, for it gave statistical validation to a view of the American economy quite different from the picture drawn using macroeconomic data. First, Birch concluded that virtually none of the job growth in a given region is due to the movement of existing firms in and out of the area. Second, a job-loss rate of 8 percent, through the deaths and contractions of existing businesses, prevailed across the *entire* economy; a region's economic vitality is due *not* to the pace at which its businesses die or shrink, but to the rate at which they are replaced. In other words, the failure to replenish jobs through firm births, through a climate amenable to entrepreneurialism, is the critical regional difference in the United States. These conclusions were accorded validity through Birch's analysis of records of nearly six million individual businesses in the United States.

But if the conventional wisdom about "smokestack chasing"— the attempts by states and localities to lure factories and branch plants from one place to another using tax breaks and other financial incentives—was disputed by Birch's birth-and-death findings, the numbers that followed proved all the more startling. The MIT researchers discovered that between 1969 and 1976 small businesses—those with twenty or fewer employees—generated two-thirds of all the new jobs in the United States. Eighty percent of the new jobs were created in young firms, under four years old—which almost by definition tended to be small—across all regions and all sectors of the economy. The key to job creation, they found, was age as well as size. The policy implications, coming at a time when the Carter Administration was vainly attempting to stimulate America's largest, declining industries, were staggering. "The job-generating firm tends to be small," wrote Birch. "It tends to be dynamic (or unstable, depending on your viewpoint)—the kind of firm that banks feel very uncomfortable about. In short, the firms that can and do generate the most jobs are the ones that are most difficult to reach through conventional policy initiatives."

Other conclusions followed: Independent entrepreneurs account for almost 75 percent of the job replacement necessary for regional growth; small firms account for higher percentages of net new jobs in *declining* areas, providing (for instance) nearly all the new jobs in the Northeast; the most successful areas of the country are those with the highest rates of innovation *and failure*, not the lowest; and goods production accounted for only 11 percent of the net new jobs created during the 1970s, with services of one kind or another generating the other 89 percent.

Birch's reputation spread rapidly. First cited in a report to Congress in 1978 (before the publication of "The Job Generation Process") titled "The Future of Small Business in America," Birch's data were promoted ceaselessly by the Council of State Planning Agencies. A policy arm of the National Governors Association, the CSPA had independently concluded that the Carter Administration's approach to economic development—which by that time had become essentially a subsidy program for large, heavily unionized industries—was ineffective and wasteful. Birch's data supported the CSPA's position, and so during 1979–80 the organization flooded Capitol Hill with the MIT studies.

The spreading of the small-is-beautiful gospel had an incalculable effect, and a variety of political factions seized upon Birch's data. Supply-side Republican Jack Kemp of New York used the MIT research to support his push for inner-city enterprise zones, tax-free enclaves inside the country's most blighted urban areas. Some progressive Democrats, notably those involved in the Congressional Northwest-Midwest Coalition, also promoted the enterprise zone concept, and exploited Birch's numbers. The neoliberals used Birch to justify their calls for development efforts directed at the rising sectors of the economy, rather than at propping up the declining industrial sectors. One of the neoliberals, Timothy Wirth of Denver, cited Birch's work in hearings before the House Telecommunications Subcommittee, which he chairs, and which was overseeing the breakup of AT&T. Birch's research is a major element in what is now an accepted piece of Democratic Party policy, the economics platform paper co-authored by Wirth and Richard Gephardt for the House Democratic Caucus. Before 1979 there is no record of David Birch testifying on Capitol Hill. Between 1979 and 1982 "The Job Generation Process" (or subsequent refinements) was inserted into committee records no less than ten times, with Birch himself appearing in person before committees or in informal sessions with even more frequency.

The impact of Birch's work, particularly the neoliberals' acceptance that the nation's postindustrial economic growth would come via entrepreneurship, represented the first breach of the exclusively macroeconomic orientation of traditional liberal ideology. But his conclusions have not been accepted without a fight. With a great deal of hoopla, the Brookings Institution—the prestigious and influential think tank associated for several decades with liberal policymaking—announced in the spring of 1982 a study that contravened the MIT findings about new, small businesses' prominent role in job generation. Former Carter Administration officials, whose smokestack-oriented economic development policy had been challenged by some neoliberals and conservatives in Congress on the strength of Birch's data, lauded the Brookings report.

Although Brookings, after further analysis, modified its conclusions, putting them more in accord with Birch's, the dispute remained a manifestation of the breach between liberals and neoliberals, the one group allied with a big labor–big industry constituency, the other group attempting to introduce incentives for entrepreneurs and small businesses into Democratic policy. The large-business versus small-business rift is consistent with—indeed, it derives from—traditional liberals' predilection to interpret economic growth as dependent almost wholly on macroeconomic policy, as against the neoliberals' willingness to look through both macro *and* micro lenses.

Is the rift significant? In May 1983, 148 House Democrats released an economic policy statement drafted by New York liberal Richard Ottinger. Their "high production strategy to rebuild America" placed the burden of economic growth on higher federal spending and lower interest rates—a purely Keynesian path to prosperity. That the report was issued at all was curious: nine months earlier, the House Democratic Caucus had put forth a policy paper, authored by two neoliberals, emphasizing three things not even touched upon by Ottinger—entrepreneurialism, risk-taking, and small business. The Democrats, it seemed, had two "official" methods of taking care of business. But even this conflict pales in comparison to the greater divide that separated old from new liberals in the immediate aftermath of the debacle of 1980: the split between the promoters of new technology and the preservers of old industries.

CHAPTER 7

"Atari Democrats"

THE SUREST METHOD of securing lasting currency for an idea, a phrase, a joke, is to plant it over a meal in Washington, D.C.—the nation's gossip capital. Take, as evidence, the January 1982 Sunday brunch at the home of writer Margaret Carlson. Among the guests were Ross Brown, currently chief speechwriter for former Vice President Walter Mondale, then a speechwriter for Senator Gary Hart (Hart's employment of a full-time phrasemaker was considered an early signal of his presidential ambitions); *Washington Post* reporter Walter Shapiro (an alumnus of the *Washington Monthly*, more recently a *Newsweek* political writer); and Christopher Matthews, administrative assistant to House Speaker Thomas P. ("Tip") O'Neill, Jr.

They were standing in Carlson's kitchen, discussing the fascination with high technology that consumed Hart and other young Democratic officeholders, when Matthews let loose with a line that would reverberate loudly in the Democratic establishment. "You know what these people are, don't you?" he asked.

A quizzical look passed over the faces of those assembled.

Answered Matthews, "They're Atari Democrats."

Laughter.

The next day, Brown told Hart's staff of the new term. More laughter. She told Hart—he'd never heard the phrase before, and he too laughed; later, he used the joke in a speech. And by some ineluctable process, less than two months later the "Atari Democrats" were christened in print by *The New Yorker*'s Washington correspondent, Elizabeth Drew.

By later in 1982, the luster had worn from the term. High-technology companies had begun sending jobs overseas; many of the neoliberals' ideas were the objects of liberal and conservative scorn. Republican Congressman Ed Zchau, a former high-technology business executive elected in 1982 to represent California's Silicon Valley, criticized an Atari Democrat as "someone who likes playing games with the economy."

Between the laughter and the opprobrium lay one inescapable fact: the neoliberals did see the future encased in silicon, the basic stuff of microchips. Although many of those so tagged would come to regret the label "Atari Democrat" for calling up visions of computer-loving politicians waltzing through fields of transistors, blithely dismissing America's heavily unionized industrial base as a sooty relic of the past, the neoliberals' early infatuation with the high-technology economy cannot be minimized. It was the first "reality" to give them a recognizable public identity.

Paeans to a postindustrial America abound in the neoliberals' speeches and writings. "The technological revolution of the 1980s will bring about changes in our economic structure no less significant than the shift from an agrarian economy of the nineteenth century to the manufacturing economy of the twentieth century," wrote Congressmen Timothy Wirth and Richard Gephardt in an early version of the economics paper they prepared for the House Democratic Caucus. Gary Hart wrote in *his* draft economics platform, "Over the past thirty years, the U.S. economy has been undergoing a transformation as significant as the Industrial Revolution of the nineteenth century. It is shifting from an economy based primarily on heavy industry and basic manufacturing to one increasingly based on advanced technology, information, communications, and services." Or, as Jerry Brown summarized, "The new reality is that wealth and power for the indefinite future derive more from the human mind than from depletable resources."

The neoliberals' adherence to the concept of the information era did not arise originally as a spontaneous intellectual recognition of the economic transition. Rather, it was, at first, the apparent solution to the dilemma of maintaining growth without befouling the environment or abusing diminishing natural resources.

Consider Jerry Brown's path to recognition of America's high-technology future. In 1980 Brown launched his second campaign for the presidency. Although there existed substantial Democratic dis-

affection with the Carter-Kennedy choice, Brown remained strictly
an odd man out.

The isolation in which much of his 1980 primary race was conducted was an unusual experience for Brown, whose life since assuming the California governorship six years before had been a public
spectacle. Shedding his California cocoon, and seeing for the first
time since he had taken office another, different part of the country—
really seeing it, unencumbered by the retinue of aides and advisers
who routinely surrounded him in Sacramento and Los Angeles—
Brown came to a stunning realization. Encountering the shuttered
textile mills and shoe factories of America's Northeast, he finally understood that not only was the rhetoric of the era of limits a politically
damaging piece of baggage, but the fact of zero economic growth was
a grim reality of industrial decay and misery. The dilemma of economic growth in an era of resource limitations now tugged at him
emotionally.

In February 1980, in New Hampshire, the solution finally revealed itself. The answer was high technology.

Brown's interest in high-technology industry was long-standing.
It was initially motivated by the role high-tech had played in fueling
the California economy. California underwent a reindustrialization
of its own during the late sixties and early seventies; always heavily
dependent on the aerospace industry, the state was rocked by a substantial employment loss in that sector, as more than 70,000 jobs
disappeared between 1960 and 1980. Because of the contraction in
aerospace, that segment of the total California economy made up of
high-technology actually shrank from 8.5 percent in 1960 to 6.5 percent in 1980.

But at the same time, a new phenomenon was occurring. Employment in other high-technology industries—computers, electronic components, scientific instruments—increased substantially. What's more,
high-tech *including* aerospace (which began to rebound in the late
seventies) accounted for more than 9 percent of California's rapid
employment growth in the critical five years from 1975 to 1980, a
time when the rest of the country was undergoing a serious recessionary
slide. Indirectly, it is estimated that high-technology job growth accounted for more than a quarter of the total increase in California's
employment in this period.

Jerry Brown's recourse to high technology, then, was natural.
Richard Reeves, writing in *Esquire* in 1978, was astute enough to

catch the import of Brown's awakening interest in a new kind of growth following the Dow Chemical incident. The governor told Reeves, "Technology and a continuous ability to generate new ideas is the only way we can maintain our present position. . . . What's driving this society? It's basically ideas . . . New ideas keep creating new wealth to add to the old wealth."

Reeves listened, and against the prevailing tide of opinion concluded, "Jerry Brown probably has a surer and more visionary grasp of that kind of future and some of its implications than any major political leader in the country."

But other commentators could not cut through the dross to the core of Brown's vision. Among those who objected to what they believed were Brown's blatant and false attempts to project a daring new-age image was Mike Royko, the irreverent columnist of the *Chicago Sun-Times* (and later of the rival *Chicago Tribune*). In April 1979, listening to the dialectical antics of the California governor, Royko called Brown "a 41-year-old intellectual hustler" who could "jabber so nimbly that nobody can figure out what he's talking about." He warned his readers that "California is threatening us with Gov. Jerry Brown, the position-leaping, buzz-wording, tripe-talking, science-fiction candidate who wants to bring his moonbeam ideas into the White House." Thanks to Royko and Garry Trudeau, creator of the comic strip "Doonesbury," Brown would hereafter be known as "Governor Moonbeam." If anything was to contribute to the deflation of his forthcoming presidential bid, and his eventual loss in the 1982 race for U.S. Senate in California, it was the ridicule associated with that nickname.

But Royko wrote before the New England winter of 1980, the third phase of Jerry Brown's political evolution. When he had come into office in 1974, Brown's concern with jobs was minimal relative to his top-of-the-list priority, the environment. The Dow debacle in 1977 ushered in a strictly political transition, in which jobs and growth were added to the formula, but were nevertheless still secondary to a new consuming interest, alternative energy, which would be the engine of (a largely undefined) progress. In 1980 growth finally became Brown's top priority. But he had not forgotten his roots, could not dismiss the values taught by the environmental movement, the lessons learned from the Club of Rome's report. Jerry Brown, of all people, absolutely could not turn his back on the long-term consequences of unbridled growth in a finite world.

Campaign '80 somehow convinced him that there was an honest

solution. "When he came home from the campaign," recalled his chief economic adviser, Michael Kieschnick, "all of a sudden it was crystal clear. His concerns had been fused: One, industrial decay; two, the resource trap; and three, high-tech."

Aides noted the change in the governor's attitude when he finally returned to California in April 1980, the presidential campaign abandoned after his loss in the Wisconsin primary—an early, if temporary, end to his national ambitions. Soon others would notice the transition. In an August 1980 article, written from the Democratic Convention in New York, Mike Royko apologized publicly for dubbing the governor with the title "Moonbeam." "The more I see of Brown," he wrote, "the more I am convinced that he has been the only candidate in this year's politics who understands what the country will be up against in the future." He concluded by declaring, "I think the moonbeam has landed with his feet on the ground."

The "Atari Democrat" tag identifies the politicians it describes as interested solely in high technology. However, high-tech is only part of the neoliberals' postindustrial vision. "The adjective 'information' is more precise than 'service' or 'post-industrial' for describing the fundamental dynamic element that will shape the economy and society of the future," wrote economist Robert Hamrin, who served briefly as an aide to Senator Gary Hart, in his book, *Managing Growth in the '80s.* Interestingly, this contravenes the assessment of Daniel Bell, whose 1973 book, *The Coming of Post-Industrial Society,* is still the seminal work on the subject. Bell rejected the appellations "service society" and "information era" as limited characterizations of the transition.

In fact, information, services, and new technology are interrelated, and all three are accepted by the neoliberals as comprising the bedrock of the present and future economy. Hamrin faulted the term "postindustrial" because " 'post' means beyond, and gives us the impression that we are leaving industry behind. This is no more true than that we left agriculture behind when the industrial era was born." True enough, and the neoliberals have taken great pains, particularly in light of the fears of workers in older industries, to stress that they are *not* promoting the abandonment of America's industrial base. Yet, although agriculture has remained a significant portion of America's gross national product, employment in agriculture has dropped steadily, from approximately 18 percent of the labor force in the World War II period to about 3 percent today. Manufacturing is expected to follow a similar course. "What I'm saying," explained Senator Bill Bradley, "is that if 25 percent of the gross national product is made up of manufacturing today, then in the year 2000 manufacturing will *still* comprise 25 percent of our GNP. But it will do it with one-third fewer workers, because of the introduction of new technologies."

A cursory glance at the statistics would seem to bear out Bradley's contention. Between 1950 and 1980 the portion of the gross national product made up of manufacturing declined only slightly. In 1950 manufacturing accounted for $131.1 billion, or approximately one-quarter of the entire GNP. In 1970, with the GNP having expanded to $1,085.6 billion, 24 percent was still in manufacturing; and in 1980, with the GNP having grown to $1,480.7 billion, manufacturing, at $351 billion, still took up 23.7 percent. Over the same period the service sector—including transportation, utilities, wholesale and retail trade, services, and government—accounted for a growing portion of the national wealth: 61 percent, or $328.9 billion, in 1950; 63 percent ten years later; and 66 percent, or $983.2 billion, in 1980.

Employment trends, however, displayed a much more marked shift. Between 1960 and mid-1981 employment in manufacturing, construction, and mining—the "goods" of "goods and services"—increased by about 5 million workers, totaling 25,683,000 in May 1981. Over the same period the number of employees in service-related jobs nearly doubled, to 65,661,000. As a percentage of the work force, laborers declined from 37.7 percent of the total in 1960 to 28.4 percent in 1981. Service workers, on the other hand, were 62.3 percent of the labor rolls in 1960, but by 1981 represented 71.6 percent.

If we look at *new* jobs, the figures are even more startling. According to MIT's David Birch, of 20 million new jobs created during the 1970s, only 5 percent were in manufacturing. A staggering 90 percent were in information-, knowledge-, or service-related fields. Trend analyst John Naisbitt, who before the success of his 1983 best-seller *Megatrends* had already promoted himself as an informal adviser to several neoliberal politicians, surveyed this data and, noting that by 1979 the foremost occupation had become the broadly defined category of "clerk," pointed out in briefings to politicians, in interviews, and in his writings that "farmer-laborer-clerk sums up the entire political and economic history of America."

This trend accelerated rapidly in the first year of the Reagan Administration, when from April 1981 to April 1982 goods-producing industries lost 1.3 million jobs, and service and finance industries gained a half-million. The shift is expected to continue. The Department of Labor projects that by 1995 manufacturing will account for 22 million jobs and services—which employed 12 million people as recently as 1973—will employ 28.5 million people.

One of the most significant features of Daniel Bell's postindustrial state he terms "the centrality of theoretical knowledge." The concept has been eagerly embraced by the neoliberals.

"The point is that the future of the American economy is in having the best thoughts, the best mental work, as opposed to having a work force that is particularly adept at making things," explained Richard Gephardt in 1982. "This is going to have to be a population that is particularly adept at thinking up things. That will result in some amount of manufacturing and production, but it will retain its competitive edge vis-à-vis other parts of the world with its superiority, its ability to be ahead on the thought-process end of things."

Gephardt is among his party's most respected economic thinkers, and his name has been attached to several items associated with neoliberalism, notably the 1982 economics platform he co-authored with Tim Wirth for the House Democratic Caucus and the "Simple Tax" legislation on which he worked with Bill Bradley. Yet Gephardt's presence in neoliberalism's leadership circle demonstrates that the neoliberals are so concerned with economic questions that they willingly overlook differences on social issues that in the past would have firmly divided Democrats.

The circulars Gephardt sends back to his St. Louis district, a white, conservative, and Catholic enclave, usually contain at least one item expressing his opposition to mandatory school busing. He voted in favor of a proposal to prohibit federal employees from paying for abortions with their government-sponsored health plans. Gephardt has opposed liberal attempts to formulate a national health insurance plan. One of his most cherished personal pieces of legislation is the unratified National Health Care Reform Act of 1980; the bill would essentially decontrol health care, presumably opening it up to increased competition. His co-author was Congressman David Stockman, who left the House to become President Reagan's budget director. In 1981, when the traditionally liberal Americans for Democratic Action gave Gary Hart a rating of 95 and Bill Bradley a 96, it gave Dick Gephardt a 45. Close associates of his say that Gephardt's secret desire is to be the Speaker of the House. But as his colleague and friend Thomas Downey, a congressman from Long Island, told *St.*

Louis magazine, "I think nationally he might have a hard time. . . . The positions he espouses [on social issues] are not the positions of my party. That is one of his drawbacks."

But Gephardt's early interest in high technology and his attempts to fashion new political responses to the economic transition have proved prescient, and he may overcome the liabilities Tom Downey notes. It was, after all, Gephardt who helped to popularize one of Washington's most prevalent contemporary clichés—that government's role in the new economy is to "manage the transition." He explained the political implications of this policy shift in June 1982. "The national government," said Gephardt, "should have a different role, a modified role, in trying to shape the economy and shape society that is less ambitious, less encompassing, more tailored, than liberals, or Democrats, or those in the more progressive wing of the Democratic Party have thought in the last twenty years.

"The transition is hard," he added. "But the new generation has been trained and is being trained for all of this. An example from my own district: Guarantee Electric, Saturday morning, opening of a new plant. President of the company, fifty-year-old engineer, started the place with his dad as an outfit that wired buildings. Took me through, introduced me to the people who are putting together all this new stuff that they're making zillions of dollars on. Each one of them is thirty, thirty-five years old. President of the company admitted to me he had no idea what they were up to. Told me, 'I know what they're doing, but I have no idea how they do it.' He said, 'If they all walked out of here tomorrow, I'd have to close my doors, because I wouldn't know how to do it. I'm a good manager, I know how to make the books come out. I understand engineering. But what I understand is twenty years behind what they understand. And it's too late for me to understand it.' "

The profusion of young engineers stemmed from Guarantee Electric's decision in the late 1970s to leave the industrial-wiring business and enter the field of computer-aided manufacturing, designing modular systems on a custom basis for the beer- and soda-bottling industry. "They've built from nothing, absolutely *nothing,* to a worldwide, multi-million-dollar business in five years," stated Gephardt. "Purely through their own ingenuity, purely through their own expertise and the hiring of talented engineers and computer people. On their own."

Of course, not *entirely* on their own. Industrial Development Bonds and Economic Development funds—money Gephardt helped to secure—were used to finance plant expansion and, along with other federal, state, and local subsidy programs, helped make it more profitable. And the government did add one element without which Guarantee Electric would not have succeeded. "The other basic contribution of government," stressed Gephardt, "was the basic research and technology that spun out of the universities in St. Louis, which allowed the firm to put a bunch of discoveries together"—that is, the government's role in education helped the company "manage the transition."

Dick Gephardt's Guarantee Electric tale illustrates one of neoliberalism's most pervasive axioms, that the postindustrial economy is "human-capital intensive," meaning that the rapid pace of industrial change demands not workers skilled at single repetitive tasks, but workers with the knowledge, education, and ability to adapt to a variety of tasks as the needs of industry shift. "Human capital" is merely the economists' term for the sum of an individual's skills. Human-capital policy is the neoliberals' pragmatic, no-nonsense method of talking about education and training.

The use of the terminology of economics and investment, consistent with the neoliberals' policy initiatives in other areas, permeates their rhetoric on education and training. Jerry Brown's major effort during his second term as California's governor was his "Investment in People" program; "Investing in Our People" was one of the highlights of the economic policy paper drafted by Gephardt and Wirth for the House Democratic Caucus in 1982. By 1982, even the mainstream of the Democratic Party had adopted the phraseology: "Investing in Human Capital" was the title of an issues workshop at the party's midterm convention in Philadelphia.

In an era when waste and efficiency are two consuming political themes, it isn't surprising that hard-headed human-capital policies should replace the "soft," socially oriented education and training programs Democrats promoted in the past. The new terminology is a way of appealing not only to liberals and traditional Democratic constituencies, but to business and industry—to the *establishment*—as well.

While education and job training have long been Democratic issues, few new initiatives were advanced in the post–Great Society years. The bulk of the party's efforts went into shielding this segment of social policy from a Republican rollback. What is striking about the reemergence of education and training is that their new economic context represents a departure from contemporary liberal theory, which has stressed not the market advantages, but the non-market benefits of education and training. Liberals have further shunned the theory of human capital because it places a value on individual worth based on individual productivity, thereby calling attention to inequalities among people. "To say that men were economically unequal was just a short step from saying men were politically unequal," economist Lester Thurow has written. Thurow has also noted the antipathy liberals have displayed toward a "technique of analysis that seemed to turn humanistic actions into materialistic actions."

Coupled with the post–World War II assumption that growth was inevitable, this philosophical predisposition allowed liberals to place education and training policy firmly within the realm of social policy, the purpose of which was to better the human condition, not to improve the nation's economy. Hence, in the 1950s and 1960s education and training fell into the category of *qualitative* liberalism, and were kept distinct from *quantitative* liberalism. John Kenneth Galbraith, in *The Affluent Society,* determined that the value of the educational investment was to enable people "to realize a dominant aspiration" and enter the "New Class," the expansion of which, he maintained, should be *"the* major social goal of the society." Because education and training were deemed to be class- or status-oriented issues, and not factors necessary for continued national prosperity, they effectively disappeared from the national agenda when other concerns—primarily Vietnam and environmentalism—buried the Great Society.

The alarming reality of economic decline during the Carter Administration led the neoliberals to adopt the traditionally conservative theory of human capital through which to propagate their ideas about education and training. North Carolina Governor James Hunt, for instance, credits conservative economist Theodore Schultz of the University of Chicago with "opening my eyes to the fact that by *far* the greatest return we have on any set of resources in this country is from education and the money we spend on it."

Acceptance of the importance of human capital in economic growth merged with the neoliberals' agreement that the postindustrial "future" is already upon us. The result has been an emphasis on science and math education in the schools. (And, as we'll see in the next chapter, these ideas also fused with neoliberal recognition of the new global economy to create a belief in increased productivity as essential to competition in the international marketplace.) Finally, because human-capital theory does indeed call attention to inequalities among people, acceptance of the theory has had the effect of liberating liberals to raise the theme of excellence alongside that of equality.

Prototypes of the transitional economy the neoliberals talk about have now sprouted. Route 128 in Massachusetts, Silicon Valley in California, Research Triangle in North Carolina are the areas in which many of the new high-tech companies have been locating. In these industrial centers the "industry" is information. Like an actual archipelago, such information archipelagos are composed of many separate islands—high-technology businesses and service firms, generally small with an entrepreneurial origin; cultural and recreational amenities for the employees; technical schools and community colleges to provide support personnel for the industries. And at the core of each stands at least one university, the hub from which springs the theoretical knowledge the archipelago relies on.

It was neoliberal politicians, particularly governors, who first recognized the import of the information archipelago and actively devised methods to encourage its growth. Governor Jerry Brown appointed a Commission on Industrial Innovation, whose final report, "Winning Technologies," issued in 1982, was directed not only at spurring further expansion in Silicon Valley, the high-tech industrial center in Santa Clara County surrounding Stanford University, but at promoting the "Silicon Valleying" of America. So consumed was Brown by the possibilities for high-tech reindustrialization that after leaving the Sacramento statehouse he incorporated the commission as a not-for-profit organization, the National Commission on Industrial Innovation.

During his first term as governor of Massachusetts, Michael Dukakis was quick to grasp the reason why the Boston suburbs along Route 128 had come alive as havens for high-tech. Massachusetts' conversion from an industrially based economy, heavily engaged in textiles, to a service economy depended in large part on the people and ideas generated at Harvard and MIT. Governor James Hunt of North Carolina has presided over the flowering of Research Triangle, an industrial park that unifies three towns—Raleigh, Durham, and Chapel Hill—and three universities—Duke, the University of North Carolina, and North Carolina State—into a service, health care, and high-tech boom metropolis. Also actively promoting cooperative efforts among government, academia, and business to create similar knowledge-intensive centers are Governors Bruce Babbitt of Arizona and Richard Lamm of Colorado.

There is no doubt that high technology is looked to as a national panacea. Microchips have been called "the crude oil of the 1980s." Possibly they might become the shale oil of the 1980s—an industry that never quite fulfills the promises made for it. But, although many states and localities are destined to fail in misguided attempts to lure high-tech industries to the exclusion of all else, the successes to date have been impressive, and they indicate the possibilities of the economic transition. They also reveal the new political responses that are necessary to establish new businesses in postindustrial America. No longer are low-cost labor, tax incentives, and cheap land the primary factors that induce a company to locate in a given area. Instead, the recipe for an information archipelago consists of five ingredients: proximity to a technically advanced, cooperative university; a reliable energy supply; availability of a trained and skilled work force, particularly of engineers and technicians; accessibility to capital to finance new technologies; and the quality of life necessary to induce an educated work force to move to the area. Establishing this sort of environment is at the heart of many of the policy considerations that have engaged neoliberal politicians in the 1980s.

The information archipelagos are junctions of information- and service-based industries with rural or small-town amenities. Traditional liberals oriented their policies toward older urban areas. Low-density urbanization, as an outcome to the phenomenon of "clean growth," has long been predicted by some demographics experts. Calvin L. Beale, a demographer with the Agriculture Department, first discerned the population reverse in the 1960s, stating then that the century-and-a-half-long movement from rural areas to the nation's cities was finally at an end. Although Beale's findings were hotly disputed at the time, the 1980 census confirmed his conclusion. The intersection of the new-technology economy and exurbia illustrates what trend analyst John Naisbitt calls high-tech's breeding of "high touch": the "lonely crowd" feeling of recent years is replaced by a new sense of community. Community, or cooperation, is one of neoliberalism's strongest underlying themes.

While the old-fashioned American value of community is resurrected in the high-tech information archipelago, an equally old-time Democratic constituency is notably absent: organized labor. Unions, which represented 24.7 percent of the work force in 1970, by 1980 represented only 21 percent of the nation's workers. Losses in individual unions—the United Auto Workers, for example, is 27 percent smaller than in the late 1970s—have not been offset with successful organizing drives in the high-technology and service industries. In Massachusetts, one of labor's earliest strongholds, not one of the 133 companies in the Massachusetts High Technology Council is unionized.

Organized labor has reacted fearfully to neoliberal pronouncements about "managing the transition." Harvard lecturer Robert Reich, a leading proponent of an industrial policy that would promote adjustment to changed economic circumstances rather than preservation of an outmoded industrial base, was attacked by union representatives at a Democratic Party economic strategy meeting chaired by Wirth and Gephardt on April 24, 1982. "You cannot glibly write off whole segments of industries," said an angry official of the United Steel Workers. Sheldon Friedman, research director of the United Auto Workers, was even more blunt. He told Reich he found his analysis "incredible." "We need both newer *and* older industries," Friedman scoffed.

A wedge has been driven between neoliberals and the Democratic Party's largest and most powerful constituency. "I think we've got to spend a lot more time communicating with labor, to make them understand what we're saying, and so we can understand what they're saying," said Gephardt in 1982. "A lot of people in labor think we're writing off the basic industries, that we don't want to make steel or cars in this country, that we're just interested in having everybody be a computer programmer. Many on our side of the equation think that labor wants to go back to 1940 or 1950 and starve out all the high-tech industries and throw billions of dollars into re-creating the 1950s."

The conflict between older constituencies tied to the industrial era's economic policies and neoliberal politicians trying to shape a policy framework for the postindustrial economy is the greatest challenge facing the Democratic Party. And the most important manifestation of this rift centers on the issue of globalism. The question for Democrats is, Will they accede to labor's desire to protect jobs from the vagaries of international competition, or will they accept the new reality and the consequences of a global economy?

CHAPTER 8

The Global Unit

IT WAS TWO DAYS after the November 1980 debacle, and Bill Bradley was trying vainly to put the best face possible on the admittedly gloomy prospect of returning to Washington as a junior member of the Senate's *minority* party. He had some thoughts on what the Democrats were missing. "I think what you need is a framework," said Bradley. "A framework of treating risk as a reward . . . of encouraging community, encouraging investment in equipment, infrastructure, people, research and development, and innovation. And placing it," he continued, his voice growing more insistent as he enumerated a series of seemingly disjointed and not overtly Democratic notions, *"in an international context."*

Bradley had spoken often, in many forums, about these issues. Risk, for instance, was the theme—certainly not a traditionally liberal theme—of a speech he had delivered the previous June to the graduating seniors at Yale University. But it was the global perspective he wanted to address at length that day so soon after the Democratic disaster. "The problems of this country are structural issues," he maintained. "What is going to be the structure of the world economy, in a world where the Bretton Woods system is under severe strain, and is deteriorating before our eyes?" Bradley was referring to the 1944 New Hampshire conference at which were forged the plans for the postwar international monetary order. "What are we going to do to improve the productive capacity of this country, so that we can compete again internationally? And what can we do about the danger we face when our lifeline"—our oil supplies, he meant—"can be cut off overnight, resulting in rampant inflation and massive unemployment?"

Global economic interdependence had become Bradley's chief concern by the fall of 1980. Finance, productivity, and energy were all globally connected for Bill Bradley. In just two short years in the U.S. Senate, his outlook had broadened considerably.

Energy had been Bill Bradley's 1978 campaign theme. His success in that election, however, his first race for public office, depended on his fame as a big-league jock. Basketball's biggest bonus baby of the day, he was nicknamed—because of the size of his contract (as well as his legendary parsimony)—"Dollar Bill." Even then, Bradley had his eye on the Senate. He had written his senior thesis at Princeton on Harry Truman's tenure in the upper chamber; and he had considered, and rejected, two political possibilities in the mid-seventies: running for state treasurer in his native Missouri and, in 1974, challenging a vulnerable Republican congressman in the Morris County, New Jersey, district to which he'd moved. If he wanted to be a U.S. Senator, friends told him privately, then *that* was the office for which he should run.

His chance came in 1978. Republican Clifford Case had held a seat in the Senate since 1953. It would be a kamikaze operation: Case—the personification of the liberal, Eastern Republican—was immensely popular, even with New Jersey's moderate Democratic majority. But Jeffrey Bell, a little-known adviser to Ronald Reagan and a supply-side theorist, by dint of hard work and a command of media strategy, benefited from the conservative drift in the Republican Party, and defeated the complacent Case in the primary. Like Bradley, Bell was young and had also moved relatively recently from out of state to run for the office. With his own potential liabilities canceled out, Bradley, name recognition on his side, coasted to a landslide victory in the general election.

During the campaign, Bradley ran heavily on the issue of alternative energy. But upon taking office, influenced by the work of the Energy Project at the Harvard Business School, he began to view the energy question not as an isolated problem but as part of a global interplay of forces. Bradley saw what is now a commonplace, that there is an interlocking trinity of issues, energy-economy-defense.

So in 1979, during his first year in office, Bill Bradley spoke not of solar energy as he had only one year before, but of the "geopolitics of oil," a new phrase, one unfamiliar to his constituents. It was the title of a series of hearings he would hold, often as the only legislator present, to determine the impact of energy issues on the domestic economy and the consequences of other nations' domestic energy policies on the United States. In short, he was endeavoring to grasp the importance of "global interconnectedness," another term he began using frequently. His big cause was no longer garbage-to-energy systems; it was a curious entity called "Spro," a beast of which few people had ever heard.

In beating the drum for "Spro"—shorthand for the United States' Strategic Petroleum Reserves, which he wanted to fill posthaste— Bradley was trying to convince his liberal colleagues that they had been approaching the energy question from the wrong end. They had spent entirely too much time debating long-term alternative sources of energy, sexy items like windmills and solar power plants, more time than they'd spent on the question of conservation. And they had deliberated upon conservation without dealing with the problem of strategic vulnerability, that is, the possibility of an oil supply interruption as severe as, if not more dangerous than, the 1973 Arab oil embargo. Bradley felt that not only was the age of cheap energy at an end, so too was the age of energy independence. That concept no longer made sense given the present structure of the energy industry and given America's involvement with its allies.

And so for a year, at every opportunity, in the Energy Committee (Bradley had won the two committee assignments he coveted, the other on the Senate Finance Committee) and in public forums, Bradley urged Congress to fill the Strategic Petroleum Reserves with as much speed as possible. Liberals, he insisted, were so enamored of technology and so concerned with the technical questions surrounding energy independence that they failed to grasp the larger, more critical problem of energy's international implications. "In the wake of the first Arab oil embargo," he would recall later, tracing the evolution of his current thinking, ". . . I realized Bretton Woods . . . was indeed the central organizing framework for the world's economy, and that we had to figure out new ways. From that time forward, I personally investigated thoughts on ways to restructure the economy."

By 1982, although still a member of the Senate Energy Committee and still publicly concerned with energy's social implications, Bradley rarely emphasized energy matters. The international financial crisis now consumed him. He devised a tax package to help spur productivity and give the United States a new international competitive edge; and every week, it seemed, he would sketch out for his colleagues on the floor of the Senate "worst case" scenarios—horror stories, really—for a possible world banking collapse.

Bill Bradley's great concern was globalism—the final element of the neoliberals' postindustrial paradigm. "The question is not that the New Deal failed," he said in late 1981. "The New Deal succeeded. And the issues that were the issues of the 1930s . . . issues of adequate basic necessities, if you will, are *not* the issues of the 1980s. The problems of the eighties are much more international in scope. They are much more related to the ability of this country to compete effectively in the *international* market, and to establish real economic growth within the context of a growing *world* economy.

"I think it's foolhardy," he concluded, "to think that we can have real economic growth while the world around us goes down the tubes."

American liberalism has always been defined in part by its internationalism and, at least since the late nineteenth century when battles over high and low tariffs were one of the most rancorous of political divisions, the internationalist perspective has found a home in the Democratic Party. In acknowledging the reality of an integrated global economic unit, the neoliberals are doing little more than reaffirming this classic liberal tenet.

But in two distinct ways, the neoliberals' globalism signifies a departure from liberalism's past. First, postwar American internationalism, particularly in the fifties and sixties, had a paternalistic hue that developed out of belief in nearly unlimited American economic and military power. If any single phrase can conjure up visions of the U.S. of 30 years ago, it is "America's leadership of the free world." As the limits of U.S. military and economic strength have become apparent, the neoliberals have jettisoned the assumptions of traditional liberalism. Instead they view the United States as a true partner among many allies. The replacement of America as leader with America as more partner and competitor has far-reaching consequences.

Second, and more important, many traditional liberals have begun to espouse protectionism, a sentiment antithetical to true liberalism. Protectionism is a political device to allay the fears of the Democrats' labor constituency, which sees uncompetitive American firms losing ground in the domestic market to stronger foreign competitors, and laying off workers as a result. "Buy American" provisions in congressional legislation provide a convenient way to reassure labor. But protectionism has become a vain policy alternative to programs that might increase American competitiveness while entailing only short-term costs.

One is tempted to interpret this retreat from classically liberal ideology as the logical outgrowth of isolationist sentiments that first appeared in the center-left during the Vietnam War. Isolationism, former Undersecretary of State George Ball has warned us, is "the other face of protectionism." Whether or not isolationism is the cause of this new protectionism, the neoliberals are in the curious and uncomfortable position of standing against a vocal minority—pessimists would say that it is already a majority—of the Democratic Party, which accepts the new protectionist creed.

However, ascribing the traditional liberals' embrace of protectionism only to their desire to assuage labor overlooks a significant intellectual split. In fact, liberals and neoliberals view the world economy differently. "I think that is one difference between [them]," economist Lester Thurow said in January 1983. "The liberals still haven't quite caught up to the fact of how integrated we are in the world. . . . Of course, the Republicans haven't either.

"We've got such a world-integrated economy that our current economic policy-making apparatus just doesn't fit," continued Thurow. "We have national economic policy and a world economy. The national economic policies put in place one by one don't work. You've really got two choices. You could build a new policymaking structure that is international in scope, or you can reduce the degree of world integration. Now, hopefully we'll do the first and not the second, although we're moving fast toward the second."

The ramifications of globalism have been hammered out in speeches, articles, and books by neoliberal politicians and advisers. As former Florida governor and former U.S. Special Trade Representative Reubin Askew said in a November 1982 speech, "A generation ago, Americans could still pretend that we could isolate ourselves from the rest of the world economy. In the aftermath of World War II, America remained largely self-sufficient, and American producers faced little economic competition, either at home or abroad. American money was spent on American goods manufactured from American resources using American energy. Strong American markets absorbed these American goods. And any occasional surplus was sold overseas, where foreign consumers clamored for the opportunity to purchase almost anything that was 'Made in U.S.A.' "

Concluded Askew, simply and devastatingly, "No more."

The changed role of the U.S. in the international economy came about in a very short span of time in the early 1970s. At least five factors were responsible: the floating exchange rates that accompanied the breakdown of the Bretton Woods system, the rise of the Organization of Petroleum Exporting Countries, the creation of the Eurodollar market, the mobility of the multinational corporations, and the industrialization of the third world.

Nineteen seventy-one was the year the world economic system collapsed. President Richard Nixon's decision to float the dollar against other world currencies on the open market removed the rock to which the world economy had been tethered since the end of World War II. In July 1944 at Bretton Woods, forty-four nations had jointly decided to fix the price of gold at $35 an ounce and to peg their individual currencies to the dollar. The system was designed to prevent countries from either promoting exports or restraining imports through the artificial method of currency devaluations, and to guard against the autarchy that had led to the collapse of the world economy in the late 1920s. The International Monetary Fund was created at Bretton Woods to monitor and govern the new cooperative monetary arrangements. Other international institutions, notably the World Bank, soon followed. The stability of the international monetary system and the reindustrialization of war-torn Europe and Japan—facilitated by the flow of strong dollars to them—fostered a world trade boom. Between 1950 and 1972 international trade grew 50 percent faster than world production. United States direct investment abroad doubled, from 4.1 to 8.2 percent.

But as the devastated world brushed itself off and regained its footing, dollars became slightly less useful. With German factories churning out Volkswagens, there was not as much need for Germans to buy American cars. The gold on which the dollar was based became more attractive by comparison. The problem was, by 1971 there were a hell of a lot of dollars out there—Eurodollars—well beyond the reach of American banking regulations. Other countries were expanding their own money supplies to meet the force of this ever-growing cache of Eurodollars, feeding a consequent expansion of the American money supply, which in turn fueled inflation in the U.S. and Europe—the classic vicious cycle. Some of the European central banks decided to suspend trading in dollars. In August 1971, fearing a run on the American gold supply—anyone could trade in $35 for an ounce of the metal—President Nixon cut the dollar's gold mooring and floated it against other currencies on the world market.

Far from halting the international inflationary spiral, the new un-predictability spurred further monetary supply growth and more inflation. Then, in 1973, OPEC froze oil exports to the West and Japan. Without a stable monetary system to absorb the shock, inflation in Europe and the U.S. zoomed higher, as did unemployment, accompanied by industrial contraction. The scene was repeated during the second oil shock in 1979. Growth in world production, 5.4 percent annually since 1961, fell to 3.6 percent. In the developed countries, those whose economic blood was oil, the rate was sliced in half, to 2.7 percent. Members of the Organization for Economic Cooperation and Development experienced average unemployment of 4.9 percent, two full percentage points higher than during the sixties.

The United States bore the brunt of the crisis, if only because it was unaccustomed to feeling pinched by forces outside its control. And the stateless Eurodollars (soon followed by Euromarks and Euroyen), OPEC's vindictiveness, and floating exchange rates were very much beyond American control. So were the giant multinational corporations, most of them with U.S. origins, which had the ability to farm out their labor—work that would have been done by Americans in years past—to third-world countries where unions and decent wages were unknown. This device is called "outsourcing," and it was used with increasing frequency as the multinationals grew an average of 10 percent annually during the seventies—twice the rate of the gross world product. Meanwhile, those underdeveloped nations, thanks to the speeding pace of technology transfer, were themselves becoming developed. First textile mills, then steel factories, finally semiconductor plants appeared on shores where, a generation before, electric generators were wildly exotic.

Each of these events was a sort of national cultural shock to Americans. The fact that the dollar was no longer the world's most stable currency was bad enough, and the idea that we could be held hostage by oil-rich Arabs was worse. But worst of all, as the eighties dawned, was the realization that third-world industrialization and outsourcing of jobs had made the United States uncompetitive in those industries—steel, autos, textiles—that had helped America to define itself almost from the turn of the century, the "American Century."

American managers and political leaders had to face an unfamiliar situation. Previously American companies had to be competitive with one another. Now they also had to be competitive with rivals overseas. Why? Because the market was no longer America; it was the world. And the producers no longer *had* to be Americans; they could be Japanese, German, Korean, Brazilian. In a scant fifteen years, beginning in 1965, world trade grew from $150 billion to $1.5 trillion, thanks to an increasing demand for consumer goods as well as for the basic materials of industrialization in nations that had previously purchased little from abroad. But over roughly the same period America's share of the world manufacturing market fell from a quarter of the total to 17 percent. As U.S. exports in all areas—agriculture, manufacturing, services—fell to 13 percent of the world total in 1980, the nation's balance of trade, which had shown a $5.4 billion surplus in the mid-sixties, now displayed a $37 billion deficit. Even more alarming, domestic consumption of domestically produced goods dropped precipitously. The nation went from producing approximately 95 percent of the autos, steel, and consumer electronics sold on these shores to making only 79 percent of the cars, 86 percent of the steel, and less than half the consumer electronic goods purchased by Americans.

Of equal importance, although less recognized, Americans held $350 billion worth of foreign assets. And foreigners owned at least $275 billion—perhaps as much as $350 billion—of American assets. This was, perhaps, the final shock: the nations of the world *owned* each other. Capital mobility, technology transfer, and lower comparative wages—all realized with a jolt during the seventies—gave a new edge to the drama, changing the role of the United States in the world.

What does it all mean? Simply that there no longer exists an independent entity called "the American economy." And that the American market is only one of many markets with which American producers must concern themselves.

The correct response to the integrated world economy, according to neoliberal theorists, is awareness that domestic policies cannot be legislated and applied in a vacuum. "The world needs to coordinate monetary policies to dramatically lower interest rates, and it needs to prevent the wide swings in currency values that make economic investment and planning impossible," asserted Lester Thurow in *The New York Times* after the rancorous 1982 Versailles summit meeting of the industrialized world's leaders. ". . . In an integrated world economy, domestic economic policies have to extend across national borders." Implicit in these remarks is criticism of the Reagan Administration's intransigence in pursuing domestic economic policies without concern for their international ramifications or their rebound effect on the United States.

The tight monetary and stimulative fiscal policies of Reaganomics, for example, contrast sharply with those of Japan, which follows loose monetary and tight fiscal policies. The yen seeps out of Japan seeking dollars, bidding up the price of the dollar and further weakening the yen. This makes Japanese goods ever less expensive for Americans to buy, and contributes at least as much to America's trade deficit with Japan (estimated at $20 billion in 1982) as the uncompetitiveness of American goods. This is but one example of how a non-global outlook imperils the United States and one of the reasons the international crises of monetary instability and debt so consume the neoliberals. "If you don't recognize that the wars of the 1980s are probably not going to be hot wars with missiles, but investment wars, where you're fighting to get a chunk of the world's capital—capital that flows across boundaries like lightning strikes across the sky," explained Bill Bradley in 1981, "then you're not going to be prepared to do battle in [the international] arena."

But it is not only the Reagan Administration that eschews the internationalist outlook; so too does the Democratic Party. The belief that domestic policies could be pursued in disregard of their global impact prevailed in the Carter Administration. A paper presented to the Treasury Department's Trade Policy Committee in June 1980 by a department official illustrates the point. "Policies designed to increase investment, research and development, and productivity, or to curb inflation, should be pursued if they will increase the domestic income and welfare, but not to meet foreign competition," wrote the official, Dale W. Larsen. *If the domestic economy is performing well, the trade accounts will take care of themselves*" [italics added].

Four years later former Vice President Walter Mondale continues to echo this theme. A product of Minnesota's progressive Democratic-Farmer-Labor Party, Mondale spent the early part of his 1984 presidential campaign repeating the dictum that the United States had to "get tough" with Japan. "The key task," he had informed a steelworkers union gathering on September 22, 1982, ". . . is to stop flying the white flag and to start flying the American flag." Scored by a horrified liberal press that of course felt no electoral pressure and therefore no compunction to rescind a free-trade tradition in order to secure labor support, Mondale protested that he remained a free-trader. But as *Washington Post* economics columnist Hobart Rowen observed, "Mondale's words—both his [steelworkers] speech and a defense of it in the *Washington Post*—were crystal clear and could not have been misunderstood." Indeed, by the spring of 1983 Mondale had unmistakably clarified his position, telling the delegates to a AFL-CIO conference that he favored legislation requiring a variety of foreign imports to contain a certain percentage of American-made parts.

It was the 1982 debate over a similar bill strongly supported by the United Auto Workers that split the Democratic Party. The Fair Practices in Automotive Products Act, more familiarly referred to as the "domestic contents" or "local contents" bill, which was co-sponsored by a majority of the House (including not a few neoliberals who know not only on which side their bread is buttered, but who actually bakes the bread), requires that *all* companies, domestic and foreign, selling more than half a million cars a year in the U.S. manufacture them with at least 90 percent American parts and labor. Companies selling 200,000 to 500,000 autos must use 75 percent domestic parts and labor. Senator Wendell Ford of Kentucky introduced the Senate version of the bill, saying, "It is only fair that foreign automobile companies create auto production and jobs in the United States since they enjoy a high volume of sales in this country." Senator John Glenn supported the bill, asserting, "[The] senseless hemorrhaging of our economy's life blood must be stopped and stopped now. Without the protection of import quotas provided by this legislation, our auto industry will have neither the time nor the resources to become fully competitive." The domestic contents bill generated more reams of editorials and analyses, pro and con, than virtually any other single piece of domestic legislation in 1982.

Neoliberals meanwhile defend the free-trade status quo. Former Special Trade Representative Reubin Askew, in opposing the UAW-sponsored domestic contents legislation, maintained, "We must not delude ourselves into thinking that we can prosper in splendid isolation from the competitive pressures of the world economy. We must not yield to a mindless xenophobia that tells us to blame other nations for all our national difficulties. We must not yield to the urge to indulge in a further, unnecessary proliferation of the import quotas, the orderly marketing agreements, the so-called 'voluntary' restraints, the 'buy American' laws, and all the other protectionist devices that already pervade the American economy."

The problem with such exhortations, and the reason for the notorious weakness of the free-trade line, especially in the face of increasingly vigorous demands for retaliation or protection, is that America's seeming economic impotence in the world market elicits an *emotional* response. Harvard University's Robert Reich argued the case for a national investment strategy geared toward international competitiveness in the Spring 1982 issue of *Foreign Affairs*. "Protections like [plant-closing legislation, industry bail-outs, hindrance of technology transfer] retard future economic growth by encumbering the movement of resources toward more productive uses, and the downward cycle perpetuates itself," wrote Reich.

Instead Reich advocates an industrial policy that adjusts to international economic conditions. However, the short-term solutions sound more convincing and powerful, easily surmounting the vain pleas for "economic reality" emanating from neoliberal quarters. Reubin Askew railed against the character of the debate in a speech before the Houston Committee on Foreign Relations in November 1982. "With total disregard for the realities of the international economy, in recent weeks America's steelworkers have actually been promised that the United States will once again make more steel than any other nation in the world. Those who believe in open trade have, by implication, been described as 'patsies' and 'suckers,' " complained Askew. "And, in an amazing leap of logic, protectionism has been equated with the salutary act of hiring a policeman to patrol the local neighborhood.

"All this," continued Askew, "not from Republicans, who have an historical affection for high tariffs and other trade barriers, but from Democrats who should know better." The tone of Askew's grievance suggests the powerlessness the neoliberals feel.

Even when a specific plan to promote free trade is advanced by a legislator, it tends to seem feeble next to reciprocity or retaliatory legislation. Senator Gary Hart took the globalist approach in piecing together the High Technology Trade Act of 1982. "High technology today, like steel before it, is seminal," said Hart in submitting the bill to the Senate, sounding the postindustrial clarion call. "It will provide the key technological infrastructure on which our economy will be built." Hart's bill was a response to the increasingly stiff trade and investment barriers American high-technology firms faced from international competitors, barriers that ranged from foreign governments anticompetitively subsidizing their high-tech firms for export purposes while subtly protecting their markets from American products, to out-and-out discriminatory tariffs.

The semiconductor industry, smarting from lack of access to foreign markets (which account for half of all world semiconductor sales), was pressing Congress for action. They wanted reciprocity, a word that connotes fairness but is actually a euphemism for tariff and non-tariff protection of the American market from foreign products—

in other words, retaliation. Florida Democrat Sam Gibbons, chairman of the Trade Subcommittee of the House Ways and Means Committee, had introduced a semiconductor reciprocity bill, the fundamentals of which had been drawn up by the Semiconductor Industry Association.

The Senate hopper held more than a dozen similar reciprocity bills. Hart and his economist, Robert Hamrin, moved in at that point, drawing up their own legislation, using the SIA's approach as a framework, but slashing through it and substituting "free trade" for "reciprocity" wherever the word appeared. Over a four-week period, Hart jawboned the SIA, the American Electrical Association, and four or five other key high-tech trade associations into supporting his free-trade version, pointing out the dangers of a retaliatory approach that could close off more markets than it would open. He eventually lined up almost the entire industry behind his method, where only half had started out favoring it.

"The general philosophy [behind the legislation]," Hamrin said in 1982, "is the way a hard-thinking pragmatic neoliberal would approach the trade issue. [It is not] emotional protectionism, which would have short-run benefits but long-term consequences." As Hart explained to his colleagues on the Senate floor, "This approach is positive; it tells the President to use the trade tools at his disposal to resolve disputes, rather than to close markets which exacerbate them."

Gary Hart's words are familiar to those who remember the liberal internationalism of the 1960s. But the world of the 1980s is quite different and the political responses it requires have changed. While old liberals continue to minister to old industries and old constituencies and to practice the politics of protection and confrontation, the neoliberals are attempting to direct their party to new constituencies that exist in the flourishing new America of high-technology industries and the service-and-information economy. On some issues—such as free trade versus protection—the neoliberals are simply sticking stubbornly to a principle abandoned by their traditionalist colleagues. But on other issues, both the principles and the practices of the neoliberals are very different.

PART THREE

Responses

SOMEHOW, IN THE DECADES SINCE WORLD WAR II, principles seem to have disappeared from considerations of leadership. Our preeminent politicians have of course always paid homage to broad values—on the right, anti-communism has long been the dominant theme, while on the left it has been a loosely defined "compassion"—but the reality is that, over the years, concern for actual first principles as the motivating force behind political action has become more and more muted. Instead, governance has come to be increasingly interpreted as a technical matter. Liberal values have become secondary to the mechanisms liberals have designed to implement policy. As a result, liberal politicians and their constituencies have grown less concerned with the principles underlying their programs than with the continuation of the old, and sometimes shopworn, programs themselves.

Neoliberalism signifies a public return to a value-oriented politics. Neoliberals insist that only through strict fidelity to their three principles—investment, appropriate technology, and most important, cooperation—can economic growth be attained in the postindustrial global economy. And growth, they maintain, is a necessary prerequisite to social justice in an era of limits.

This concern for growth as the bottom line of politics causes the neoliberals to speak a peculiarly mechanistic-sounding language. In the lingo of high technology and economics, the crucial measure of a program seems to be costs-benefits analysis. The neoliberal issues—infrastructure decay, consumption taxes, human-capital policy, industrial policy—sound dry, unappealing, even frightening to the interest

107

groups that comprise the traditional liberal coalition. Indeed, the Democrats' 1984 presidential nominating process has been dominated by these fears, as the special interests—nuclear-freeze advocates, blacks, feminists, gays, organized labor—seek to raise their individual concerns to the top of the Democratic agenda. But while the interest groups are unwilling to surrender the programs through which they have benefited, the neoliberals do not wish to compromise their principles.

For all these reasons, the proposals that do evolve out of neoliberalism's three principles—such as national service, military reform, the "Simple Tax," an innovation-based industrial policy—are opposed by many traditional liberals. The proposals threaten too many vested interests. Traditional liberals and their constituencies have been well served by the system created during the past three decades, in which "big government," dependent on the techniques of systems analysis, has gradually obscured the goals of liberal programs. How and why this occurred, and how certain members of the liberal community reacted against the trend toward a politics without values, is an essential part of neoliberalism's critique of traditional liberalism.

CHAPTER 9

Big Government and the Cult of Expertism

BIG GOVERNMENT WAS AN ENEMY successfully targeted by Ronald Reagan in 1980. Like the conservatives, the neoliberals also criticize big government, but their analysis is more specific. First, they assert that liberalism came under the thrall of systems analysis in its efforts to solve society's social ills; second, they believe that the dependence on systems analysis allowed public policy to be taken over by a class of experts who were removed from the pressures of representative democracy; and third, they maintain that government of, by, and for the experts resulted in a fragmentation of public policy which in turn allowed politics to become dominated by special interest groups. The results were that policy development and implementation were driven further from the values that initially motivated public concern, and a bureaucracy was created that fed off itself, becoming ever larger and ever more feckless with each passing year. The rubric "redefining the role of government" is a primary axiom of neoliberalism, signifying the neoliberals' belief that government has grown too ineffective, too large in some senses, too removed from the people it is intended to serve. Many traditional liberals have vilified their revisionist colleagues for what they perceive to be an abandonment of the principle of affirmative government. The neoliberals do not accept the Reagan framework of reducing government's role in rectifying social inequities. However, in their willingness to incorporate market solutions and decentralization of authority into their policy formulations, they reveal their desire to redefine liberalism without the clamp of big government.

Two strains of thought competed among progressives in the 1960s

and on into the 1970s. Daniel Patrick Moynihan, the intellectual sire
of social programs in the Johnson and Nixon White Houses and currently the Democratic senator from New York, in his book *Maximum
Feasible Misunderstanding,* identified the two strains as "the shiny,
no-nonsense, city-as-a-system Robert S. McNamara style," and "the
shaggy, inexact, communitarian anarchism of the [radical historian]
Paul Goodman variety." Historian Samuel H. Beer is more concise;
the dual revolution of the 1960s, according to Beer, involved two cur-
rents of thought: the technocratic and the romantic.

The counterculture of the sixties revolted against the technocratic
mindset. Sam Brown, a Harvard Divinity School drop-out who assembled Students for Eugene McCarthy in 1967–68 and a year later
helped to organize the nationwide Moratorium against the Vietnam
War, pinpointed this tension in a 1970 article. Brown condemned the
"pragmatic" Americans for Democratic Action liberals who had, in
order to secure their social goals, accommodated themselves to the
prevalent 1950s–60s Cold War mentality to the point of starting and
accepting the Vietnam War. "The last generation of liberals made an
ideology of effectiveness," charged Brown, "and finally came to believe in their own tactical compromises."

Postwar liberalism had, according to this analysis, fallen into dis-
array because of its "ideology of effectiveness." Brown's criticism
mirrored a charge made a half-century ago by Horace Kallen, a former disciple of the philosopher of pragmatism, John Dewey. "[Prag-
matism] dissolves dogmas into beliefs, eternities and necessities into
change and chance, conclusions and finalities into processes," wrote
Kallen. "Men have invented philosophy precisely because they find
change, chance, and process too much for them, and desire infallible
security and certainty. Pragmatism . . . calls for too complete a dis-
illusion."

Daniel Patrick Moynihan noticed in the Great Society "the increasing introduction into politics and government of ideas originating
in the social sciences, which promise to bring about social change
through manipulation of what might be termed the hidden processes
of society." Indeed, the beginning of the Johnson era saw a veritable
explosion in the social sciences that continued unabated during the
Nixon-Ford years. From 1964 to 1975 the number of Ph.Ds conferred
annually in the hard sciences increased from 2,320 to 3,611—a modest 64 percent. But the number of doctorates in the social sciences
jumped an astounding 386 percent during the same period. More significantly, at the same time the amount of federal spending on ap-

plied social science research went from $235 million to nearly $1 billion.

But it was the "pragmatic" premise underlying applied social science that allowed the folly of "big government" to flourish. The basic assumption of the discipline, as summarized by Samuel Beer, was that "by controlling certain inputs, one could bring about mass behavioral results." No better example of the sixties technocratic liberal mindset exists than a memo written in 1965 by John H. Rubel, then a corporate vice president of Litton Industries and director of its economic development division, to Sargent Shriver, director of the Job Corps, one of the Great Society's flagship programs. "I think of the Job Corps as a complex transforming machine of many internal parts," wrote Rubel, a former Assistant Secretary of Defense under Robert S. McNamara. "The input—the raw material—that is fed into this machine is people. The output is people. It is the function of this machine to transform these people." The primary tool of the new era, the device that would enable liberals to solve the challenge of abundance, was called "systems analysis." John Rubel praised it as "a way of inventing your way to a solution." It was a method by which a "pragmatic," liberal government could now attempt to play God.

Systems analysis, policy analysis, costs-benefits analysis, quantitative analysis, and econometric analysis are different guises for what is essentially the same thing: the evaluation of either existing or proposed programs according to quantifiable standards of efficiency. These standards involve the construction of "models" of the real world—generally on a computer—through which variable sets of data can be tested. While systems analysis has been an invaluable aid in determining the effectiveness of various government programs, it also suffers from inherent limitations. Its models tend to be unidimensional, restricting the universe under scrutiny rather severely. Additionally, certain kinds of variables simply cannot be quantified, such as the human reactions to unknown stimuli. Government's growing reliance on systems analysis led it increasingly to ignore the purely political considerations of policymaking, which in turn fomented a fragmentation of public policy and of the national interest at the hands of special interest groups which came to dominate an enlarged, yet weakened, federal government.

Systems analysis had its roots in the New Deal, when the first centralized regulatory bureaucracy, exemplified by the National Recovery Administration, was established by the federal government. Although the New Deal's operations were the result of pragmatic, rather than theoretical, considerations, there was a joining of the new Keynesian economic theories to the policies already being developed to save the nation's economy, as FDR's advisers became more attuned to the theoretical justification for their activities. Out of this juncture grew a science of economic management, which, because of the invention of the computer, could for the first time in man's history apply economic theory to programmatic tests. Thus was born econometrics.

By the 1950s a more sophisticated econometrics had spread to the private sector. It was formally reintroduced into public sector management by Robert McNamara, when he left the presidency of the Ford Motor Company to become John F. Kennedy's Secretary of Defense in 1961. President Johnson was so impressed with the application of econometric analysis in the defense field that he issued an executive order that all agencies in the executive branch employ policy analysis. Thus the new system spread beyond the confines of the Department of Defense into other areas more directly affecting social welfare.

The White House saw systems analysis as a method of discerning the constraints and discovering the costs and benefits of all actions. Significantly, *human beings were assumed to be quantifiable systems.* Congress, to retaliate, began extending its own bureaucracy. In part, it was a defensive measure: the legislators needed some method of coping with the increasingly technical and sophisticated material with which the White House and its agencies were bombarding them. But the result was the creation of a new policy-analysis bureaucracy in Washington, one that has come to be called government's "fourth branch." Thus were planted the seeds of big government.

The model-makers took on the role of priests in the high church of government. Former Navy Undersecretary R. James Woolsey has even referred to analysis as "a reigning theology." Elected representatives were ceding more and more of their authority to a "professional fraternity" which, in Woolsey's words, had "its own rituals, its own stylized forms of well-worn argument."

The most notorious instance of the misuse of systems analysis was Robert McNamara's handling of the Vietnam War. Former Undersecretary of State George Ball has recounted McNamara's assessment after his first visit to Vietnam in 1962—"Every quantitative measurement we have shows we are winning the war"—and noted that "the very quantitative discipline that he used with such effect as Secretary of Defense did not always serve him well as Secretary of War. . . . He could not help thinking that because the resources commanded by the United States were greater than those of North Vietnam by a factor of X, we could inevitably prevail if we only applied those resources effectively—which is what our government frantically sought to do for the next ten years."

Out of the ashes of the Vietnam debacle arose what has since become known as the military reform movement, one of the programs most closely associated with today's neoliberalism. "The reform movement," explained James Woolsey in 1982, "includes a strong dose of emphasis on institutional biases, on institutional tradition, on morale and strategy—all the things you weren't allowed to talk about during much of the sixties and seventies in defense, because 'it couldn't be modeled in the computer, so how could it be important?' " And so in rejecting systems analysis as a pragmatic principle of big government, the neoliberals embraced military reform.

CHAPTER 10

Military Reform

THE MILITARY REFORM MOVEMENT originated as a counterattack against the systems analysts, the "best and the brightest" who embroiled the United States in Vietnam during the same period their technocratic colleagues in the federal government's social policy sector were using their expertise to create a welfare-state bureaucracy. Although the reform movement cannot be characterized as an attack on "big government"—national defense is, after all, indisputably the federal government's responsibility—the neoliberal criticisms of the military bureaucracy and their suggested solutions mirror the neoliberal attack on big government in other areas.

The reformers' focus on "maneuver warfare," for example, is a military application of the principle of resource limitations. The reformers accept the fact that the era of abundance has ended, that America's economic foundation has changed so that our industrial base can no longer supply the massive amounts of hardware necessary to conduct a war of attrition, thus necessitating the adaptability and maneuverability of military systems.

The demands of the new economic era are human-capital intensive. In economic policy this means a better-trained and better-educated work force and a more cooperative attitude from other sectors of society. In military matters, this leads to the neoliberals' insistence on manpower, unit cohesion, and company morale as essential factors in the country's ability to fight and win wars.

Finally, because the new technologies have integrated the world economy, creating close economic dependencies between nations and enforcing a sense of "global interconnectedness," there is a need for a maritime strategy to replace the continental strategy that has dominated American military thinking for most of this century.

The military reform movement has drawn Democrats and Republicans, both liberals and conservatives, into its fold. For the young Democrats, especially, who were attracted early to the movement, it represents a departure from the traditional liberal attitude toward defense, which since the Vietnam War had been staunchly dovish, noninterventionist, and anti-military.

The military reform movement's first article of faith is an insistence on a maritime strategy to supplant the reigning continental strategy of the armed forces. This theme originated with Republican Senator Robert Taft of Ohio and was picked up by neoliberal Colorado Democrat Gary Hart when he entered the Senate in 1975. (Hart became so closely identified with the maritime cause that he was nicknamed "the admiral from Colorado.") "A basic strategic fact is that the United States is a sea power, not a land power," wrote Hart, Taft, and defense analyst William Lind in their "White Paper on Defense." "Our traditional dependence on the sea has grown as our economy has become more dependent on imports and exports."

The neoliberals have no foreign policy distinct from the Democratic Party's foreign policy; which is to say, aside from a lukewarm obeisance to the notion of human rights and a confused acceptance of the concept of a nuclear freeze, their foreign policy seems to consist of little more than opposition to the Reagan Administration's intransigence on arms control and its intervention in Latin America. One of the prevalent criticisms of the military reform movement is that it too lacks a context by which its doctrinal reassessments can be applied. "They're going about things ass-backwards," charged *The New Republic*'s Morton Kondracke, an early chronicler of the new liberalism. "The reform movement is attempting to define a military strategy without first expressing a foreign policy into which it would fit. They aren't saying *what* American power is for, *where* they would be willing to intervene."

To a large extent, Kondracke is correct. Gary Hart's facile assertion that American foreign policy should follow the dictum "Never seek hegemony" is the closest thing to a foreign policy doctrine to emerge from the neoliberal camp, and a significant departure from liberal thought, which since Woodrow Wilson's day has defined itself by its active, interventionist internationalism.

But the maritime strategy is based on a foreign policy consideration, and like most, if not all, of the neoliberals' interests, this one too is economic. The maritime strategy firmly recognizes the economic connections of the industrialized world. "Despite our important relationships with Canada and Mexico, we are essentially an island nation," wrote Hart in *A New Democracy*. "Our trade in raw materials moves by sea. The importance of control of the sea is growing, not diminishing, as world economic interdependence grows."

The maritime strategy has three parts. It proposes a greater number of smaller, less expensive aircraft carriers than the naval force currently relies upon; the introduction of high-speed advanced-technology ships, such as hydrofoils; and a larger fleet of conventional submarines instead of the current focus on the large nuclear attack subs. In other words, the military reform sea-power doctrine emphasizes flexibility, maneuverability, and adaptability—three qualities that not only define neoliberal military reform in general, but neoliberal responses in such areas as industrial policy and human-capital policy as well.

Neoliberal industrial policy advocate Robert Reich speaks of America's new "flexible-systems economy," in which industry's basis is no longer the long runs of standardized product lines that characterized the industrial era, but more specialized items made in smaller batches. Reich stresses the need for American industry constantly to adapt to changing contingencies to retain its competitive advantage, and advocates educating and training workers to be more maneuverable within the job market. The same rhetoric and similar images apply to the military reform movement and its maritime strategy. The reformers oppose the continued introduction of large aircraft carriers because they represent an enormous thirty-year commitment of resources, which along with their size limits their long-run versatility. If the character of warfare or the nature of America's international relationships changes, U.S. reliance on a fleet based on thirteen massive carriers could place the nation at a strategic disadvantage. Furthermore, the carriers' bulk makes them militarily vulnerable; indeed, Soviet naval strategy is founded upon incapacitating them, prior to aircraft deployment.

But far from suggesting the elimination of the aircraft carrier as the basis for American naval strategy, the reformers stress its importance. Carriers are flexible: their role can be revised quickly by changing the planes they carry. Aircraft can be employed at sea or on shore; they can carry missiles or bombs. And they can strike fear into enemy hearts without ever having to fire a single weapon.

The pregnability of a few lumbering ships has moved the reformers to advocate an additional force of smaller, less expensive aircraft carriers, not to replace the baker's dozen but to buttress it. The older carrier fleet would be maintained and modernized, but the bulk of the navy's strategic hopes would be placed in a larger, "reconceptualized" fleet, built to be adaptable (through the use of modular, easily upgradable on-board weapons systems and sensors) and used as a replacement for a portion of the fleet's traditional warships—cruisers, destroyers, frigates.

Because of their focus on smaller, cheaper systems, the military reformers have been criticized by the Pentagon's reigning powers for being anti-technology and for promoting quantity over quality. But in fact, what looks to be opposition to technology is actually a restatement of the theme of appropriate technology. "I think you want to use technology intelligently, to improve reliability, to reduce cost," said former Navy Undersecretary R. James Woolsey in 1982. "I think the electronics revolution gives you an opportunity to do that, if you handle it right. What you want is the military analogue of your small, new twelve-dollar pocket calculator that doesn't break down and only needs a new battery every couple of years, instead of the military analogue of the desk calculator of six years ago, which cost hundreds of dollars, didn't do very much, and kept breaking down." In short, the more advanced the technology, the smaller and simpler the systems can be. This is a far cry from the typical conservative pro-defense stand, which President Reagan's Defense Secretary Casper Weinberger exemplifies. The hawks continue to stress a reliance on large nuclear submarines, while military reformers insist that technology has improved diesel electric power so that smaller submarines have become not only feasible but a desirable addition to the naval fleet. As Gary Hart summarized at a meeting of the Council of Foreign Relations in New York on June 11, 1981, "Far from being obsolete, conventional subs are quieter on patrol than nuclear subs, less detectable by active sonars, and better in shallow waters. They also cost about one-quarter as much as nuclear attack-submarines, so we could afford larger numbers in a mix with nuclear ones."

Appropriate use of technology, in military reform theory, also requires a greater emphasis on manpower. James Woolsey, in the defense policy segment of *The New Republic*'s March 1982 "Democratic Agenda for the '80s," asserted that technology could increase weapons reliability and decrease costs; enable us to further efforts in space and under the sea; improve the ability of current forces to conduct electronic warfare; and aid in designing adaptable weapons systems. Such systems, he concluded, require an emphasis on "innovative and demanding training and realistic maneuvers for our forces," and on "forces that emphasize agility and ability to maneuver."

The concept of maneuverability permeates the military reform movement. The second major component of the revisionists' vision is the doctrine of maneuver warfare. Mainly this means that in a war America must "outthink" its enemies; in speeches and texts, that word is a beacon identifying reform sentiment. James Woolsey in *The New Republic:* "We will not be able to overwhelm the Soviets or their clients on the European mainland. We must *outthink* them and exploit their weaknesses." Gary Hart to Bill Moyers in June 1980, enumerating the ways to overcome an enemy: "There's another factor also. I think we've got to *outthink* them." This emphasis on outthinking and outmaneuvering the enemy issues from a canon of neoliberal economics: the belief that the U.S. industrial base, the tireless producer of virtually infinite supplies for the better part of a century, can no longer manufacture enough material to enable the nation to outlast an enemy in a bullet-to-bullet, bomb-to-bomb, tank-to-tank, man-to-man war.

Military reformers of all stripes seem to agree that the doctrine of attrition warfare, whereby an enemy is defeated by the use of massive firepower, is obsolete. As military historian Edward N. Luttwak of Georgetown University noted, with frustration, in the conservative Heritage Foundation's anthology *Reforming the Military,* "Against Soviet forces we could rarely expect to obtain a firepower advantage, while on the other hand, the rigidities of Soviet tactics should offer much scope for methods of agile maneuver." American reliance on attrition warfare, charged Luttwak, is due to the Pentagon's insistence on "cost-accounting debates and the fancier bookkeeping of 'systems analysis.' "

The reformers like to quote the ancient Chinese philosopher Sun Tzu's ranking of the four ways to defeat an enemy as justification for their theory. Lowest on the list is to destroy the enemy soldiers— attrition warfare—because the difficulty of mounting and completing the task without losses is enormous. Up one notch is the destruction of the enemy's logistics. Much better is the attempt to destroy the enemy's alliances. But the best tactic is to destroy the enemy's strategy— to crush the mind of the opposing leader.

If future battles are to depend more on outthinking the enemy, on the ability of commanders to disrupt, frustrate, and outmaneuver the opposition, and on the capacity of troops to adapt to changing situations, then recruitment and training must reflect these new doctrines. For officers this means education, command ability, and the ability to think.

The reformers fault the military education and promotion process, which disgorges bureaucrats instead of thinkers. Gary Hart explained the problem to the Council of Foreign Relations in 1981. "Our current military system gives remarkably low priority to ideas about warfare," he said. "The military education system—through the service academies, the command and staff schools, and the war colleges—emphasizes study of management, not the art of warfare. A cadet can graduate from the service academies with only one semester of military history. And, overall, our promotion system reinforces the inadequate education. The services promote the manager, tolerate the troop leader—at least in the junior ranks—but have little room for the theorist."

Some simple solutions have been suggested to correct what Jim Fallows, author of *National Defense,* has termed "an army that [has] sacrificed its military values to those of the career rat race." In the Vietnam War, careerism resulted in "ticket-punching"; commanding officers served six-month tours with their troops, after which they rotated out and up. Jumping from command to command was the path to career advancement. Eliminating the rotating command system was one tactic recommended by military reformers. And, beginning in 1981, the Army took several steps to increase unit cohesion.

Smaller, more cohesive units that are more agile and maneuverable are growing more popular in today's military. As Steven L. Canby, a West Point- and Harvard-educated lieutenant colonel in the Army Reserve and a leading figure in the reform movement, wrote in the Heritage Foundation's *Reforming the Military,* "Good tactics . . . are as much a function of the manpower system as they are of doctrinal concepts. . . . A sound manpower system supports good tactics by providing cohesive units, lean organizations, and all-level command initiative." Manpower, asserted Canby, "must be viewed as part of an organic whole."

The military reform movement is a microcosm of the new liberalism. On defense matters in particular, liberals have been uncomfortable with dwelling on goals—preferring instead simply to oppose the conservatives' "spend, spend" philosophy—and thus have ignored the need to approach military affairs strategically. Burned once by the technocrats who drove them to overapply force in an unwinnable war, liberals withdrew from defense policy. The neoliberals, having rejected the technocratic approach, can look at defense in terms of ends *and* means. "This group," said Larry Smith, who until 1982 served as Gary Hart's administrative assistant, "believes you can outthink a problem more effectively and more predictably than you can simply overpower a problem. And I think that is directly derived from Vietnam."

Out of the burnt cinders of the Vietnam era arose the notion of integration of separate concepts—postindustrialism, appropriate technology, globalism—into a unified doctrine of military reform. "In my mind, in Gary Hart's mind," said Smith, "this is the earlier, competing idea of the American character. Namely, that somehow there is something especially ingenious and smart and inventive about America."

CHAPTER 11

The Rise of Appropriate Technology

SYSTEMS ANALYSIS NOT ONLY CREATED a military bureaucracy unable to adapt to change, it also helped to provide a social policy bureaucracy in government that could not cope with the problems of the 1970s and 1980s. Future neoliberals began condemning the situation as far back as a decade ago, to the consternation of their liberal brethren. In 1974 there began the curious spectacle of young, purportedly liberal Democrats running for office and lambasting "big government." Gary Hart opened his campaign for the U.S. Senate that year with his famous pronouncement, "We're not a bunch of little Hubert Humphreys." Traditional liberals misunderstood this as a rejection of government *in toto:* as late as 1980 Arthur Schlesinger, Jr., interpreted Jimmy Carter's criticisms of the federal bureaucracy as "campaign demagoguery."

But there are distinct differences between the conservatives' and the neoliberals' critiques of big government. By 1980 the Republican Party had officially adopted the philosophy Barry Goldwater espoused on the campaign trail in 1964: government is the problem, the *only* problem. Ronald Reagan honed this message, opposing the federal government's activities on behalf of social welfare, equality of opportunity, affirmative action, environmental and occupational safety—on everything, it seemed, except national defense.

Although the neoliberals have also found fault with big government, they readily promote the necessity and efficacy of *affirmative* government. The federal government is indeed the solution to many of the ills that beset society; it must, they maintain, serve as the guaran-

121

tor not only of freedom, but of opportunity and equality. But they further hold that government, under the thrall of a "you can have it now" philosophy driven by pseudoscientific systems-analysis techniques, has promised too much. Its inability to deliver on those promises has led to an unhealthy disillusionment that seeps through society, fragmenting it. As a consequence special interests claim the allegiance people rightfully owe to the nation as a whole. From this critique has sprung the neoliberals' revisionist query, "What is the proper role of government?"—a question liberals had not asked since the 1930s. The neoliberals' answer—that government *can* decentralize certain functions, that the market *has* a place in reform—sets them apart from the traditional liberals, who have long cherished centralization as an article of faith and disputed any reform role for the market.

"The goal of liberalism," historian Eric Goldman has said, "is to put itself out of business." By the mid-1970s, lulled by the prosperity and security of the preceding two decades, it had accomplished exactly that. Liberals had abrogated their philosophical requirement to experiment, promote change, and hasten the future, in favor of a rigid system that appropriated all problem-solving functions to a federal government under the control of a technocratic class of experts. By the late 1970s, however, with the "new realities" of growth within limits, information technologies, and globalism pressing upon them, the neoliberals—particularly those who sat in the nation's statehouses—had rejected the unyielding centralization of authority for a more pliable approach to government, one that harked back to an almost-forgotten creed: decentralization.

Decentralization is a natural response to the postindustrial paradigm. MIT's David Birch concluded after looking through his "new microscope"—his term for the records he has gathered of six million businesses—that the macroeconomy to which government policy has long ministered bears only a slight resemblance to the microeconomy he was uncovering of small, entrepreneurial, information and service businesses. The macro-to-micro shift implies the need for a more decentralized approach to the economy's problems; or, to use Richard Gephardt's words, a "more tailored" methodology.

"Information is decentralizing, incredibly decentralizing," affirmed trend analyst John Naisbitt in 1981. "The model to look at is the telephone system. It's a huge, monstrous machine, but it's decentralized down to the individual. Only you or I can access it, only you or I can control the information that goes out over it. . . . Information is the least controlled thing there is, and it's the most decentralizing." Unlike, say, John Kenneth Galbraith, who thought new technologies compelled centralization and bureaucracy ("technostructure" in his words), the neoliberals see just the opposite. "Technology is a force for decentralization," asserted industrial policy advocate Robert Reich in 1982.

The New Deal, the Fair Deal, and the Great Society each concentrated greater power in the central government, as a response to economic crises and the social inequalities generated by an overreliance on local responsibility and the unregulated market. Most of the criticism of central government during the 1930s, 1940s, and later, in the 1960s issued from the right or the radical left. Liberals learned to react to such censure with a near-automatic affirmation that federalization is good and federalism is bad. But the price of that affirmation was bureaucracy.

Citing but one example, Arizona Governor Bruce Babbitt noted in 1982 that "public education has become bureaucratized beyond belief. It has become bureaucratized in the name of equal opportunity, in pursuit of some undeniably [beneficial] social justice aims. But we've become careless about the way we've let the bureaucracy take over the public school system, and reduce it to a big fat book of procedural rules, and less content."

Babbitt is one of the new political breed who simply cannot be defined by traditional liberal or conservative criteria. He serves a conservative, historically Republican state, a fact that has certainly enabled him to challenge liberalism's shibboleth of centralization with relative immunity from electoral prosecution. Yet, as he stated to an audience at Princeton University in February 1983, he still considers himself very much a progressive: "I am a liberal . . . I am a social activist . . . I am also a realist." After receiving a degree in geology from Notre Dame and a law degree from Harvard in 1965 (the year he participated in the giant civil rights march in Selma, Alabama), Babbitt served as an assistant to the director of VISTA (Volunteers in Service to America, the "domestic Peace Corps"), and then as a lawyer for the Office of Economic Opportunity in rural south Texas. His knowledge of Spanish (until the election of Toney Anaya as governor of New Mexico, Babbitt was the only current chief executive in the country fluent in the language) served him well in both jobs. In fact, although little noticed by the Anglo press, his long-standing involvement in and sensitivity to issues of concern to Hispanics has made him a major figure in that community nationally.

Babbitt seems, at first blush, a curious mixture of 1960s-style social liberalism and liberalism-within-limits sentiment. One of the few Democrats to risk a public call for the progressive taxation of Social Security benefits, Babbitt went so far as to try out his pitch at a senior citizens center in Phoenix in December 1982. Asked later about the response, he smiled and replied, "I immediately regretted my indiscretion." But he has continued with his pleas, telling his Princeton audience, "After fifty years of social change and government intervention, we have reached an era of limits."

These limits don't mean that neoliberals seek to replace the federal government as the locus for action with a system of decentralized units. Richard Gephardt, in 1982, maintained that "eighty percent of what needs to be done to keep the economy in order comes under the heading of macroeconomic policy," which is inherently a federal responsibility. Rather, the neoliberals are willing to entertain solutions that do not involve the centralization of authority; they simply seek to answer the question, "What is the *appropriate scale* for our activities?"

"There will be some areas which are so clearly imbued with the national interest that it will be appropriate to have a national response," Bruce Babbitt said in May 1982. "But we have lost the ability to ask that threshold question: 'Is this a matter for national concern?' We've had a pell-mell rush to assume in any situation that a quick federal law is a net benefit, even though it destroys our ability to have variegated, inspired, and different solutions in the process." Applying his theory of decentralization to the problems engendered in education by the federal bureaucracy, Babbitt asked, "Wouldn't [it be better to have] a federal law, a one paragraph federal law, saying that, in lieu of all this federal aid . . . states must have basic foundation plans for support to equalize the resources devoted to education in every school district in the state?"

Rather than devise a process in Washington to promote a given principle, and mandate the application of that same process in every area of the country, neoliberals believe that, in many cases, a more appropriate role for the federal government is to specify the goals to be achieved, while allowing the states to design the best methods for reaching them. "Instead of mandating things," said Babbitt, "by pouring all this easy-act federal money all over the place, I would ask whether we can't get the same effect in a less intrusive, less mandating way—the same effect in equality of treatment, and equality of resources. It's a far preferable way of getting equality without the deadening overlay of all the federal stuff.

"I don't quarrel with the tremendous strides that have been made through Congressional and judicial intervention," he added. "We've really made some tremendous steps toward social justice. But we've brought with it a bureaucratizing of the system. My question is, isn't it now possible, now that we have a quickened sensitivity about these issues, isn't it possible to lift some of the deadening bureaucratic hand? While at the same time saying to parents and students and communities, 'Your access to a federal court for protection against serious, basic infringements remains absolutely intact'?"

Babbitt was an early supporter of President Reagan's "new federalism," a set of programs designed to return jurisdiction over a variety of social programs to the state governments. But Babbitt quickly soured on the program. "Reagan has an essentially nostalgic view of government," he explained. "The reason that he missed the opportunity to sort all this out and establish a system in which there is vitality up and down is because of this nostalgic view, this anecdotal view of the world. . . . He says the federal government has no responsibility—'I deny the need for a national government, except to raise armies and print money . . . and not very much of that!' So his credibility is eroding rapidly, because there are issues that require attention in the twentieth-century economy.

"The trick," continued Babbitt, "is how you devise the litmus test. This is an important issue, a political philosophy that allows you to dip the litmus paper into a political issue, pull it out, and say, 'Well, if it's red, that's a national issue; if it's blue, that's a local issue.' " His comment closely reflected the position taken by Congressman Gephardt at *Esquire*'s 1981 dinner for neoliberal politicians and advisers. In response to a question about federal versus state welfare programs Gephardt replied, "Whatever program you have in place should be a national program, rather than a continuation of what we have. I don't know whether I'd go as far as a negative income tax, but the program we have now is fragmented into a lot of different pieces—we have food stamps, we have state welfare programs, we have AFDC, we have a number of other subsidy programs, like Social Security and SSI. It would make sense to me to consolidate that. Of course, that's easy to say and difficult to do.

"But there are other places where I'd get rid of government," continued Gephardt. "I would get rid of government in health care. I would get rid of government in education to a much greater extent than we have. I would discharge those responsibilities either to the private sector or to the states. I guess it's a way of saying I don't think you can take a theory, such as 'Liberals are for government doing lots of things,' or 'Neoliberals are for government doing lots of things.' You almost have to go area by area and say, 'What is your decision in that area? Why? Why do you think that government should have a role or should not have a role?' We may differ, obviously, on these different areas. But I think what you will find among this group and people like us, is that we do not have a dogmatic approach that government does it better, or that government shouldn't do it at all."

The mere willingness to consider decentralized solutions to social problems, the entire idea of a "litmus test" to determine federal and state responsibilities, is a drastic departure from the liberalism of the past. And decentralization (along with the macro-to-micro shift) represents one of neoliberalism's strongest themes, appropriate technology. Because appropriate technology is a neoliberal cornerstone, it's worth briefly investigating here.

At its most fundamental level, appropriate technology simply means that there are proper methods of achieving any desired goal. Overapplication of resources can be as damaging to the reaching of that goal as underapplication or underfunding. Appropriate technology is relevant to every area of policy—military reform, tax restructuring, energy programs. But always there is an awareness or an intuitive knowledge of limits.

In his 1977 dissertation on appropriate technology, *Many Dimensional Man: Decentralizing Self, Society, and the Sacred,* social philosopher James Ogilvy invokes the same rejection of technocracy and expertism that drives the neoliberals. "The intention," Ogilvy writes, "is to demystify technology, to render access to sometimes arcane tools that otherwise remain in the hands of the specialists and professionals only too eager to turn their knowledge into a saleable commodity."

In seeking to return technical expertise to a loosely-defined "the people," appropriate technology favors the entrepreneur over the technostructure, the microeconomic view over strictly macroeconomic interpretations, the smaller unit over the large unit, and decentralized decision-making over centralization.

Once the concept of appropriate technology is understood, the neoliberals' attacks on "big government" are certainly not "anti-government," as traditional liberals charge. Their criticism of bureaucracy, their interest in decentralization, their concern for "human-scale" politics, might best be termed a quest for appropriate *political* technologies. Gary Hart's speech to the Western Electronic Manufacturers Association on April 20, 1976, slightly more than a year after he took office, is an example not of an anti-government bias, but of an anti-technocratic inclination.

Through a cursory sketch of the numbers, Hart dispelled the myths that the federal government, in its efforts to solve the great problems of the sixties, had either grown too large or spent too much. Statistics simply did not verify these assertions. In 1955, 14 out of every 1,000 persons were civilian employees of the federal government; twenty years later, the ratio was exactly the same. In 1950, 16 percent of the federal budget was taken to pay them; in 1975, the percentage had declined to 13 percent. The smotheringly large agencies of the bureaucracy? The Department of Defense was far and away the largest, with 3.2 million people, and two-thirds of them were in uniform. The Department of Health, Education and Welfare, by contrast, employed only 139,000 people. Taxing and spending? Defense, with 64 percent of the personnel, spent a quarter of the budget.

Hart was among the first liberals to point to the exponential growth of middle-class entitlements as the reason behind the escalating rate of government spending and taxing. Social Security and Medicare for the elderly, no matter what their individual financial status, consumed five times as much federal money as all other welfare programs taken together. "The three popular villains of big government are largely mythical," Hart recapitulated for the manfuacturers. "The federal bureaucracy is not an expanding octopus. On the contrary, it has remained about the same size. Federal spending has grown in proportion with the economy and inflation—maintaining a roughly constant share of our output of goods and services. The overall federal tax burden also has not grown, but it has shifted from business to individuals."

Isn't this a typical liberal oration—a defense, even, of big government? No. There was indeed a problem with big government, asserted Hart. However, it would not be found in the conservative canards.

"The central problem of big government springs from our attitudes and expectations," he declared. "The problem of big government is big promises that cannot be backed up by performance. The problem of big government is inflated expectations that generate disillusionment rather than hope and progress. The problem of big government is the myth that it can solve every problem and meet every challenge. The problem of big government, frankly, is the demand placed upon it by every interest group in our society."

The problem of big government, implied Hart, was caused by the technocrats, the qualitative liberals, the promoters of "you can have it now." "When problems are exiled to Washington for solution, people become 'clients' of government programs rather than sovereign citizens to whom government must be accountable," he said. "The result of this process over the years is that people are stereotyped and stripped of humanity to fit into a cold definition of program categories. Real people become 'recipients,' 'consumers,' 'clients of health-care delivery systems.' What we need are citizens and human beings. . . . This nation must grow beyond the arrogant and ill-considered promises that government could 'whip' inflation, immediately win a 'war on poverty,' or guarantee 'world peace.' "

A critique of liberalism's past was the theme of Gary Hart's first campaign for the Senate in 1974. A chiseled-featured, even-tempered, thirty-seven-year-old upstart who had never run for office before, he launched that race with billboards that declared, "They've had their turn. Now it's our turn." To this day, there are many old liberals who still have not forgiven him.

Traditional liberals will imply that their antipathy toward Hart is based on his management of George McGovern's spectacularly successful drive for the 1972 Democratic presidential nomination and of the equivalently unsuccessful general-election campaign. As in his 1974 Senate race, Hart was without credentials, at least on paper, for the role of campaign coordinator in 1972.

A Kansas native, the son of conservative and religious—and Republican—parents, Gary Hart attended a small Methodist college, married his college sweetheart, and entered Yale Divinity School in 1958 bent on a teaching career in religion and philosophy. But the 1960 presidential race was for Hart, as well as for many other leading neoliberal politicians, a turning point. John F. Kennedy did not fit this Midwesterner's image of a Washington politician, that of someone too old and too doctrinaire to be a useful model. After volunteering in the Kennedy campaign, Hart switched vocational directions and entered Yale Law School, befriending there another former theologian, Jerry Brown, the son of the governor of California.

Because of John Kennedy, Hart came to a conclusion that would carry him through his subsequent career: that power—even power within a single ideological discipline, such as liberalism—must be wrested by each generation from its predecessors, who have grown complacent and conservative, and will fight internal change. To Gary Hart, the 1960 election, particularly the primaries, proved this point. They convinced him that, even among liberals, the divisions were deep. He saw the ideological old guard, what he still refers to as the "Eleanor Roosevelt wing" of the Democratic Party, the segment that considered itself the rightful and lineal heir to Franklin Roosevelt's mantle, futilely pushing Adlai Stevenson for a third try at the presidency, throwing up test votes in the U.S. Senate to verify their claim that young Kennedy was "not liberal enough." But Kennedy, the man who lit the flame of activism in the cerebral divinity school student, represented something new, different, and appealing: pragmatic liberalism. "I believe that John Kennedy was the bridge from Roosevelt and Truman and the New Deal to something beyond," Hart said in 1981. "I think he was the generational bridge to the post–New Deal era, and that that bridge was destroyed by the assassination."

To some, the disillusionment that followed upon Kennedy's death ended their political involvement. To others, though, the torch had indeed been passed to a new generation and they intended to keep it. Gary Hart went to Washington and served briefly as a special assistant to Interior Secretary Stewart Udall, then left for Denver, where he toiled away at his law practice. He did issues work for the Democratic Party and worked for Bobby Kennedy, in 1967–68. In 1970 he helped shepherd George McGovern around Denver when the senator came to deliver a speech to the annual Jefferson–Jackson Day gathering of the state's Democrats. As McGovern prepared to leave, he told Hart, "I've decided to make the race for the presidency, and I'd like to have your help." It was only later that Hart discovered he had signed on not as western states coordinator, but as manager of the entire campaign.

While the subsequent two years provided Gary Hart firsthand knowledge of how power struggles between supposed ideological confreres can destroy a campaign, it also brought him insights that ten years later help to explain the current turmoil within the Democratic Party. Those who had labored so assiduously to the very end to block McGovern's nomination, claiming that he was not a true representative of Democratic liberalism, dealt a fatal blow to his eventual candidacy; they represented not the mainstream of the Democratic Party, felt Hart, but what was by that time a fringe, mired in the past. They were clearly kin to the ideologues who had attempted to deny John Kennedy the top spot in 1960.

The signal lesson Gary Hart learned in 1972 was that change, although inevitable ("as certain as the transition of generations themselves," he wrote in his chronicle of the 1972 race, *Right from the Start*), had to be worked for, had to be organized for, had to be fought for. Probably thinking of his own impending Senate campaign, he wrote in his memoir of the McGovern years, "The forces of change and progress must develop a new generation of leaders who can instill confidence and demonstrate competence."

But it would be wrong to view the new liberalism of the 1980s as merely a generational struggle for power. While shared experience is a critical part in the formation of any generation's world view, especially in the political arena, it does nothing to explain the extreme ideological disparities that always exist between people of the same age. Neoliberalism is more than just the common bond of experience and activity. It arose because certain individuals recognized that, as inevitable as change in politics was, and as important as organization would be to effect it, the crucial element was missing: ideas.

For Gary Hart and other Democrats then too young to make an effective difference within the party's hierarchy, this was the blinding revelation of the McGovern campaign. "McGovern somehow brought to the surface a whole new generation of political organizers, the best the country has seen for many years," Hart wrote in 1973. "But he did not bring out a new generation of thinkers. He did not because it isn't there." The fount, he concluded, had run dry: "The best thinkers of the 1930s, 40s, and 50s, and even the 1960s, were not producing." He let fly a thought that many of McGovern's young supporters, veterans of the antiwar movement and flushed with their success at nominating a candidate, might have considered heresy: "By 1972 American liberalism was near bankruptcy."

Nature would provide the new blood, but new ideas required an arduous rethinking process, part of which included a questioning, if not a rejection, of recent politics and cherished liberal notions. Mainstream Democratic politicians had, of course, begun to do this in the late sixties, when the conduct of the Vietnam War (and Lyndon Johnson's de facto abdication) forced them to reconsider many of their beliefs about American supremacy, the new internationalism of the 1960s, the post–World War II doctrine of containment, and the nature of the authoritarian regimes the United States was supporting in order to defy an equally noxious totalitarianism. But none would dare to dismiss the Democratic Party's *domestic* policies of the 1960s. That was thought to be political suicide.

That is until 1974, when Gary Hart successfully challenged the prevalent maxims. "The pragmatism of the New Deal has become doctrine—if there is a problem, create an agency and throw money at the problem," he charged in a stump speech on his way to the Senate. "We have lost that sense of pragmatism over the years, and what were once viewed only as experiments have now become articles of faith." To compound this infidelity, Hart deigned to list specific Johnson-era programs that had not delivered on their promise. "The ballyhooed war on poverty succeeded only in raising the expectations, but not the living conditions, of the poor," he insisted. "The federal housing program has been a miserable failure." The obvious solution to such flops was to toss them out, but the marriage of bureaucracy and technocracy allowed the instinct for self-preservation among government workers to prevail. Furthermore, it fostered the creation of interest groups so tied to specific government programs that they would fight strenuously for their continuation, even if the programs no longer served the needs for which they were created. "If you want to get government off your backs," Hart told a crowd of middle-class Coloradans during that first campaign, "get your hands out of government's pocket."

After he took office, Hart honed this theme, eventually joining with other young Democratic officeholders in expressing the belief that there were limits to what government could accomplish. What's more, the limits were natural; it was the expectations that had been artificially raised—by the analysts, the technocrats, the Whiz Kids. The experts. The liberals.

And so neoliberalism developed in part as a revolt against "expertism," and as a reassertion of the politician's right to hold to values and to demand effective execution of programs designed to meet those values. This fundamental aspect of the neoliberal critique was well illustrated at one of the breakfast gatherings sponsored by Hart and Texas Congressman Martin Frost during 1981–82. These morning sessions became a meeting ground for congressional neoliberals during their early efforts at coalition. Wandering in late to one of the Hart-Frost breakfasts, Bill Bradley took a seat and listened to the discussion already under way. His colleagues were going over the possibility of persuading some well-known *philosophe* to lend intellectual credibility to their opinions and prescriptions. Arthur Schlesinger? James MacGregor Burns, perhaps? One of the congressmen turned to Bradley and asked, "Well, what do you think, Bill?"

Replied Bradley, "We don't need a rabbi."

In rejecting the cult of expertism, analysis, and bureaucracy, Bradley talks of "rabbis," James Woolsey of a "reigning theology," and Larry Smith—Gary Hart's former administrative assistant and an expert on arms control—of "priests." The religious symbolism is significant because of its prevalence. "We hold to these values," affirm the neoliberals, "and we *don't* need experts to validate them for us." Larry Smith described the traditional stance: "In my own field, I've seen debates organized on defense policy, and within three hours the discussion turns to, 'Should we have an F-18? Can the AWACs be countered?' I'm saying, wait a minute, I don't want to pay *my* senator to talk about whether that radar will work. I'm perfectly willing to let a radar engineer decide that. What I want, if the Republic is going to work, is my senator to state his basic purpose for which we might use force. Then I want him or her to engage in a judgment, a subjective judgment, on the character of threats, and on the war itself which may have to be fought. Because I think those are imponderables. And on the basis of *that,* I'm willing to have him say, 'I want an AWACs because it fits into this.' "

But, added Smith, liberalism during the 1960s and 1970s was the victim of a "Ph.D. culture . . . whose unstated premise is that these matters are expert matters which the public can't get involved in." Because the public was shut out from decisions over military matters, then over social policy and regulation, it finally turned against the promoters of these programs, voting many liberals out of office. "When the neoliberals complain, as they do, about the 'pointy-headed theoreticians,' " said Larry Smith, "they are simply recognizing the vulnerability their values had to counterattack—which is partly a product of fragmentation, itself derived from an underlying assumption that public policy is derived from expertise."

Big government, in short, arose from the liberal belief that leadership was a technical question. The more intractable a problem became, the larger the government grew, as more agencies were created and additional experts hired to study the deepening crisis—even if more appropriate political responses to the problem existed. The neoliberals assert that this unquestioning acceptance of centralization and the cult of expertism was one of liberalism's chief failures.

"What I think the Bradleys and Harts and Gephardts are saying," concluded Larry Smith, "is, 'Look, we're tough enough and smart enough—in fact, the electorate itself is tough enough and smart enough—to deal with these matters at other than just the declaratory level.'"

CHAPTER 12

Using the Market for Reform

THE PRINCIPLE OF APPROPRIATE TECHNOLOGY encompasses not only decentralization but another key aspect of the neoliberals' policy apparatus: using the market for reform. Neoliberals are less sanguine than traditional liberals about the utility of top-down economic controls in promoting progressive social goals. Neoliberals don't accept the conservatives' belief that a competitive free market will always assure the public welfare more efficiently than federal regulations, but they do express a readiness to explore market mechanisms to solve many of the problems previously dealt with by regulations.

In January 1982, then New York Governor Hugh Carey delivered a speech that exemplified the market-reform aspect of appropriate technology. During his tenure in Congress, Carey had personified the street-smart, interest group—beholden New York City liberal. He had never questioned the increasing centralization of economic authority advocated by his party in the 1960s. He was, explained the *Almanac of American Politics,* "a product of the Democratic Party . . . that in [New York] practically invented the welfare state as we know it in America." But as governor from 1975 through 1982, Carey was forced to contend with his state's economic decline and its transition from an industrial to a service economy, changes to which traditional policy did not speak. He hired as deputy director of the state's Office of Development Planning a former Rand Corporation economist named Roger Vaughan, a prominent member of neoliberalism's policy subculture. Gradually, through Vaughan's influence, Hugh Carey became a neo-liberal.

His January 1982 speech on economic recovery, authored by

Vaughan, was a solid piece of liberal heterodoxy. He argued that Democrats must "redefine the role of the federal government in regulating the marketplace." Carey, then entering his final year as New York's chief executive, elaborated. "In a capitalist system, competition is essential for efficiency, innovation, and protection of the consumer," he said. "Unfortunately, the structure of regulation that evolved at the federal level and in many states during this century was designed to suppress, rather than encourage, competition. It operated not to protect the consumer, but to protect established firms. It often engendered extreme inefficiency.

"In the long run, free and unsubsidized competition will best serve the national interest," he concluded, adding, ". . . I recognize that the language of economic deregulations has sometimes seemed unfamiliar, and sometimes uncomfortable, to many of my liberal Democratic colleagues."

Unfamiliar? To traditional liberals, deregulation is downright *unholy*. And conservatives, although they talked a good game, have been just as adamant about protecting their favored constituencies with a suffocating web of regulation.

In assessing the American regulatory predilection in *The Zero-Sum Society,* a theoretical bible to neoliberals, Lester Thurow pointed out that of the two types of regulations available to limit adverse "externalities" and "income effects"—attempting to control the quantity of goods or services produced, and trying to affect the price—the nation's political leaders and interest groups have more often than not opted for the former, even though it can be empirically proven that these "quantity" or "q" regulations are generally less efficient and more stifling to competition over the long run than price or "p" regulations. The usual objection to market solutions—price—is that producers, if given the option, will gladly pay for the right to, say, pollute, and that they will simply pass the cost of the regulation on to the consumer anyway. But Thurow argues that resistance to regulation is not intrinsic to one category or the other; rather, resistance will occur in any case. To ensure the public welfare one must adopt that type of regulation that will induce the greatest degree of compliance, be least disruptive to economic efficiency, and spur the development of new techniques by which the needs of producers and consumers are adequately met. Price mechanisms are the best way to accomplish these goals, says Thurow. But, he cautions, "Getting to a set of 'p' regulations after a set of 'q' regulations has been adopted is going to be one of the major challenges of the 1980s."

At the risk of making a complicated issue sound simple, the willingness to consider price regulations over quantity regulations distinguishes the neoliberals from liberals as well as conservatives. The neoliberals believe that in many areas, the market is a better allocator of net benefits than a set of top-down, central-government controls. Decontrol of prices and, for example, the imposition of effluent charges are by their very nature decentralized. Like the simplified tax schemes advanced by some neoliberals, they imply that once artificial distortions and the smothering hand are removed, and individuals are allowed to make their own choices about investments and purchases based on market considerations, then they will make the choices that are in their own best interests and, collectively, in society's best interests.

Arthur Schlesinger, Jr., has accused the neoliberals of finding "great virtue in the unregulated marketplace," but in fact, this is far from true. While they profess skepticism toward old liberalism's rush to regulate, neoliberals find the Reagan Administration's knee-jerk dash to deregulate equally faulty. In a 1983 case, a Federal Trade Commission economist argued against recalling a product in which defects had been found, suggesting that victims could sue for compensation. Congressman Albert Gore, Jr., responded, "Some screwball thought market forces could be defined as lawsuits by widows and orphans!"

Although in many ways he personifies an "Atari Democrat," Gore has worried about the labels attached to politicians who speak his language. "I wouldn't say I'm advocating a high-technology future," he cautioned in the summer of 1982. Gore feared that politicians bunched under these titles would be seen "as having a synthetic substitute for compassion that was intellectually base." He paused, then laughed. "You know—all right hemispheres with hypertrophied left hemispheres."

Gore had reason to be concerned about the implications of neoliberalism. For most of his political life he'd been consumed with the thought of following his father's path to the U.S. Senate. Gore's opportunity came when Senate Majority Leader Howard Baker, a fellow Tennessean, announced in 1983 his intention to retire the following year. Immediately Gore became the front-runner for Baker's seat. Now the tall, hawk-nosed Gore had more reason than ever to be cautious about alienating Tennessee's tobacco growers and factory workers with indiscriminate talk of high-tech.

Nevertheless, Gore had spent four years chairing the Congressional Clearinghouse on the Future, a powerless, ad hoc, bipartisan advisory committee dedicated to instilling a longer-term perspective—"future awareness," in his words—on Capitol Hill, so it was difficult for him to avoid the subject of technology for any length of time. "Genetic engineering, computers, robotics . . ." Gore ticked them off one by one on his fingers. "These are the components of the scientific revolution that has mutated into this process of change unlike *any* we've seen before." And for Gore, these elements of future awareness demand at least a partial rejection of the past. "Out of that four-year series of conversations, dialogues, speeches, and seminars," he said, referring to his clearinghouse tenure, "I've come to share the conviction of many in this country that we are in the midst of an accelerating scientific revolution, and that we are *kidding ourselves* if we pretend that tinkering around with the mechanisms created in another age is going to deal with a world where a lot of the key assumptions are changed."

Again, the famous banner: *The solutions of the thirties are not going to solve the problems of the eighties.* The irony is that Gore's father was one of those who helped to invent those old mechanisms. Senator Albert Gore symbolized the new South of the postwar era, a territory where a populist tradition of economic progressivism at long last joined a moderate social liberalism. As senior senator from Tennessee, the elder Gore established himself as one of Congress's staunchest supporters of Lyndon Johnson's Great Society, as well as an early and ardent opponent of LBJ's Vietnam War. Both factors helped lead to his defeat in 1970, after thirty-two years in Washington, eighteen of them in the upper house.

Gore *fils* went to Harvard, and afterward attended divinity school—like such other leaders of the neoliberal vanguard as Gary Hart, Jerry Brown, and Sam Brown. He then went to law school and served in Vietnam. (He is one of the very few Vietnam veterans in Congress.) In 1976 he succeeded the man who had taken over his father's House seat when the elder Gore moved to the Senate in 1953. And now he waits to complete the circle.

"A lot of us," said Gore in 1982, "believe now that government has to play a different kind of role, to try to channel the forces in our society and our economy, rather than try to dam them up. We believe that government can play a leveraging role, a logarithmic role." He smiled. "Rather than a manhandling, bureaucratic, regulatory approach, we believe that it's a kind of *jujitsu* approach to the forces that shape the economy and shape society."

Part of the transition from "manhandling the forces of change" to the "jujitsu approach" to social policy entails accepting the market's role in that policy. A good example is Gore's own legislative handling of the relationship between hypertension-induced heart disease, the nation's leading killer, and the high salt content of the foods that make up the American diet.

"A traditional, New Deal kind of approach might have been to have a government program, or at least a law, mandating that the sodium content of various foods be no higher than a certain level," contended Gore. "I opted to take a different, two-pronged legislative approach. To mandate labeling of the amount of sodium per serving— there is still a government role, and a forceful role, but it is at the point of contact, the point of leverage—and to stimulate as much discussion and education as possible in the country about the connection between sodium and high blood pressure." The reasoning, he explained, is simple. "You marry increased awareness with the increased information flow. And at that point you begin to see the forces of the marketplace solve the problem for you."

In an earlier era liberals spoke of competition as a form of social insurance, but by the sixties and seventies top-down regulations and controls became the order of the day. The Carter Administration took great strides toward economic deregulation, with the aid of traditional liberals like Senator Edward Kennedy, deregulating the airlines and beginning attempts to deregulate the trucking industry. But Carter's halfhearted efforts to moderately decontrol energy prices met stiff opposition from old liberals like Senator Howard Metzenbaum and Kennedy, whose 1980 primary challenge to the President rested on a platform advocating wage and price controls and continued regulation of energy prices. The frustration of trying to storm the old liberal blockade of controls and regulations moved economist Alfred E. Kahn, the administration's designated inflation fighter, to remember his job as exasperating. "No one had a more sobering experience than I," he said, "in dealing with inflation and understanding the failures of the traditional program and the problems of dealing with the traditional constituencies." Not only did Kennedy's attack from the outside hinder the administration's efforts, but inside the White House Vice President Walter Mondale also proved himself a strong opponent of the efforts at deregulation supported by other members of the administration. "There wasn't a time I tried to do anything about Davis-Bacon, [the law requiring the government to pay prevailing union wages on federal projects] or minimum-wage exemptions for young, inexperienced workers, or eliminating dairy-price supports and acreage limitations," recalled Kahn, "where it wasn't Mondale's office that absolutely put the kabosh on it."

Job training and retraining and energy policy provide the best examples of how neoliberals would use the market for reform. They maintain that our economic health as a nation depends on increased government investment in education and training, but they further believe that to operate at peak efficiency, training institutions must be subject to the demands of the market. Proposals for training vouchers are thus garnering attention in Democratic circles, despite the fact that vouchers are traditionally associated with conservative policies.

Economist Pat Choate of the Business Roundtable, has developed a plan for Individual Training Accounts that would operate much like the popular Individual Retirement Accounts. IRAs, unlike company pension plans, are tied to the individual and not the job, thereby providing a high degree of personal security. ITAs would function according to the same principle. They would be composed of savings plus equity, and financed by equal contributions from the employer and the employee, up to a maximum amount. Choate suggests a maximum contribution of $3,000 to $4,000 each from employee and employer, for a total ITA of $6,000 to $8,000, plus interest, to be collected over a period of six years.

The ITA would remain with the worker, drawing interest, until retirement. If the fund is never drawn upon, then at retirement both worker and company would have returned to them their shares of the investment, plus accumulated interest. If the worker is displaced, then the ITA would become available in the form of a voucher that could be used at eligible institutions. The federal government would bear the responsibility for certifying training establishments at which veterans of future economic wars can use their vouchers, just as it accredited schools under the original G.I. Bill. Workers would still be entitled to unemployment insurance, but after a specified period of time (Choate suggests twelve to fourteen weeks) would be required to begin use of the ITA for retraining and/or relocation. Upon reemployment, contributions to the ITA from both the worker and the new employer would resume, until the threshold was reached.

Choate's proposal has advantages beyond the obvious ones of providing security in a time of economic instability and allowing the displaced worker the right to decide his or her own future. Because both the worker and the employer have an equity interest in the ITA, there is an incentive for the individual to be more prudent about the use of the funds than he would be with a flat federal grant, and for the business not to dismiss summarily an employee who might otherwise be retrained and retained within the firm. In addition, the aggregate ITA funds would increase the real level of savings in the nation, providing a boost for the economy, and the savings would be targeted specifically for human-capital investment, while also remaining available as a new source of government borrowing.

Versions of Choate's plan have been advocated by some neoliberals. Bill Bradley, in a lukewarm opinion piece for *The New York Times,* suggested that "one way [to help workers upgrade skills] might be to create an insurance program under which workers displaced by technology or foreign competition could cash in their policies and use the money to acquire new skills," a clear reference to the ITA proposal. Gary Hart, in *A New Democracy,* specifically endorses Pat Choate's proposal.

Hart also recommended a similar program devised by economist Roger Vaughan. Vaughan, a former adviser to former New York Governor Hugh Carey, has designed a much more comprehensive and ambitious program for job vouchers to finance training and retraining, incorporating them into a complete restructuring of the federal training system.

Vaughan has proposed a "G.I. Bill for the American Worker" that would guarantee all workers the right to be retrained for jobs. This right would be exercised through the issuance and redemption of job-training vouchers. Workers would earn credit for vouchers for each month of employment, from a maximum entitlement of $50 a month for those in jobs paying $10,000 or less annually, and sliding down in increments of $5 for each additional $2,000 of earnings, to a minimum entitlement of $5 per month credit for workers with yearly earnings of $30,000 or more. In addition, the maximum credit of $50 a month would be earned for each month a person is on unemployment, and welfare recipients would be eligible for an automatic voucher of $2,500, repaying it by taking no credit for the first three years of work. One of the hidden values of Vaughan's voucher system is that it places the disadvantaged, the unemployed, the underemployed, the displaced, and even the working person under the same tent, removing the stigma that in the past has been attached to public employment and training programs like CETA (Comprehensive Employment and Training Act).

Vaughan also sets a $3,000 limit on the value of a voucher. Like Choate's ITA, the vouchers could be redeemed at any accredited public or private institution for education or training, including programs set up by firms to upgrade the skills of their own workers—providing, in effect, an incentive in the form of a partial subsidy for employers to retrain their employees rather than displace them. Vouchers could only be used to pay 90 percent of a program's cost, ensuring some amount of individual responsibility, and a person would not be eligible to participate in more than one voucher-supported activity in any five-year period.

Vaughan's voucher system departs significantly from liberal job-training programs of the recent past, not only because, organizationally, it attempts to redress the fragmentation of earlier programs by providing a coherent framework for *all* training and employment policy, but at a more fundamental level because it allows the individual freedom of choice and responsibility for decisions, while promoting and enhancing the role of an active government. In this sense, a voucher system fosters a traditionally conservative ideal within a traditionally liberal context. "Public resources—financial and technical—are harnessed with the individuals' resources," affirmed Vaughan and economist June Sekera in a human-capital policy paper prepared for the Corporation for Enterprise Development. "They are not used to suppress initiative and substitute for individual responsibility. Education and training institutions would have to compete to attract vouchered individuals. This would encourage innovation and would reduce the institutional inertia that often characterizes agencies protected from marketplace pressures by public subsidy."

The market is also fundamental to neoliberal energy policy. Neoliberals argue that a carefully decontrolled energy market can be used to promote conservation and the use of renewable resources and discourage use of depletable energy sources.

In *Energy Future,* the critically acclaimed 1979 treatise on energy policy, editors Daniel Yergin and Robert Stobaugh of the Harvard Business School detailed a series of assumptions that, they said, would direct energy and growth policy in the United States for the foreseeable future. First was the natural transition in the world's energy production and consumption patterns caused by the depletion of natural resources and the industrialization of underdeveloped countries. Second was the belief that the market—the power of supply and demand—necessarily molds the degree and shape of economic growth. And third was the understanding that in a democratic society economic costs of energy decisions could not be considered in a void; social costs must be factored in. Given these three realities, energy policy must promote conservation and renewables as the "key sources," the surest path to energy security for the United States over the coming decades. Underlying this argument is an inherent comprehension of the politics which of necessity are involved in the formation of a national energy policy. "We try to explore energy questions pragmatically, from the bottom up," wrote Yergin and Stobaugh in the introduction to *Energy Future,* "examining not only the technical and economic obstacles and opportunities, but the political and institutional realities as well."

It was Richard Nixon who first shackled the nation's energy producers (and consumers) with the manacles of heavy regulation as a protection against the vagaries of the new international energy realities. Yergin and Stobaugh were among the first popularly received theoreticians who argued from a liberal position (that is, out of concern for the lower classes and for equity considerations in general) that *decontrol* of prices was a necessary element in an equitable energy future. This put them at odds with traditional liberals, such as John Kenneth Galbraith, who nevertheless reviewed their book favorably. (Ironically, Galbraith used his review of Yergin and Stobaugh's work in the *New York Review of Books* to advertise his idea for a federal rationing program that included taxing the price of gasoline up to $5 per gallon and issuing gasoline stamps to consumers to offset the hike, violating *Energy Future*'s adamant stance against controls. The famed economist sloughed off the issue of the bureaucracy that would inevitably be necessary to administer such an undertaking. "Nothing, alas, can be done without people," he quipped.)

While Yergin and Stobaugh cautioned against an overreliance on the market, recommending a gradual "detoxification" plan to cure the country's addiction to depletables, their primary suggestions, *contra* Galbraith, were based almost entirely on phased decontrol of energy prices. Admitting that "the country certainly cannot afford to ignore measures that *might* marginally increase domestic supplies," they favored continuation of efforts begun during the Carter Administration to decontrol domestic oil and gas prices—including the price of the "old" gas not decontrolled under the Carter plan—coupled with targeted assistance for low-income groups and elimination of the windfall profits tax on newly found oil, to encourage exploration. "We favor reliance on the market," *Energy Future* asserted emphatically.

Yergin and Stobaugh's recommendations in favor of energy price decontrol were echoed by several neoliberals in the early days of the Reagan Administration. In a speech to the New York City Bar Association in April 1981, Gary Hart advocated decontrol as a method of limiting oil consumption and as a means of spurring exploration for new oil. "The government," said Hart, "ought not to set artificial prices or establish relative energy prices. Decontrol of oil [during the Carter Administration] was the right step for this reason."

New Jersey's Bill Bradley went further. Bradley argued vociferously against the traditional liberals' and conservatives' notion that America could conserve and produce its way out of an energy crisis. Responding to an editorial written by former Carter Administration domestic policy chief Stuart Eizenstat in *The New York Times,* Bradley said that "the calls for Government subsidies for commercializing synthetic fuels, solar energy, and conservation" and "the calls for Goverment allocations and Government agencies to administer them" are "a response to the wrong problem." Bradley was one of only two Northeastern Democrats in the Senate (Paul Tsongas was the other) to vote in 1981 against reimposition of controls on domestic oil. "Because domestic oil was kept lower than the market price, we encouraged consumption," Bradley explained in Senate debate. "Because oil production in the United States was not increasing, we bought more exports."

Bradley's own response (aside from his never-ending call for the U.S. to fill its Strategic Petroleum Reserves) was contained in his Emergency Preparedness Act of 1981, introduced in September of that year. Bradley's bill was a replacement for the soon-to-expire Emergency Petroleum Allocation Act, passed in the heat of the first Arab oil embargo in 1973. The Bradley legislation reflected his conviction that "relying on market forces would be far more effective in reducing economic distress during an oil supply cutoff than government attempts to control prices and supplies." It called for price controls to be replaced during an emergency with immediate tax cuts and transfer payment increases to offset the effects of the crisis on poor and middle-income citizens, and the rapid distribution of emergency block grants to all fifty states to help low-income people hurt by an oil cutoff. Although supported by other neoliberals, the Bradley proposal lost in committee.

Paul Tsongas, who supported the Bradley bill, stressed in *The Road from Here* that liberals "must accept the reality of decontrol," but added that "the liberal must argue for shock absorbers to cushion the impact on low- and middle-income citizens." The mugwumpian mixture of deregulation with tax breaks and transfer increases recommended by neoliberals like Bradley and Tsongas led political writer

Robert M. Kaus to quip, "Conservatives decontrol; liberals decontrol and send checks."

The strategy put forth in *Energy Future,* and the program by and large accepted by the neoliberals, is very similar to the "soft energy path" of Amory B. Lovins, a wunderkind out of Harvard and Oxford's Merton College, who began his career as an international consulting physicist in 1965 at the age of eighteen. Under the auspices of the Friends of the Earth, Lovins started developing alternative energy policies in the early 1970s, publishing *Soft Energy Paths: Toward a Durable Peace* in 1977, at about the time the new liberalism truly awakened. Although revealed in his writings as a bright-eyed optimist whose vision of a cooperative pluralistic society working happily within the bounds of new appropriate energy technologies obscures the sometimes messy political bargaining necessary to create policy, his sketches of the soft path have helped define the parameters of the neoliberals' energy program.

The soft path differs markedly from the avenue of energy policy pursued by the U.S. government. The governmental "hard path" is characterized by many of the same elements common to traditional policy—whether liberal or conservative—in a host of areas. It assumes an inevitable correlation between energy consumption and economic growth and for the most part relies on depletable resources, notably Arctic and offshore oil and gas and strip-mined coal, to fuel the engines of growth. The hard path presupposes that these resources will continue to be used in enormous centralized power systems (coal-burning electricity-producing facilities, nuclear-fission breeder reactors, and the future fusion breeders). The massive application of technology is extremely capital-intensive, and for that reason potentially inflationary and certainly subject to the slightest inflationary pressures.

The most salient feature of the soft path, aside from its basis in renewable resources and conservation rather than in depletables, is its emphasis on the application of technologies less centralized than those in the hard path. Often referred to generically as "solar," these technologies are defined by Amory Lovins as flexible, resilient, sustainable, and benign. In 1980 the federal expenditures on soft-path strategies totaled $1.5 billion—less than the amount spent nationally *each week* for imported oil.

The transition away from the hard path and the continuation of conservation efforts can be achieved with a relatively passive government strategy of using the market for reform. The other primary soft-path goal, the shift to renewable resources, depends upon a more active approach, albeit one that still stresses market forces. Daniel Yergin and Robert Stobaugh think that the correction of inherent market distortions favoring oil and gas consumption is the initial step toward a transformation to a national solar program. The price of imported oil fails to approximate its true costs, including its very real social costs, but attempts to impose the kinds of tariffs necessary to discourage its use meet with violent opposition. Therefore, say the *Energy Future* editors, the politically viable alternative is to use incentives to promote solar energy, coupled with deregulation of the prices of conventional sources. "The carrot," they conclude, "makes for better politics and more acceptable change than does the stick."

Amory Lovins adopts the same approach, arguing for economic incentives, rather than additional regulations, to promote soft energy. Among the incentives he recommends are the gradual increase in efficiency standards for home appliances and automobiles and cogeneration (the production of electricity using the waste steam produced in many factories) for commercial use. "Though economic answers are not always the right answers," wrote Lovins in 1976, "properly using the markets we have may be the greatest single step we could take toward a sustainable, humane energy future."

The soft path relies upon appropriate technology. For this reason energy reform is an adjunct to the military reform debate. Like the military reformers, soft-energy advocates explicitly condemn the development of policy in the political vacuum created by systems analysts. "It is tempting to subordinate the democratic process to elitist technology, to substitute 'we, the experts,' for 'we, the people,' " wrote Lovins in 1978. "That is gratifying for the experts, but after a while it does tend to lead to a loss of legitimacy."

Like supporters of the military reform movement, who oppose the headlong rush to build more technologically sophisticated and complicated weapons systems in favor of using technology to simplify armaments, soft-path advocates believe that "the challenge" (in Lovins' words) "involves making things sophisticated in their simplicity, not in their complexity." It is, then, no wonder that an alliance would be forged between the military reform and soft-energy movements. And such a compact indeed exists. The introduction to Lovins' 1981 book, *Energy War: Breaking the Nuclear Link* (co-authored with his wife, Hunter), was written by Admiral Thomas H. Moorer, a conservative and the former chairman of the Joint Chiefs of Staff, and former Navy Undersecretary R. James Woolsey, an avowed advocate of appropriate technology in military policy. Admitting that "efforts to stereotype the [Lovins'] approach in terms of the traditional national security debate will prove to be a difficult exercise," Woolsey and Moorer nevertheless interpreted the Lovins' recommendations—greater efficiency and decentralized, simple, and renewable energy sources—as very much a part of that debate:

> The vulnerabilities [of centralized power facilities] are so numerous—to the weather, to accidents arising from complexity . . . to a handful of terrorists, to the detonation of even a single smuggled nuclear weapon—that denying the plausibility of such threats is unlikely to prove persuasive. The authors' recommended solutions . . . thus appear in a very different light than that in which such recommendations have often appeared before. In the hands of the authors, these are not solutions that derive from a desire to take to the hills with a bag of Krugerrands to abandon a decaying society, nor are they steps to resist the use of modern technology or demand special subsidies. The Lovins seek rather to persuade us not to resist what the free market and millions of citizens and local governments are already doing in their own self-interest.

"Do not resist the free market." In his wildest dreams, no pundit of twenty years ago would ever have predicted that this dictum would again define a liberal program, let alone energy and defense policies. In the eighties, the neoliberals have allowed it to guide them.

CHAPTER 13

The Entrepreneurial Economy

THE YEAR 1983 IRONICALLY marked the centenaries of both John Maynard Keynes, the intellectual theorist of New Deal liberalism, and Joseph A. Schumpeter, an Austrian who spent his last years teaching at Harvard. In a cover story for *Forbes,* Peter F. Drucker, the noted author, political scientist, and management consultant, bemoaned the fact that Keynes's birthday was being celebrated with conferences, seminars, and plaudits throughout the West, while his contemporary's anniversary was passing virtually unnoticed. "It is becoming increasingly clear," wrote Drucker, explaining his displeasure, "that it is Schumpeter who will shape the thinking and inform the questions on economic theory and economic policy for the rest of this century, if not for the next 30 or 50 years."

The neoliberals would agree. Their willingness to accept the efficacy of market forces in promoting liberal goals represents not only the importance of appropriate technology, but what is perhaps their most significant departure from contemporary liberal theory: the shift from Keynes to Schumpeter. From this *other* economist's work derives neoliberalism's concern for risk, innovation, and entrepreneurship, as well as the neoliberals' attempts to replace the politics of redistribution with the politics of investment.

In Schumpeter's economic theory, risk is the essence of progress, and creative destruction is the product of risk-taking. Risk has entered the mainstream of new liberal politics. The acceptance of Schumpeter, who was ignored during the ascendancy of Keynes from the 1930s through the 1970s, has gone hand in hand with the apotheosis of the entrepreneur. Among neoliberals, the promotion of entrepreneurialism dates at least as far back as Taylor Branch's 1970 warning about the dangers of no-growthism in the *Washington Monthly*. For years, however, Branch's article remained an anomalous example of entrepreneurial fervor. But beginning in the late 1970s, promotion of risk-taking and entrepreneurship among a class of politicians and advisers increased, soon becoming the norm.

Significantly, this new push was accompanied, in many cases, by explicit condemnations of the riskless society that traditional liberal policy was charged with creating. In a 1976 editorial in the *Washington Monthly*, Charles Peters disparaged young people's preference for security, and had the temerity to attack one of the era's plenipotentiaries. "They are children of the television, shopping center, consumerist age," wrote Peters of contemporary youth. "Their knight in shining armor has been Ralph Nader, the protector of those who buy things."

Other leading Democratic advisers have joined in the vilification of risklessness. Writing in *The Economist,* the influential British news magazine, in 1981, New York investment banker Felix Rohatyn, whose push for a new Reconstruction Finance Corporation is among the most controversial ideas floating around in Democratic circles, harshly observed:

> The New Deal and the Great Society were the great liberal economic watersheds of this century; they were fundamentally different in their aims and results. The New Deal sought to put people to work and curb the excesses of the 1920's; it also saved the capitalist system in America. The RFC, CCC, REA, TVA all aimed at stimulating production and employment; they succeeded. The SEC, Social Security, the Federal Reserve Board, the FDIC, anti-trust legislation aimed at regulating excesses and protecting the public; they succeeded. The Great Society, on the other hand, aimed at cradle-to-grave security, income transfer, elimination of poverty, pervasive regulation; to the extent it failed, it did so largely because America cannot afford it. By attempting to reduce the element of risk it succeeded in eliminating many of the incentives to create wealth.

To a large extent, Lyndon Johnson and his Great Society have been blamed for much more than their share of contemporary economic ills. The Great Society's signal accomplishments—the Civil Rights Act and the Voting Rights Act, for instance—were clearly successful in extending the right of participation in U.S. society to minorities who had been unjustly and illegally kept from sharing in the American dream. To look at these programs, or LBJ's push for education, or even Medicare, as attempts to induce "cradle-to-grave security" is a distortion of the Great Society's intent. Furthermore, much of what Johnson is faulted for in the areas of excessive regulation and income transfers is traceable to the Nixon-Ford years. Nevertheless, the social planners in the Republican White Houses and the Democratic Congresses were seen—and saw themselves—as continuing in the tradition of the Great Society. The result of that presumed mandate, in the eyes of the neoliberals, is a society without risk. And no risk means no growth—as simple as that.

The evolution of the now-disparaged riskless society is based upon the unquestioning acceptance of Keynesianism. Economists tutored under Keynes's theories came to believe in economic equilibrium as the ideal state, and further held that misallocations in capital and labor would be corrected the closer the economy moved toward equilibrium. This indeed underlies the unwavering adherence to macroeconomic policies as the all-sufficient answers to inflation and unemployment that has characterized the Keynesian domination of liberal governments. It also explains Reaganomics, its mix of monetarism and supply-side tinkering, which, although it departs from the Keynesian demand-stimulation imperative, nevertheless is, in Peter Drucker's words, "[a] desperate attempt to patch up the Keynesian system of equilibrium economics."

In his *Theory of Economic Development* and *Business Cycles,* Schumpeter posited that innovations, which he defined broadly as "the setting up of a new production function," are the fuel of economic evolution, igniting irreversible changes in the way activities are accomplished, and resulting in not only new products, but new markets and new organizational forms. Historically, innovations tend to arise in clusters; when one entrepreneur believes the risk of introducing a new innovation is safe enough and proceeds to bring it into the production process or the market, his success leads others to do likewise. Additional financing then becomes available. But, since all cycles must have downturns as well as upturns, the entrenchment of innovations lowers their prices; goods produced by the new processes then glut the market. Profits fall, and the entrepreneurs take fewer risks. Eventually, the market contracts and venture capital disappears, resulting in fewer innovations . . . until, of course, the next cycle. In other words, "entrepreneurs appear en masse," as does capital investment, and vice versa—ebb and flow.

Schumpeter's conclusions cut to the very core of neoliberal economic thinking: Innovation is the essence of economic progress; profit is a motor of economic growth; capital formation is essential for investment, which finances the productivity increases necessary to generate new wealth. What's more, these hypotheses strike at the heart of Keynesianism by prizing disequilibrium over equilibrium, and by asserting that innovation, far from being an external variable, an "outside catastrophe" in Keynes's words, serves a vital function. And where Keynesianism's focus on the macroeconomy raised the economist-policymaker to saintly status within the liberal pantheon, asserting that only he had the knowledge and ability to control the levers that created wealth, the Schumpeterian system esteems the businessman, the entrepreneur, the innovator, the individual microeconomic actor, who in fact *himself* controls the macroeconomy.

The theoretical shift to Schumpeter from Keynes flips our familiar policy considerations on their head. Noted Peter Drucker:

> The basic question of economic theory and economic policy, especially in highly developed countries, is clearly: How can capital formation and productivity be maintained so that rapid technological change as well as employment can be sustained? What is the minimum profit needed to defray the costs of the future? What is the minimum profit, above all, to maintain jobs and to create new ones?

Liberals had never asked these questions. But, as has been obvious at least since the publication of Lester Thurow's *The Zero-Sum Society,* from now on, the neoliberals would. "From biomedical applications to alternative energy technologies we see signs that innovation and invention are still very much alive in our economy and hold promising signs for our future," maintained Congressman Timothy Wirth in a February 1982 speech to the Rocky Mountain Inventors Conference. "But the problem now is encouraging an atmosphere which will aid inventors in turning better ideas into products which produce jobs and economic growth."

Much of the influence of Schumpeterian theory on the neoliberals can be traced to the work of the Council of State Planning Agencies, a policy development arm of the National Governors Association, and particularly to its former director of policy studies, Michael Barker. It was the CSPA that first publicized David Birch's MIT research on small-business job generation, the CSPA that opposed the Carter Administration's large-industry-oriented economic development policy, the CSPA that argued for the market's place in liberal economic policy. In the end, it was the CSPA under Barker that assembled many of the economists who would comprise the leading edge of neoliberalism's policy subculture.

Michael Barker worked in the Planning Office of Massachusetts Governor Michael Dukakis, a tough, no-nonsense neoliberal first elected in the Watergate year of 1974, only to be defeated in 1978, then reelected in 1982. Barker left Dukakis' administration during the governor's first term, however, to become associate director for community and economic development of the CSPA in Washington.

Just prior to his arrival, the CSPA had been blessed with a $350,000 federal grant. Barker made a decision that would have an important effect on the development and transmission of neoliberal thinking: he opted to use the money to publish a series of pamphlets aimed at the developers of public policy, soon expanding the scope of his audience to include not only the men and women in governors' suites, but members of House and Senate crews, employees of executive agencies, and staffers in state legislatures as well. The intent was to saturate with information those people, as Barker defined them, "who wanted to understand more about economics, but didn't have the time to drop out and go to the Kennedy School, or develop a friendship with someone at Brookings."

In casting about for a methodology for his books, Barker recalled the frustration he had felt in the Massachusetts governor's office over the lack of coherence in the state's development strategy. Tax policy was drawn up independent of education policy, which was designed apart from banking legislation. There was little that connected the individual areas to an overall plan for economic growth; consequently, the traditional policies employed by state governments (following the federal government's lead) had, he saw in Massachusetts, almost no impact on economic development. "I did strongly feel that there wasn't a body of theory that addressed how we could solve the problems of the *real* economy," he said. "There was too much macro policy, not enough micro policy. We really did feel that everything that had gone before was bunk or useless." So he chose to deal with policy development from the standpoint of basic markets in land, labor, capital— what economists call factor markets. "Traditional programs," he pointed out in 1983, "were just *swamped* by the market. They didn't make enough of an influence."

But what *did* make an influence? Coming from Massachusetts, Barker had been aware of David Birch's MIT research on small-business job generation for several years. Governor Dukakis' 1975 economic development report cited Birch's statistics in affirming the need for a policy aimed at the entrepreneur. In Washington, independent studies confirming Birch's thesis were falling into Barker's hands. Michael Kieschnick, for example, had done a master's thesis at Harvard's Kennedy School on the profitability of small manufacturing firms that was "very exciting"; and so Kieschnick was commissioned to do a CSPA report. But federal government policy, dominated by traditional liberals and the interest groups that controlled them, did not touch the job-generating sector of the economy. The capital markets were operating inefficiently; small business couldn't get the money it needed. Labor markets were not working—trained personnel were not available, and people looking for work were unprepared for the open jobs. And still the Carter Administration's economic development policy consisted of subsidizing the *cost* of capital for large firms— even though capital costs were only a fraction of the cost of doing business, even though large firms were not part of the developing sector, and even though those operations that would grab the money would be dying businesses in the older manufacturing industries.

The CSPA declared a print war against the Carter Administration. It was to be small business against large, new business against old, venture capital against subsidized capital; *correcting the market imperfections against creating new ones*. A ceaseless publicist, Barker mailed out tens of thousands of releases about the CSPA's policy books, worked to plant excerpts on op-ed pages in *The New York Times* and *Washington Post,* and then sent photocopies of the resulting editorials by the thousands to legislators, executives, and their staffs. The council's monthly Xerox bill at one point totaled $15,000.

Much read, the CSPA's books and reports exploded many of the macroeconomic myths promulgated by the New Economics of the 1960s, creating in the process a new conventional wisdom. There was *not* an almost infinite universe of branch plants waiting to locate in any state whose tax policies were the most lenient; in their special "Series on Development Policy," the CSPA's economists revealed that business location decisions almost never depended on explicit state development policies of any kind, including taxes. Instead, they relied upon other tangibles not usually thought of as part of development policy, such as an educated work force and availability of transportation, both of which had generally been considered under the rubric of *social* policy. The current, almost universal, skepticism of government officials toward the ability of tax abatements to attract business is due in large part to the CSPA's work. Recognition of the inability of industrial revenue bonds to help generate new business and new jobs—the effectiveness of IRBs had long been an article of faith among liberals—could also be traced to Barker's efforts.

Use the markets, asserted the CSPA, don't subvert them. *Investment* guides economic growth, the council maintained. The use of pension funds for economic renewal was the theme of one CSPA book. The role of venture capital in urban development—who had *ever* thought the two were connected?—was the subject of another. The council developed its own National Investment Bank proposal in 1978 (well before the idea of a revived Reconstruction Finance Corporation had received much attention) in anticipation of the sunrise versus sunset industry debate it saw in the offing. The entire current obsession with investment in infrastructure to halt the precipitous decay of essential public facilities can be traced to the CSPA's *America in Ruins,* by Pat Choate and Susan Walters. David Birch's research identifying new, small businesses as the source of most new jobs in the economy was publicized again and again in a series of CSPA books and leaflets. And the role of regulation in influencing economic development was analyzed and dissected. "There was a tendency in the sixties and seventies to propose new regulations every time a problem was found," recalled Barker. "You got the feeling there was a core group of bureaucrats who sat around developing all-purpose regulations that could be adapted to any purpose. . . . Those regulations have done lots of good. But they were not anywhere the ideal solutions." Such liberal infidelity was compounded by the conclusions of many of the reports. "There is considerable evidence," noted one, *State Taxation and Economic Development,* "that market considerations are the most important single factor in explaining . . . differences in economic development."

At one point, circa 1979, it all came together: the obvious ineffectiveness of the traditional programs; David Birch's conclusions in his MIT study about job generation; the independent studies, like Kieschnick's, that verified Birch; the need to add a "micro" forcus to the "macro" viewpoint. Small business. Micro policies. Markets. *Entrepreneurs.* "An emphasis on entrepreneurship is a crucial factor in differentiating an American 'industrial policy' from those of Japan or West Germany," wrote economist Roger Vaughan in a report issued by the council. "The willingness of individuals to take significant risks and start a business is the closest thing to a unique characteristic of the U.S. economy."

Nothing in liberal orthodoxy scorned entrepreneurs, although, in Michael Barker's words, "There had been a tendency to view them as greedy, and to look at profit as somehow dirty." Rather, traditional liberal policy had ignored the entrepreneur. But now, thanks in large part to the CSPA, entrepreneurship would again be a Democratic concern, vying with the big labor orientation of the party. Michael Kieschnick would carry the entrepreneurial message out to California, becoming Governor Jerry Brown's chief economist in part on the basis of his CSPA work. Roger Vaughan would write about entrepreneurs for the CSPA and convert New York's Governor Hugh Carey from an old liberal to a neoliberal. Later, Kieschnick, Vaughan, and Barker would form their own independent policy advisory group, the Gallatin Institute, to continue the neoliberal attack.

But entrepreneurialism implied something else totally unfamiliar to liberals. It required *risk*. Wrote Roger Vaughan in his CSPA pamphlet, *Economic Renewal: A Guide for the Perplexed":*

> The evolutionary process requires risk taking. "Efficient" risk taking requires both high rewards for the right decision, and a high rate of failure for the wrong decision. Any strategy that either discourages risk taking or that limits failure will stultify development. If we protect a financially troubled firm, we are thwarting the growth of better managed or even "luckier" firms that are producing goods and services more in tune with the nation's needs. Saving a dying corporation does not provide more jobs than allowing its demise. More efficient rivals and new business will provide the jobs at much lower cost.

Vaughan took care to distinguish between true risk, "an unavoidable aspect of evolution," and uncertainty, which he characterized as a deterrent to evolution. Fluctuating public policy, the kind developed in a fragmented bureaucracy, is the single greatest source of uncertainty and effectively prevents risk-taking, because of the entrepreneurs' fears that the ground rules will be changed, that the dice will figuratively be loaded against them. "The process of 'creative destruction' should not be blocked through public policies," wrote Roger Vaughan, summoning Schumpeter's theories. And with that assertion, published and promoted by Michael Barker of the CSPA, the New Economics of the 1960s would fade away, to be replaced by entrepreneurial economics.

The new entrepreneurialism could, did, and does make for some strange bedfellows. The bible of supply-side conservatism, *Wealth and Poverty* by George Gilder, published in 1980, is replete with tributes to Joseph Schumpeter and paeans to risk. Gilder had even written for the *Washington Monthly*. Like Charles Peters, Gilder blamed the change in our society's basic incentive system for a deleterious restructuring of the U.S. economy. "As the enterprising spirit is channeled increasingly into law and other professional schools," he wrote, "and thence into government, its lobbies, consultant groups, and organized clientele . . . the crucial inducement to invest once again sinks below the attractions of other wealth." At other points, Gilder was redolent of Lester Thurow: "Perhaps the central secret of capitalist success is its ability to convert the search for security, embodied in savings, into the willingness to risk, embodied in enterprise." Michael Barker, citing a pre-publication excerpt of *Wealth and Poverty* that appeared in *Inc.,* the small-business magazine, said, "There was very little in there that the neoliberals disagreed with. There was very little in there that *I* would disagree with!" And, returning the bow, Gilder's review of Robert Reich's 1983 *The Next American Frontier* was boldly laudatory. "After a decade of Democratic fantasies about the end of economic growth, the 'threat' of new technology, the exhaustion of natural resources, the impending great depression, the need for 'reindustrialization,' the mandate for a 'new protectionism,' " wrote Gilder in *The Wall Street Journal,* "Mr. Reich is making an unabashed case for Schumpeterian 'creative destruction' and economic rivalry and growth."

Disagreements—*significant* disagreements—do of course exist. The new liberals say that Gilder distorts Schumpeter. Supply-side conservatism remains insistent on ministering to the macroeconomy by extrapolating from tax cuts to productive investment. But the greatest difference between neoliberals and supply-siders is this: to Gilder, risk-taking and investment are induced by insecurity, but to neoliberals, following Schumpeter, risk and investment are rational processes and a degree of *security* is necessary to induce them. However, the neoliberals add (in contravention of traditional liberal thinking, which ignored the market effects of its social programs), policies designed to produce security must not distort the market such that risk-taking and investment are thwarted. "Transfer payments, training programs, targeted procurement policies, and affirmative action initiatives are among the efforts used to redress economic imbalance. These programs are central to any conception of economic equity," asserted Roger Vaughan, clearly differentiating the neoliberal philosophy from prevailing Reagan policies. *"However, the structure of many of our redistributive programs discourages rational economic behavior and therefore reduces market efficiency."*

This latter assertion places the neoliberals squarely in opposition to one leading left-liberal group, the Economic Democrats, the latest incarnation of the 1960s student left, who appear to be gaining support among traditional Democratic constituencies, particularly organized labor. The Economic Democrats deny any role for risk-taking in the growth process, and dispute the contention that regulatory and redistributive programs can seriously warp investment. At a January 1982 forum on industrial policy sponsored by the Democracy Project, economists Bennett Harrison of MIT and Barry Bluestone of Boston College, leading Economic Democrat theorists, homed in on this point.

"Before we can embark on any major planned structural transformation of the economy," asserted Bluestone and Harrison, "we are going to have to reject the claims of those who would deliberately promote insecurity as a matter of policy, find ways to re-establish the social safety net, and *extend* the range of the regulatory system to make that net even more secure." Bluestone and Harrison left little doubt that the private initiatives the neoliberals find crucial to economic growth have no place in their scheme; investment decisions, they argued, are the province of "community (and union) researchers, together with advisory councils of rank-and-file workers and consumers." By omission, the two economists specifically reject a role for individual risk-takers and entrepreneurs. The neoliberals are caught straddling a Reagan right which declares any and all efforts to promote security a blight upon risk-taking and investment and a reconstituted left which flatly opposes the notion that too much security can be dangerous to our wealth.

The subject of risk is frequently addressed by leading neoliberal politicians. "Americans have to begin to treat risk more as an opportunity and not as a threat," Senator Bill Bradley explained in 1982. "What I think happens is that people look at their own lives, and see that there's a certain richness to betting on themselves. That is what risk is. There's a certain exhilaration to working as hard as you possibly can to realize the fruits of that risk-taking. And that doesn't mean, in my view, only in the economic area. For example, I think business managers have managed much too frequently for the bottom line *next year*. They aren't willing to take the risk in their business career to put aside money for research and development, and make the investment out of corporate funds for what will pay off five years from now. They've managed for next year's bottom line because that's how they were promoted."

Two years earlier, in a speech to the graduating class at Yale University, Bradley had addressed the same subject. "The growing preference for a relatively risk-free existence is, I believe, undermining the drive and creativity and sense of unlimited possibilities which have helped to renew our communities, our economy, and our personal lives," he told the Elis. "The point is, there are costs, real costs, to our generalized and increasing preference for risk-avoidance as a society: lower productivity, less innovation and creativity, greater inefficiency, and a lowest-common-denominator approach to too many aspects of life." Bradley reaffirmed the personal and public requirements to insure against certain risks, such as illness and loss of life, but charged the students to seek out "some of the productive ones which challenge us to achieve excellence."

Smoothing the path to entrepreneurship involves, to a large degree, improving the investment process. Government investment in research and development to provide the raw material—ideas—upon which new ventures are built is a key policy of neoliberal entrepreneurial economics. So is increased government investment in human capital, particularly in bolstering education in mathematics and science to correct a failure in the labor market, the lack of adequately trained personnel. The neoliberals' tax policies, which center on the removal of artificial distortions that prevent capital from flowing into productive enterprises, is yet another tenet of market-oriented, entrepreneurial economics. Neoliberal efforts to open foreign markets and fight protection of the American market have met with the approval of entrepreneurs. State policies to link university R & D to private-sector business development—in effect, facilitating the rise of the information archipelago—have been endorsed by the National Governors Association, whose 1982 Task Force on Technological Innovation was chaired, not surprisingly, by California's Jerry Brown, along with Michigan Governor William Milliken.

Other policies, particularly those structured to remedy flaws in capital markets that hinder the ability of small businesses to obtain financing, are more specifically designed to meet the needs of the entrepreneurial class. Chief among these is the elimination of the capital gains tax on *productive* assets—defined as "tangible property used in the production of goods and services"—and a concomitant increase

in the tax on *unproductive* assets. Explained Roger Vaughan in the
CSPA's "Beyond Supply Side Economics": "This will encourage entrepreneurs to use their resources to start new enterprises and will also
encourage formation of new venture capital corporations that will increase the availability of capital to new firms." The reform is aimed
at stemming the tide of capital currently washing into nonproductive
assets (yachts, furs, paintings, stamps) as well as into real estate
speculation, which has grown to flood proportions since the advent of
Reaganomics.

As governor of California, Jerry Brown introduced a reform of
his state's tax code—designed by economist Michael Kieschnick—to
conform with the entrepreneurial credo. Brown's Targeted Capital
Gains Tax Reform Act of September 1981 eliminated the capital
gains tax on investments in small, privately held businesses. (California defines a small business as any operation with no more than
500 employees, a headquarters in the state, and securities which are
not publicly traded at the time of acquisition. Acquired stock must be
held for at least three years to be eligible for the exclusion.) At the
same time, the California plan raised the state's capital gains tax on
nonproductive assets, thereby introducing a shift in the incentives built
into the code. Coupled with this, the state lowered the deduction investors can take on capital gains from nonproductive assets from 35
to 30 percent; nonproductive assets include jewelry, antiques, coins,
and stamps. State officials estimated an increase in the state's venture
capital pool of up to $50 million as a result of this reform.

Finally, more than two dozen states have developed public agencies to close the capital gap between entrepreneur and investment.
Connecticut, for instance, has both the Connecticut Product Development Corporation and the Connecticut Innovation Development Program. The decade-old CPDC, which has a $10 million capitalization,
finances development costs in existing new firms with grants and loans,
for which it receives a limited royalty, generally 5 percent of sales,
decreasing as the loan payment is reached and surpassed. Through
1982, the CPDC had earned more than $800,000 through its funding
of fifty-seven individual projects. Its support has helped to create 300
new jobs and $11 million in product sales in the state. Its success
helped to spur the creation of the CIDP in 1981, the purpose of which
is to promote new high-technology innovations by small and medium-
sized manufacturers by providing for working capital loans at below-
market interest rates. The CIDP's initial capitalization was $2 million.

Massachusetts, Indiana, Michigan, and New York have also created similar public financing mechanisms to aid entrepreneurs.

The high-tech banks, the capital gains tax reductions, the talk of risk, and the other proposals that comprise entrepreneurial economic policy all aim toward one goal: the creation of new wealth. Without new wealth, there will be no new jobs, and the battle for social justice and equity will be that much more arduous. Creating new wealth requires investment—another of the key tenets of neoliberalism.

CHAPTER 14

From Redistribution to Investment

THURSDAY, SEPTEMBER 16, 1982, was a humid late-summer day in Washington. The document that was released to the press in Room 1732 of the Longworth House office building that morning spelled out no major reforms or—superficially at least—seriously threatened any vested interests. What it did (although it is questionable whether any of the dozen or so sleepy reporters attending the session fully recognized it) was shatter precedent. For the Democratic Party had assembled behind a report that meekly yet unmistakably replaced the politics of redistribution with the politics of investment.

The paper, "Rebuilding the Road to Economic Opportunity," was the first in a series of planned platform initiatives drawn up by the House Democratic Caucus. Its principal authors were two neoliberals, Richard Gephardt of Missouri and Timothy Wirth of Colorado. Wirth and Gephardt were rapidly engraving their names on Democratic economic policy, co-chairing not only the caucus's economics subcommittee, but an economics task force for the Democratic National Committee as well. Neither effort proved easy.

By the time of its release the congressmen's paper was something of a joke among party watchers. For more than a year, drafts of it had circulated back and forth between members of the party's Committee on Party Effectiveness, a diversified group that represented such a variety of faiths and ideologies that the word "incompatible" would be too weak a description of it. From conservative "Boll Weevil" Kent Hance of Texas to ultraliberal Parren J. Mitchell of Maryland flew the Wirth–Gephardt proposals. And time after time, back they would sail, with the admonition from caucus chairman Gillis Long of

Louisiana to make the damn thing just a *little* more palatable to the Democratic mainstream. After much compromise, the entire caucus finally signed off on the report.

Tim Wirth—a tall Westerner with impeccable Eastern credentials (Exeter, Harvard), a Ph.D. in education from Stanford, and a history of White House service under former Secretary of Health, Education and Welfare John Gardner, a liberal Republican—led off the discussion at the September 16 press briefing by invoking the elements of the postindustrial paradigm. "We've tried to define in the paper what the basic challenges are," explained Wirth. "The change in the basic nature of the economy from a fundamentally industrial economy to one that is increasingly technology- and information-based. And there's the basic change in our economy, away from a domestic economy to an increasingly international economy."

Wirth's knowledge of the subject was broad. As chairman of the House Energy and Commerce Committee's Subcommittee on Telecommunications, he was on the cutting edge of the technological revolution. His exposure to postindustrialism, and his political ambition—Democrats in Colorado like to say that Tim Wirth began running for President the day he was inaugurated into the House—had brought about a shift from many of the traditionally liberal stances he'd taken in the past. An advocate of energy price controls early in his career, in 1977–78 Wirth began preaching a more popular free-market line, arguing for decontrol. Along with Gephardt, Leon Panetta, and Norman Mineta, he was part of the "Gang of Four," a collection of neoliberals, who drafted their own version of the 1981 budget as a compromise between the Reagan plan and the Democratic leadership's budget. Tim Wirth was well versed in struggling with alternative political responses, and he addressed himself to the demands by the new economic paradigm. "We're moving away from the politics of redistribution to the economics of growth and opportunity," he said, "with a very clear sense of the *investments* we must make in ourselves and our future."

Caucus chairman Long asked Gephardt for additional comments. Gephardt responded, "We are setting a *very high priority* on those economic investments. We see them as central to having a bright economic future."

One of the reporters needed a bit of elaboration. What is this "politics of redistribution" you're moving away from? she asked. It was, answered Wirth, the "ad-hocery" that had dominated Democratic politics in the 1950s, '60s, and '70s, after the formation of the

Roosevelt electoral coalition, the attempt to—"buy off is too strong a word," he said—reach out and keep under the tent this group and that group and the other group with this, that, and the other piece of legislation. "We've tried to make a dramatic shift away from that," concluded Wirth. "The Democratic coalition is sound, the Democratic coalition is there, but it does not have a coherent theme."

And so, in September 1982, investment became their signature. "Democrats have been concerned for too long with the distribution of golden eggs," Senator Paul Tsongas wrote in *The Road from Here*. "Now it's time to worry about the health of the goose." This was also the message of "Rebuilding the Road to Economic Opportunity" (better known as "The Yellow Brick Road," a nickname derived in part from the report's yellow cover), whose central informants (although not named in the paper) included such leading members of neoliberalism's policy subculture as economist Roger Vaughan, MIT professor David Birch, and industrial policy advocate Robert Reich. According to the paper, "growth and fairness" are the "cornerstones of the Democratic vision." Yet most of its recommendations are directed, firmly and strictly, not to fairness, but to growth. The one method of achieving it is hammered out page after page: "Increasing Investment in Our Economy," "Investing in Our People," "Investing in Public Infrastructure," and "An Environment for Investment." The redundancy is intentional; investment, believe the Democrats, is a theme that can carry them to victory in the eighties.

The shift in party concerns has not necessarily been met with applause, or even with silent acceptance. The *Washington Post* was the first to launch what would become the customary traditional liberal salvo against the new liberalism, attacking the Wirth–Gephardt proposals in an editorial entitled "Skirting the Fairness Issue." The newspaper marveled at the speed with which much of the ideas about reindustrialization, as late as 1979 considered fringe notions, had replaced what it termed "such core Democratic issues" as welfare and national health insurance. The *Post* was not amused:

> What is truly striking about the document, in fact, is how far the pendulum has apparently swung. Most of the social issues that used to consume Democratic interest have actually been gathered up and put in a box labeled "women's issues." To judge from the document, health care, welfare, nutrition, private pensions and fair access to employment—items that used to be thought of as investments by the nation in all its human capital—apparently need only some fixing up to make sure that women get their fair share of the benefits.

The *Washington Post*'s stiff reaction to "Rebuilding the Road to Economic Opportunity" contrasted sharply with the tepid recommendations in the report. But, in fact, Wirth and Gephardt *had* ignored many of the issues that Democrats had spent years debating. "The Yellow Brick Road" was a political document as much as it was a policy statement, and politically, the middle constituency that had deserted the Democrats for Ronald Reagan needed to be wooed more strenuously than those constituencies already in the Democratic camp; hence the emphasis on economics, rather than on social issues. Traditional liberals had a right to be angry. Investment had never been *their* theme. Yet their complaints meant little. When the House Democrats issued their comprehensive ninety-page campaign document in January 1984, a blue cover replacing the bold yellow of the preliminary versions, investment, budget deficits and the nuclear arms race were the party's chief themes. "We must set the terms of the debate as the Republicans did in 1980," maintained Gillis Long. The Democratic transition was in full public view.

This concern for investment flows naturally and inexorably from the neoliberals' recognition of globalism. International competition hit the U.S. economy like a speeding Datsun, and was one of the most significant "new realities" faced by the new liberals as the eighties dawned. In the ten-year span 1969–79, the ratio of imports to the final sale of goods in the United States rose from 8 percent to 21.2 percent. Likewise, while only 8 percent of America's goods were exported in 1969, by 1979 it had leaped to 17 percent. In selected industries, the differences over the twenty-year period beginning in 1960 were even more telling. In autos, imports jumped from 4.1 percent to 21 percent; steel, from 4.2 percent to 14 percent. But the insistence on the domestic marketplace as the sole focus of American industry prevented politicians and businessmen alike from seeing that the reverse was also true: the strength of the American economy, for the first time in the country's history, depended on the competitiveness of American goods in the international marketplace.

The world, all of a sudden, had opened up, and America, the benevolent big sister, who had rebuilt her vanquished enemies after World War II, was being beaten by them. One of the reasons, beyond the discordance between America's fiscal and monetary policies and those of its trading partners, was an issue not recognized, or even terribly important, in 1970: the productivity problem.

As a public issue "productivity" began to leave strictly economic circles and come into general circulation around 1979. From the

Harvard Business Review to *The New Republic* to the *New York Review of Books* to *The New York Times,* analysis of the productivity problem spread. American products were not competitive in the international marketplace—indeed, they were not competitive at *home*—because it took more man-hours to produce them than it took the nations with which we traded, allowing our global comrades to make and to sell cars, steel, electronics, and clothing for less than we could.

By around 1980, as the Carter Administration's failure to deal with the problems of a rapidly declining American economy was being confirmed, MIT economist Lester Thurow released a compelling and influential analysis of the productivity problem and the international economic structure, couching it within the context of a prescription for the U.S. economy. *The Zero-Sum Society* immediately upon its publication became as much the bible of neoliberal economics as *Energy Future* was on resource policy and *National Defense* would soon be on military matters. Swiftly, a library of Democratic ideas was rising from the embers of the party-in-demise.

Lester Thurow calls himself a liberal. He went from the mines of Montana, his native state, to Williams College, to Oxford on a Rhodes scholarship, then on to graduate work at Harvard, and later served on the staff of Lyndon Johnson's Council of Economic Advisers. Overnight, he became the economic guru of the emerging movement, a John Kenneth Galbraith for the 1980s (albeit without Galbraith's stunning wit and glib intelligence).

Thurow had been a participant in the debacle that had highlighted the breakdown of Democratic ideology nearly a decade before. He had helped to develop the proposal for "Demogrants," a $1,000-per-person guaranteed annual income scheme with which 1972 Democratic presidential nominee George McGovern wanted to replace welfare and several other fragmented entitlement programs. The proposal, introduced in May 1972 on the eve of the California primary, was a disaster, slapped together in a last-minute rush to prove that McGovern's base of ideas was broader than simply his opposition to the Vietnam War. Neither the candidate nor his economists were able to describe fully their program's contents or probable results; McGovern's inability to define its costs on a nationally televised debate tainted him as a shoddy, scattershot thinker. His campaign manager, Gary Hart, recalled the day the Demogrants program was announced as the specific point when he realized that liberalism was near bankruptcy, the day he knew that "the background work wasn't there." Lester

Thurow (whose nickname during his undergraduate days had been "Less Than Thorough") learned from the experience that "ideas need time to kick around, so the rough edges can be worn off."

Introducing ideas into the soccer game of politics was a role Thurow hoped to play with *The Zero-Sum Society*. It served the purpose admirably. He angered traditional liberals by destroying many of their shibboleths, and maddened conservatives with reasoned attacks on their pet notions. To the former, he pointed out that wage and price controls simply could not exist without a massive bureaucracy to administer them; that the corporate income tax was inefficient and that it discouraged needed investment; and that the strict approach to anti-trust had failed to take into account the degree of cooperation necessary to compete in the international marketplace. To the latter, he disclosed that the no-regulation, no-tax "free market" they craved would not, in itself, help business; that a degree of economic planning was justified and necessary to compete in the new, global economy; that social spending and government intervention did not impinge on economic success; and that "big government" had nothing to do with economic efficiency or inefficiency. To both liberals and conservatives, his message was an application of Lincoln's dictum, "There are few things wholly evil or wholly good. Almost everything, especially of Government policy, is an inseparable compound of the two, so that our best judgment of the preponderance between them is continually demanded."

This, indeed, was the essential message of *The Zero-Sum Society*, implicit in its title. "Intractable problems are usually not intractable because there are no solutions," wrote Thurow, "but because there are no solutions without side effects. . . . It is only when we demand a solution with no costs that there is no solution." His theme throughout the book was that individual Americans, and the interest groups to which they belong, held to a "cover your own ass first" philosophy; this, coupled with the political leadership's willingness to follow the whims of the special interests, had produced an arrangement that was decaying from within, a system in which a debilitating political entropy was halting the process itself. *The Zero-Sum Society* was, underneath the charts and tables, an attack on the "you can have it now" approach liberals had been promoting for at least two decades.

The grand zero-sum game was an international contest, Thurow realized, and playing it to win required increases in productivity. "How can we increase the supply of goods available for private consumption, corporate investments, and government expenditures?" mused Thurow, restating the implicit goal of *all* government policy, the raising of the standard of living. "To find an answer, we must find a way to accelerate the growth of productivity."

Thurow was one of the first to bring the productivity problem to national attention. From the end of World War II until the mid-1960s, productivity grew an average of 3.3 percent a year. It slowed to an annual increase of 2.3 percent from 1965 to 1972, and 1.8 percent during the next five years. But 1977 marked the opening of the first period in American history with both rising output and *no* productivity growth.

While mainstream liberal economists had heretofore focused almost exclusively on stimulating demand, they neglected the inescapable fact that heightened demand could just as easily mean the purchase of more Toyotas and Volkswagens as it could the buying of Buicks. New wealth must be created in America; "new wealth," in fact, became a rallying cry for the new liberals. The way to create it, they understood, was to raise the national level of productivity, to increase the value of each man-hour of work. Raising productivity, explained Thurow, means retooling America's basic industries, thereby making them more efficient, and shifting resources away from low-productivity to high-productivity activities—or, in the parlance, from sunset industries to sunrise industries. The key to accomplishing this is investment.

Thurow had created a new political language. "Sunrise," "sunset," "productivity," "investment"—the words began to flow from the lips of the neoliberal politicians like water over Niagara. The politicians adopted Thurow as a mentor and began spreading his views. When Bill Bradley began anchoring a national affairs program on cable television back home in New Jersey, his first guest was Lester Thurow, talking about investment and the productivity problem. Reflecting on the osmosis of political ideas, the MIT economist said in 1981 that it is important "to have some of these ideas floating around in the public domain for a couple of years, so you see what can be sold and what can't be sold. But also, simply, if an idea's been around for a long time, it doesn't scare you." He pointed to the example of supply-side tax-cut theories, which Ronald Reagan had first introduced as a campaign theme four years earlier. "It has to be like Kemp-Roth, where it's been floating around for five years, and everyone's kind of vaguely heard about it," said Thurow. "In some senses, Kemp-Roth is just as scary as McGovern's Demogrant program. But it didn't sound scary. It had been around so long, it had become familiar."

Emphasizing investment—focusing on the supply-side of the public policy ledger—necessarily implies a certain spurning of Keynesian demand-stimulation policies. In looking at the United States as a massive macroeconomic machine, liberals since Roosevelt's day have thought across-the-board prosperity to be a function of the animation of demand, which in turn would control the rate of supply-side expansion. Through the 1960s, spending, rather than savings, was the primary concern of government policy.

The recessionary period that opened with President Nixon's first term of office should have indicated the need for a different response, one that would have restrained demand, at least to a degree, in order to increase savings and then investment in new plant and equipment. But both liberals and conservatives had grown uncomfortable with, or unaccustomed to, supply-side and restraint-oriented proposals. They held stubbornly to their demand-stimulation policies. The outcome of the ever-increasing rush to spend was inflation, which contributed as much as any other single factor to the rejection of Democratic policies in 1980 and the presumed mandate to supply-side conservatism.

Ironically, Democrats had already begun to shift to an investment-directed, supply-side program during the Carter Administration. Alfred Kahn, chairman of Carter's Council on Wage and Price Stability, is a microeconomist by training, a former student of Joseph Schumpeter's at Harvard. He correctly saw stimulation of investment as one of the best ways to counter the limitations on government's resources and the inflation problem. Industrial deregulation, one of the halfhearted principles of Carter's economic policy, was viewed by Kahn (who oversaw airline deregulation as chairman of the Civil Aeronautics Board) as one sort of investment-oriented activity, in which the removal of artificial and unnecessary distortions would foster private investment in industry, leading to increased growth. While traditional liberals applauded some of these moves (Senator Kennedy played an important role in guiding airline deregulation through the Senate), they opposed others. Kahn's frustration with the liberals' adherence to what he considered discredited policies—continued regulation of energy prices below the market rate, wage and price controls, an expansionary monetary policy, and increased government spending—led him to charge in *The Economist* that "what these proposals have in common is that every one of them in effect denies the existence of a scarcity problem." The old liberals' "reactions to the painful manifestations of the economics of scarcity," maintained Kahn, ". . . are largely romantic in both rhetoric and substance."

The focus on investment, and the rebuff to Keynesian demand management, presents a clear division between old and new Democrats. The liberals' response to Robert Reich's 1983 argument for an investment-directed industrial policy, *The Next American Frontier,* was lukewarm. But the reaction by George Gilder, the philosopher of Ronald Reagan's supply-side conservatism, was positively euphoric. "It sounds like supply-side economics to me," wrote Gilder in *The Wall Street Journal* of Reich's plan. ". . . Mr. Reich's program closely resembles the President's." On one significant count, at least, Gilder's assessment was very wrong. Although industrial policy and supply-side conservatism both hinge on investment stimulation rather than demand management, the Republican program, which is based on across-the-board tax cuts, holds to the old macroeconomic picture of the universe, assuming that manipulation of marginal tax rates will miraculously lead everyone suddenly to save and invest. The low rates of savings and of investment in new plant and equipment subsequent to President Reagan's exercise in tax-cutting have exposed the fallacy of this supply-side theory. Industrial policy, which might be called "supply-side liberalism," takes a much more microeconomic view of where and how investment must be directed, focusing (in the neoliberal arrangement) on specific encouragements to entrepreneurs, and on areas like investment in human capital that are almost wholly ignored by Gilder and other supply-side theorists.

However, the apparent similarities have been enough to alienate old-school liberals. Replying to Lester Thurow at a January 1982 Democracy Project forum on industrial policy, economist Stanley K. Sheinbaum, a long-time national and California Democratic Party activist, noted, "What I do see is that the demand side is being completely ignored as we get caught up with the supply-side effects of saving and investment. . . . We have to remember that investment is a function not so much of savings as of demand. If the demand is not there, the investment will not occur." Referring to the beginning of the contemporary inflationary spiral—Lyndon Johnson's waging of the Vietnam War without the imposition of tax increases to finance it—Sheinbaum cautioned, "Keynes didn't fail; LBJ did."

Even the problems of American business management are subject to neoliberal scrutiny. By the late 1970s neoliberals were connecting the falling U.S. productivity rate to American business management.

While investment and investment-related competitiveness were now recognized as affairs of state, they had *always* been part of management's province. And management had shirked its duties. Badly.

The fault lay with society's incentive structure, which had directed an upwardly mobile generation into the wrong pursuits. "Productivity will not be improved," wrote New York investment banker Felix Rohatyn, a leading Democratic adviser, in his own "neoliberal manifesto" in *The Economist,* "when the sons of factory foremen increasingly want to grow up to be lawyers and management consultants instead of engineers and chemists." Lester Thurow, shedding the economist's traditional cloak of neutrality in one of his *Newsweek* columns, also tied the productivity problem to the managerial inefficiency of American business. "America is becoming a white-collar bureaucratic nation," he wrote, "partly because our education system is supplying vast numbers of new workers who are trained to be bureaucrats." How vast were the numbers? Colorado Governor Richard Lamm dwelled on one of the neoliberals' most frequently cited statistics in a speech to the Denver Rotary Club early in 1982. "Are we training our students for the right things?" Lamm asked. "The United States has 535,000 lawyers—Japan has 15,000. The United States has two and a half times the number of lawyers in 1981 than in 1951. One lawyer per 700 population in 1951 and one for every 410 now." In his 1983 report to Harvard's Board of Overseers, an assessment that drew national press attention, university president Derek Bok quoted the same set of figures. (What made Bok's critique of the lawyerly layering of America so startling and impressive was that before assuming Harvard's helm he had been dean of its law school.)

As the recognition grew that liberals had forsaken growth and its components—science, research, exploration, business—there arose as well an awareness that the ethic of innovation had also died. Liberalism and bureaucracy had become so intertwined as to be indistinguishable in the public sector. But worse, in the private sector, lawyers and MBAs, those without experience in the production side of the economy, were now commanding the troops. Predicted Lester Thurow, "We are going to have to save ourselves on the office front."

The neoliberals received early statistical validation of their belief that a misguided management ethic was at least partly to blame for the country's economic malaise. The seminal piece of literature was an article in the July/August 1980 issue of the *Harvard Business Review* by two Harvard Business School professors, William J. Abernathy and Robert H. Hayes, entitled "Managing Our Way to Economic Decline." "It gave substance to [the neoliberals'] sense that business was responsible for our malaise," recalled the Gallatin Institute's Michael Barker, "that there was a difference between the bureaucratic managers of large corporations and the individual entrepreneur out creating new businesses from an idea with his own sweat and efforts."

In their research, Hayes and Abernathy quantified what Lester Thurow had been saying, that business success required a commitment to compete technologically. But whereas Thurow concentrated upon the broad national and international issues of the need for investment in new technology to spur industrial revitalization for competitive purposes, the Harvard professors brought this problem down to a much more tangible level.

"Our experience suggests that, to an unprecedented degree, success in most industries today requires an organizational commitment to compete in the marketplace on technological grounds—that is, to compete over the long run by offering superior products," they wrote. "Yet, guided by what they took to be the newest and best principles of management, American managers have increasingly directed their attention elsewhere." Private sector managers, concluded the professors, displayed a preference for "analytic detachment rather than the insight that comes from 'hands-on' experience"; furthermore, they concentrated on the short-term profit picture rather than on the long-term benefits of technological research and development. "It is this new managerial gospel," they wrote, "that has played a major role in undermining the vigor of American industry."

The neoliberals' critique of management separates them from Republican conservatives. President Reagan faults only the government in hindering investment; he absolves the private sector from blame. The neoliberals, although pinpointing distortions created by contradictory government policies that interfere with business's ability to invest, are quite specific in blaming the short-term perspective of today's business managers for the lack of productivity-enhancing investment.

Who are these managers? Harvard lecturer Robert Reich, who has gained notoriety as an advocate of an innovation-based industrial policy, refers to them as "paper entrepreneurs"—wealth rearrangers rather than wealth creators. Although he dedicated a chapter of his 1983 best-seller, *The Next American Frontier,* to a history and critique of paper entrepreneurialism, he first launched his attack in the *Washington Monthly* in 1980. Reich identified them as the accountants "who manipulate tax laws and depreciation rules to produce glowing . . . annual reports," consultants for whom mergers are the highlights of existence, financiers who wax eloquent over mutual funds, lobbyists "skilled at obtaining government subsidies," and "the corporate executives, trained in law and finance, who hire all of the above."

And, of course, they are the lawyers, always the lawyers, "whose briefcases bulge with statutes, opinions, depositions, interrogatories, motions, and prospecti," the lawyers who serve as amoral hired guns for the existing corporate interests, whose raison d'être is the rearrangement of the pieces of the existing pie, using tactics ranging from the threat to the delay. They have bottled up the system without adding to its largesse; they draw salaries and commissions beyond the wildest dreams of factory workers, yet they produce infinitely less than those same workers in terms of real wealth. The neoliberals' contempt for lawyers is palpable, a latter-day version of Dick Butcher's gleefully murderous declaration of intention in Shakespeare's *Henry VI, Part 2:* "The first thing we do, let's kill all the lawyers." They are the prime pie-slicers, says Reich, and their interests are opposed by those who want to enlarge the pie.

And although neoliberals and conservatives may sound alike in speaking of the need for investment, they part company on the question of the role of the public sector in the investment process. Republicans reject a government role. Not the neoliberals.

"There are a lot of factors that affect real economic growth, and government is one of those factors," said Bill Bradley in 1981. "I would argue that private investment is *necessary*—we need new plants, new equipment—but not sufficient. If we are going to get economic growth, we require two other kinds of public investment. We also need investments in the economic infrastructure, railroads and ports, so we can take advantage of, say, our comparative advantage in coal, and export it; and investment in human capital, older workers who need to be retrained for newer industries, and minority youth in the cities, who have no stake in society unless they have some skills."

All these issues—investment, productivity, management—have been traditionally associated with the Republican Party, which has long been characterized as the party of business interests. But the neoliberals' acceptance of the postindustrial paradigm, particularly their recognition of globalism, forced them to depart from traditional Democratic complacency toward business and management issues. Improvement of productivity is essential to renewed American global competitiveness. And that, assert the neoliberals, requires managers who understand the requirements of the international marketplace as well as government policies designed to foster an economic climate favoring investment. One of these proposals also appears to be traditionally Republican: lowering taxes. But in neoliberal politics, Republican looks can be quite deceiving.

CHAPTER 15

A Tax Policy for Investment

CAPITAL INVESTMENT, investment in infrastructure, and human-capital investment are three technical-sounding pieces of jargon that neoliberals toss around. Translated, they stand for the amount of money available for business to invest in plant and equipment, and for government investment in rebuilding public works and in training and educating American workers. Neoliberals are particularly concerned with the government's role in stimulating formation of this capital.

The neoliberal concern about investment has been bought wholesale by the Democratic Party's leaders, older, traditional liberals who nevertheless realize that "investment" is a politically attractive theme in the economically distressed eighties. Under the guise of "investment in human capital," education and training have reemerged after a decade's dormancy as issues of public concern in 1984. "Infrastructure decay" has recently turned into one of the nation's most dire problems. But while traditional liberals have been willing to recognize the crises in human capital and infrastructure brought to the fore by the neoliberals, they have insisted on treating them with traditional solutions. Only in the area of tax policy have the old liberals accepted a neoliberal response.

Nothing threatens established political interests more than tax reform, and although Democrats—much more than Republicans (1981's supply-side tax cuts notwithstanding)—have long publicized the need to clean up the system, little has been done or even attempted. "Democrats," charged California Congressman Leon Panetta in 1982, "are always talking about plugging loopholes, about tax reform. But it never went anywhere. Why? Because in fact, a lot of our members were bought and sold by the same special interests who structured the system as it exists. So while we were talking on one side, we were doing something very different on the other. It is that endless kind of charade that needs to be stopped."

Neoliberals—Panetta among them—have tried to stop the "endless charade" by introducing several tax reform measures all founded on the principle that the tax system should be employed only for revenue-raising, and not to engineer specific social responses, a clear departure from standard liberal policy of the 1960s and 1970s, which advocated targeting of tax breaks to aid favored constituencies (a ploy of conservatives as well). Neoliberal proposals to replace the current loophole-ridden personal income tax with either a progressive consumption tax or a radically simplified income tax are based solely on a view of the economy's investment needs, as are two other staples of the neoliberals' tax platform, the integration of the corporate and personal income taxes and the institution of first-year write-offs for business expenses.

Investment requires a higher national savings rate. Savings, in turn, implies reduced personal consumption. Hence the recommendation advanced by Lester Thurow, Robert Reich, Gary Hart, and others that the personal income tax system be supplanted by a consumption tax.

While proponents of the consumption tax emphasize the fairness of the system as one of its benefits, its real appeal lies in its ability to encourage savings and investment, which would increase the nation's net productivity and thus its ability to compete in the global economy. One of the prevalent criticisms of the current system of income taxation is that it discourages savings by, in effect, taxing them twice, the first time as income and the second time as return on investment. The maze of the tax code has led to the proliferation of tax shelters that tend to reward unproductive investments—even investments that incur losses—as well as borrowing. "A penny earned is a penny taxed, a penny saved is a penny taxed twice," quipped *The Wall Street Journal*'s Susan Lee. "But a penny spent or borrowed, ah, now that's a penny. In fact, it's pretty close to a nickel."

Consumption taxation was the cornerstone of the early drafts of Gary Hart's "Economic Platform for the 1980s," and although he has backed away from his initial forceful advocacy of it, it remains a part of Hart's final campaign platform, contained in his book *A New Democracy*. A consumption tax, wrote Hart, is "simple and fair; it . . .

also promote[s] savings and investment." Hart proposes taxing only income that is spent, exempting that which is saved or invested; all current deductions would be eliminated, except for a standard write-off of $10,000–$15,000 depending upon family size. It is not, he insists, a national sales tax or even a value-added tax, a fear often called up when the idea of consumption taxation is raised. "It is simply a tax on personal expenditures, which are easily calculated as the difference between income and net savings," he wrote, specifying "net savings" as the amount saved or invested in assets and the amount borrowed during the same period.

Hart and Lester Thurow have both stressed that, just as there is nothing inherently progressive or regressive, liberal or conservative, in income taxation, neither is a consumption tax by nature one or the other. (One of the most comprehensive proposals for a consumption tax, in fact, and a clear influence on Hart's plan, was contained in a January 1977 Treasury Department study, "Blueprints for Basic Tax Reform," undertaken at the behest of outgoing Treasury Secretary William E. Simon, an archconservative.) In Hart's plan (which he labels a "savings-incentive tax" in his 1983 book, a rhetorical departure for his earlier citations) a rate schedule that would rise with the amount of individual consumption, and indexing of the rates, presumably against the Consumer Price Index, would guard its progressivity. One of the dangers inherent in a consumption-tax plan, the ability of taxpayers to gather fortunes that they then pass on, tax-free, to their offspring, would be circumvented by treating bequests as expenditures.

Would that it were so simple. A "savings-incentive tax" would raise the tax burden on the young and the old—those who spend more to establish themselves in life, and those who take advantage of accrued savings in the "golden years"—while benefiting the middle-aged, who statistically form the bulk of the country's savers. And whether a consumption tax is, in reality, as uncomplicated as its advocates paint it is debatable: defining consumption is at least as difficult, and as open to special-interest wrangling, as defining income under the current tax code.

Moreover, the consumption tax suffers from one major, nagging flaw: the lack of empirical data to suggest how people would react under it. Bill Bradley, when he turned his attentions away from energy and toward tax policy in 1981, found this to be the stumbling block that caused him to dismiss consumption taxation as a useful alternative to the current system.

Bradley opted to work within the framework of income taxation.

He enlisted the aid of Richard Gephardt, and together they defined the parameters for their new tax proposal: It would have to encourage savings and investment; it would have to be simpler than the old system, so that taxpayers could understand it; it must strive for neutrality; and it must be progressive—the values of a traditionally liberal program.

Soon, however, there emerged a consensus on three not-necessarily-liberal items. In order to achieve simplicity and efficiency, all earnings would have to be taxed in the same way, whether investment income or ordinary income. Embodied in this proposal is the principle that taxes *not* be used to elicit specific kinds of social and economic behavior; targeting of tax breaks and credits, in short, would be eliminated. This represented a clear departure from conventional Democratic wisdom, and even violated much of what Bradley had himself tried to accomplish in energy policy, when he shepherded through the Senate a series of tax breaks aimed at spurring conservation and the use of renewable resources. And accepting what they considered to be political reality in the eighties, Bradley and Gephardt decided not to attempt income redistribution through their new comprehensive tax system. "Over the years, the tax code has become a vehicle for political favoritism and social engineering," Bradley would explain to Democrats gathered for the party's June 1982 midterm convention in Philadelphia. "It is now far too complex. It is blatantly unfair. And it distorts responses to new economic conditions and hampers our efforts to become more competitive in world markets. That complexity, unfairness, and inefficiency in our tax code have become symbols of everything that is wrong with government."

Bradley and Gephardt first considered a flat tax. The appeal of the flat tax mushroomed during the late 1970s and early 1980s as the complexity of the current tax code became an increasingly bothersome burden on the average taxpayer. In the fifteen years following 1967, the number of credits, deductions, exclusions, deferrals of liability, and preferences built into the code more than doubled, with the federal government's revenue losses exceeding $250 billion. Ultra-conservative populist Republicans like Senator Jesse Helms of North Carolina and Congressman Ron Paul of Texas, as well as moderate Democrats, came in with flat-rate plans to diffuse a system that was rightfully seen as benefiting the rich, who are better able to take advantage of the maze. (One of the most detailed flat-tax plans is neoliberal Leon Panetta's Tax Simplification Act, which would tax all income at 18 percent but allow tax credits—to be subtracted from taxes owed rather than from gross income—for each member of the household.)

The problem with flat-tax proposals is that, although indeed simple and efficient, they are far from fair, because they reduce the tax liability of the wealthiest segment of the population. Bradley and Gephardt took a different tack, advancing in mid-1982 the most comprehensive and realistic tax reform package currently before Congress, and the one most likely to be at the center of the Democratic Party's platform for 1984 and beyond.

Referred to alternately during its brief history as the Simplified Tax and, oxymoronically, the Progressive Flat Tax—but ultimately called, simply, the Fair Tax—the Bradley–Gephardt plan proposes to generate the same revenues currently raised under income taxation by lowering the rates and broadening the tax-paying base. A flat rate of 14 percent would be imposed on single taxpayers with incomes up to $25,000 and couples with incomes up to $40,000. Progressive surcharges of 12 to 16 percent would be applied to incomes above those levels. While the top rate on personal income would drop from 50 percent to 30 percent, additional revenues would be taken in by the elimination of all credits, deductions, and exclusions, except those deemed politically necessary—for charitable giving, home mortgage interest, Social Security, veterans' benefits, certain medical expenses, and state and local taxes. The personal exemption would be $1,600.

According to Bradley, this sort of comprehensive tax would lower the tax burden on well over half the tax-paying population. Yet it would retain the distribution of tax liabilities, increasing the amount of tax paid by the small percentage at the upper end of the income scale, particularly by eliminating the capital gains exclusion and the dividend exclusion, adding markedly to the adjusted gross incomes of those who take the greatest advantage of current loopholes and shelters.

In what way does the Fair Tax proposal spur investment? The plan's sponsors make a behavioral assumption that a fair and simple tax system will promote participation rather than evasion. "If people can understand the tax system—which they certainly cannot today with all the exclusions, deductions, and loopholes—they will be more likely to support the tax system," said Gephardt on May 27, 1982, the day of the program's announcement. "And with the growing size of the cash or underground economy, we need a system which has widespread support."

Gephardt's hope that a simpler system will encourage people not to utilize the underground economy—the growing use of barter and cash transactions, for example—is naïve. Until proper enforcement procedures are devised, it will remain relatively easy and painless to subvert the tax system. Nevertheless, the same optimism that drives the neoliberals to believe that the market can be used for reform also pervades their predictions for the Fair Tax. The neoliberals assume that removal of the distortions currently built into the tax code will naturally guide people to invest in the most productive enterprises, not those which provide the greatest shelter. "In between the investor and the investment comes the tax code," Bradley explained in September 1982. "It diverts rates of return and skews investment not to what has real value in the marketplace, but to where Congress thinks it should go. You clean it up and let a person decide what he or she is going to invest in, based on what the real value [of the investment] is in the marketplace."

The goal of spurring productive investment rather than aiding the proliferation of tax shelters also impels the suggestion that the corporate and personal income taxes be integrated. Advocated by Lester Thurow and Roger Vaughan, among others, the proposal was also made—in what must surely rank as one of the decade's greater ironies—by President Reagan in January 1983. Reagan's comment, an apparently off-the-cuff remark to a group of Boston businessmen, sounded so similar to a recommendation that the corporate tax be *eliminated* that it immediately met with a rash of Democratic opposition, which effectively quelled all further talk, Republican or Democratic, of the idea. Yet the President indeed advocated integration— the passing on of corporate income to the stockholder and the taxing of it at the personal rate. Such integration, wrote Roger Vaughan in "Beyond Supply Side Economics," a brief prepared for the Council of State Planning Agencies, "would have far-reaching consequences for the structure of industry. It would encourage individuals to invest in commercial and industrial assets rather than in residential property. . . . It will change the form of ownership of corporations, reduce the tendency toward conglomerate ownership, and encourage longer-term planning." Needless to say, all three results are consistent with the neoliberals' general priorities for the information era.

The corporate income tax is largely a myth. As Lester Thurow indicated in *The Zero-Sum Society,* the notion that, under the current system, the entity being taxed is a corporation is largely simplistic. "[Corporations] simply collect money from someone—their shareholders, their customers, or their employees—and transfer it to the government," wrote Thurow. "There is no such thing as taxing corporations as opposed to individuals." Another argument against the existing corporate tax structure is similar to those advanced against the loophole-ridden personal income tax. Coupled with existing depreciation schedules, it provides little incentive for saving or investment, and because interest on debt is tax-deductible, it actually favors borrowing.

Integration of the two taxes would lead to the correction of these flaws. Shareholders in corporations would be taxed at the personal rate on all income, whether retained or paid out, earned by the corporation on behalf of the shareholder. At the end of the calendar year, the shareholder would receive a form, similar to a W-2 form, informing him how much income is to be added to his total income for the year, and how much tax has been withheld. Pressure would be placed on corporations by shareholders to pay out dividends; and shareholders would be encouraged to plow dividends back into stock because earnings will be distributed, rather than retained, thus promoting wider ownership of the nation's productive capacity.

"If we can all participate in the growth process," said New York Governor Hugh Carey in 1982, when announcing his support for integration of the two taxes, "we shall all become more productive and energetic in our pursuit of the most efficient ways of organizing production." Not only that, but the increased flow of money from households into equity investments, claims Roger Vaughan, will stimulate new business development, which has traditionally favored central cities. "With the distribution of corporate income in the form of dividends, [investment] decisions would be made by millions of individuals," he concludes, "who would be less prone to 'write off' unfashionable urban areas and Frostbelt regions."

Integration of the corporate and personal income taxes thus serves to remove distortions that inhibit efficient investment decision-making, the same principle that guides another item on the neoliberals' tax platform. They call for the replacement of the Reagan Administration's Accelerated Cost Recovery System (ACRS) for business depreciation—also known simply as "10-5-3" because it allows write-offs for buildings in ten years, for machinery in five years, and trucks in three years—with the First Year Capital Recovery system developed by Professors Dale W. Jorgenson and Alan J. Auerbach of Harvard.

ACRS was one of the two cornerstones of President Reagan's tax bill (the other was the Kemp-Roth three-year, 30 percent tax cut). The 10-5-3 program was passed in order to provide incentives for business to invest. But in 1982, under ACRS, investment by American business in new plant and equipment dropped to approximately $165 billion from a previous average of $175 billion a year. Much of the savings accrued to business by the institution of ACRS have gone to pay dividends, reduce debt, and finance mergers and acquisitions, which skyrocketed in 1982–83.

The Jorgenson-Auerbach plan seeks to correct the distortions built into 10-5-3, thus rectifying the channeling of capital into unproductive investments by allowing write-offs for the actual present value of an asset, according to a schedule of thirty categories, in the year the investment is made. Its primary virtue, one that calls up the value of the Bradley-Gephardt personal income tax scheme, is its simplicity. "Rather than choosing among a range of asset lifetimes and a number of alternative depreciation formulas for tax purposes, taxpayers would simply apply the first-year capital recovery allowance to their purchase of depreciable plant and equipment," Jorgenson and Auerbach have written. "No records of past purchases would be required to substantiate capital consumption allowances in a given year."

Like the Fair Tax, First Year Capital Recovery assumes that investments, when freed from the direction of artificial distortions, will by nature flow into the most productive areas. Thus it is much more market-oriented than the Reagan Administration's supposedly "free-market" approach and places greater faith in the individual decision-maker. Bradley-Gephardt and Jorgenson-Auerbach, in short, are both more free-market than Republican proposals, testimony to the neoliberals' faith in the marketplace.

CHAPTER 16

Education: Investment in Human Capital

THE NEOLIBERAL THEME of investment also shines forth in another policy area that has burst into public awareness recently: education and training. Called "human-capital policy" by the neoliberals— terminology adopted by the Democratic Party as a whole—creative education and training programs were being pursued vigorously by several neoliberal governors before human capital became a national issue. The major initiative of Jerry Brown's second term as California governor was his ambitious "Investment in People" program. In the South, Governor William Winter of Mississippi pushed through a set of extraordinary amendments to his state's constitution allowing for raises in teachers' pay by 10 percent and for the establishment of a state kindergarten program; Governor Robert Graham of Florida has shepherded through his legislature minimum high-school graduation requirements for his state. But the most far-reaching human-capital program, and the one most specifically tied to economic growth and the visions of a postindustrial America, has been in North Carolina. That's because education is in the governor's blood.

James Baxter Hunt, Jr.'s mother was the sort of schoolteacher you remember until the end of your life, the kind who would take the troublemakers, the tough kids, or those who had simply flunked English, bring them over to the house and, on her own time, tutor them. Jim Hunt remembers that she wouldn't take a penny for it, and that when she taught, they learned. "Toughest guys in the school," he recalls, "and they learned."

Hunt's father also worked for the government, as a soil conservation agent. He would take his little son to grange meetings, where the six-year-old would fall asleep listening to tobacco farmers declare how Roosevelt had saved them. Growing up in a government family in Rock Ridge, near Greensboro, the younger Hunt was bred with FDR's name in his ear, brought up to believe that it's natural for government to do things, that programs can make a difference, that politics serves the good of the people.

The message stuck. North Carolina, an eminent historian has said, is the only state in the Union where every man is born a politician. In Hunt's case, this was almost certainly true; Joseph Grimsley, now secretary of natural resources in Hunt's administration, remembers that when he first met Hunt, at the age of fifteen, he was told by others that "from the age of five, they've been saying Jim'll be governor someday." From those formative years, Hunt's politics was built on education and the land, both of which controlled the rate and quality of economic development in the South.

North Carolina has had a long-standing romance with public education, and if Hunt came by his interest hereditarily, that concern was buttressed by a widespread cultural attitude that makes his state almost unique among the fifty. Ever since Governor Charles Brantley Acock built the public school system at the turn of the century, public education has been a top-of-the-list political issue in the state. Today, officials boast that 95 percent of the state's youth are enrolled in *public* schools. "There's been a political tradition of education in this state. It's been a passion for a whole strain of governors," said Ferrel Guillory, editorial page editor and columnist for the *Raleigh News-Observer*.

By the time James B. Hunt, Jr., became governor in 1976, desegregation had receded as an issue in North Carolina. Federal activism had succeeded in opening up—legally, at least—avenues of progress and a whole generation of Democrats who had been weaned on the integration battles of the 1960s had taken over the reins of government. Ironically, this created political problems for the new leaders. "Once you ethically cross the rubicon of integration," mused Ferrel Guillory, "what then do you do? The answers to that question are not easy, and that's what has confronted Jim Hunt as governor."

Legally and morally, desegregation is no longer an issue in the South. Practically and politically, however, race relations and equal opportunity remain contentious questions. Immediately upon assuming office, Governor Jim Hunt faced several racial and labor problems that were tarnishing North Carolina's progressive image. Human capital was the issue he took on to maintain political unity. Hunt is a master politician, a talent he learned from two decades as a member of his party's inner circle, beginning as a Young Democrat in college at North Carolina State. When America's best-known North Carolinian, Senator Jesse Helms, threatened to dominate the state's internal politics with his nationally financed, powerful, right-wing Congressional Club, Jim Hunt whipped the state's Democratic Party into shape, oiled his own machine with doses of campaign savvy, political patronage, and money, and sent his forces against Helms's in the 1982 congressional races. Hunt's soldiers won in every contest. He is expected to unseat Helms in the 1984 U.S. Senate race, a campaign that promises to be the most expensive, and perhaps the bitterest, in Senate history.

Jim Hunt knows the value of an issue. Human capital brought blacks and whites together when the Wilmington Ten controversy, in which a group of black activists was convicted of criminal conspiracy and a series of bombings, promised to divide them, and got businessmen and social activists talking despite long-simmering disputes over unionization. And human capital just might be the issue to topple Helms. "[Education] happens to be the way you pull society together," Governor Hunt said in Raleigh in March 1983. "You need to be always looking for these issues that don't divide us or pull us apart, but bring us together, teach us to be cooperative and to work together."

But underlying Hunt's education policies is the economic issue. "When I travel outside our state, people ask about our universities, our community college system, our public schools, our North Carolina School of Science and Mathematics, our Research Triangle Park, and our Microelectronics Center," noted Hunt in his January 1982 State of the State speech to the legislature. "They ask me: How does North Carolina do it? And I tell them: Our strategy is to invest in education and economic growth." A year later he repeated the theme in an interview: "I wouldn't hesitate to do what has to be done to get growth, and you get growth through education." With Hunt, stressed Ferrel Guillory, "Education is *always* linked to economics."

The Hunt program has been bold and expansive, particularly for an era marked by austerity and shrinking budgets. Hunt told his legislature in early 1982, "The limits on our financial resources do not mean that we have to limit our vision, our dreams, and our aspirations for North Carolina. . . . We don't have to have more money to do what we need to do in North Carolina." Nevertheless he had the temerity to recommend across-the-board salary increases for state employees, especially teachers, training grants for teacher improvement, aides in every early elementary school classroom, and the hiring of a "lead teacher" on a year-round basis in every subject in every North Carolina high school, in addition to a proposal to increase public investments in Research Triangle, the state's own Silicon Valley. Time and again, at home and in national forums like the National Task Force on Education and Economic Growth, Hunt repeats his message: Education equals growth.

"I have concluded through a process of thinking and study and seeing how things work in the political economy that *this* is the issue, the thing we can do that works best, economically," Hunt said. "This is the thing we can do to pull people together, almost all of them, so they'll understand each other, respect each other. So the nation can work."

Concludes Hunt, "Economic growth has to be our primary purpose. . . . I proved to myself through rigorous economic analysis that education was the best way to spend money, in terms of growth."

Education equals growth is a neoliberal equation. And although education has been a Democratic issue for decades, the economic context in which it is currently couched represents a dramatic departure from the 1960s, when education was considered a social issue, the cornerstone of the Great Society.

"Investment in human capital," which encompasses job training, retraining of employees already in the work force or displaced by new technologies, and education of future workers, is the fourth stage in the postwar cyclical romance with education. The GI Bill, which sent tens of thousands of veterans of World War II to college, was envisioned as a social equalizer, a method of expanding the middle class in America—an unarticulated goal of the New Deal and the Fair Deal. The second phase began in 1958, in the aftermath of the Soviet launching of Sputnik, when education, particularly in math and science, was interpreted as a priority for reasons of national security. Significantly, education programs in the late 1950s and early 1960s were aimed at producing scientists, teachers, and others on the top rung of the human-capital scale, rather than concentrating on the competence of the work force as a whole.

Education and training were two mainstays of the Great Society, the third stage in the postwar education push, but here, as with the other major components of President Johnson's program, such as voting rights and civil rights, the issue was *access,* that is, availability of educational opportunities to all citizens.

But while the policies of the 1960s may have sufficed to fulfill the immediate goal of guaranteeing access, the neoliberals believe that these policies are no longer sufficient. They argue that the liberal education agenda fails to address the new economic realities, and in some cases an education bureaucracy has developed that is counterproductive to the goals of the 1980s. The early efforts in math and science education and the general expenditures for research and development, for instance, were directed at bolstering the space program and defense technology. To this day, defense-related expenditures dominate federal outlays for R & D. The structure devised to funnel money from government into R & D to sponsor innovation has proved difficult to adapt to current needs. It is, as Governor Hunt told the American Academy for the Advancement of Science, "too federal." Innovation for the purpose of economic growth can best be organized at the state and local level, Hunt believes, and so a redefinition of the federal and state roles in technological and human-capital development is required.

One of the paradoxes of the 1960s and 1970s was that centralization of authority led to a fragmentation of policy. In few cases is this as evident as in the education and training programs of those two decades. By 1965, before the Great Society was overwhelmed by Vietnam, these initiatives had already been strewn among more than a dozen agencies and departments, each with its own mandate, its own style, and its own agenda.

The legacy of this fragmentation was sadly underscored in a 1979 General Accounting Office report on the federally sponsored programs for employment and training in a single jurisdiction, Tidewater, Virginia. All told, $22.4 million was being spent annually in Tidewater, in no less than forty-four separate programs, which involved more than fifty local administering agencies, five federal departments, and three independent federal agencies. Concluded the GAO: "No federal, state, or local organization was responsible for coordinating all of these manpower programs." Today, authority over federal job-training programs is still the province of four federal agencies, which operate independently of each other. There are currently twenty-two separate programs to aid displaced workers.

The errors of recent education and training programs have been revealed by the unmet needs of the private sector and by anticipated shortfalls in workers expected in the near future. Because of the birth dearth that followed the baby boom, tomorrow's workers—three-quarters of the employment pool for the year 2000—are already in school. Yet the schools are not preparing them for the postindustrial society.

Structural unemployment, according to a Congressional Budget Office report, had displaced between 840,000 and 2.2 million workers by January 1983; another 10 to 15 million jobs stand to be lost before decade's end. Yet there also exists a potentially crippling skills shortage, with workers not properly trained to fill the 17 to 25 million new jobs expected by 1990. The Department of Labor has reported that the United States dropped from second to seventh in the world in the measured "skill endowment" of its work force over the last several years. And the Reagan Administration, which has publicly decried the low level of math and science attainment, has taken no steps to increase the number of teachers. It has eliminated virtually all of the primary and secondary school science programs sponsored by the National Science Foundation. "Far from attacking these inadequacies, America is in retreat," maintained the American Academy for the Advancement of Science in a 1983 report. "The Federal Government appears to be abandoning any serious efforts to help upgrade the quality of American education."

The neoliberals expect to address this array of problems with a series of initiatives that stress decentralization, public/private sector cooperation, and adaptation to the realities of an increasingly technological society. Some of the programs involve simple reaffirmations of ideas once present on the liberal agenda but forgotten in the social turmoil of the past two decades, such as raising the status of the teaching profession, encouraging excellence in the schools, and increasing teacher pay. Others involve fundamental additions to the traditional agenda; for instance, economist Roger Vaughan's proposal that job retraining, like universal public education, ought to be considered a right of citizenship.

The training/retraining voucher system advocated by Vaughan and fellow economist Pat Choate, and supported by officials like Senator Gary Hart, is one method of attacking the human-capital crisis. A training/retraining entitlement is worthless, however, unless the government can provide adequate guidance to individuals about where jobs are and where they are expected to be. The United States is the only nation in the industrialized world without compulsory notification of job vacancies. The existing data system is woefully deficient.

"The present projections of the Department of Labor are incomplete and untimely," charged Choate, "and are produced at such a high degree of aggregation, covering such large geographic areas and populations, as to be of little use in identifying potential jobs and potential workers to fill them."

In the absence of federal action, some states—notably Oklahoma, South Carolina, and North Carolina—have instituted their own employment data banks to assemble information and projections on job availability. "There isn't any reason to run a vocational program at a community college unless there's a demand for that skill at the end of the course. It took us a little while to learn that," said Betty Owen, North Carolina's secretary of education. "We turned out an awful lot of beauticians and auto mechanics and typists, and found out at the end that there weren't any jobs for those people." As a result of the skills mismatch, North Carolina created the Labor Market Information System. "We can now say, there will be so many jobs in robotics in 1985. And we can say to our community colleges, you get your house in order and put in courses to train people in robotics," said Ms. Owen. "Not only does the education system need to know, but the banks need to know it. The telephone company needs to know it. And government needs to know it, to do good planning." Nevertheless, state and local initiatives are not sufficient. Elected officials at these levels are generally disinclined for political reasons to publicize jobs that might be out of state. Only a carefully maintained federal system, operated in such a way as to augment state data banks, will serve the primary information needs of the job seeker.

Because many states have well-developed community college systems (North Carolina's network, which was unified under Governor Terry Sanford, includes fifty-eight community colleges and technical institutes for its one hundred counties, with at least one institution within thirty miles of every resident), elected officials have begun to look at this arrangement as the natural training ground for the post-industrial economy. Increasingly, vocational education will be moved out of the secondary schools, which will concentrate more and more on basic educational skills, and job training will become the province of the community colleges, which in turn will be viewed as a two-year extension of public education.

Progress toward this goal has been made not only in James Hunt's North Carolina, but in California's community colleges (coordination of the system as a postindustrial vocational-training arena was part of

Jerry Brown's "Investment in People" program), in Arizona under Governor Bruce Babbitt, and in Colorado under Governor Richard Lamm.

One of the most insistent neoliberal education themes is public-private partnership, a part of neoliberalism's final, all-embracing motif, cooperation. Neoliberals believe that in the postindustrial society the private sector's requirements are not for skilled workers per se, but for educated workers who have the intellectual wherewithal to adapt to a variety of tasks and increasingly sophisticated industrial systems. As Jerry Brown was fond of repeating throughout his second term, "We must augment our traditional concern for the '3 Rs' with a new focus on the '3 Cs'—computing, calculating, and communicating through technology."

The reaffirmation that economic growth is a precondition for true social justice has led to the addition of technological literacy to the definition of the educated American. Public/private sector advisory councils, such as Brown's California Commission on Industrial Innovation (dismantled by his Republican successor, George Deukmejian) and Hunt's National Task Force on Education and Economic Growth (which he co-chairs with Dr. David Hamburg, president of the Carnegie Corporation), have transformed technological literacy into the burning educational issue for the coming decade. Businesses have responded to the lack of technological knowledge in a variety of ways, engaging in "adopt a school" programs, in which they lend personnel and facilities to troubled school districts, and providing grants and awards to outstanding teachers. Recommendations for further cooperation include the guarantee by businesses of summer employment to teachers of math and science, to enable the public schools to retain teachers who might otherwise leave to pursue higher salaries in the private sector. At the same time, far from calling for government to abdicate its role in education, as has been charged, several neoliberals have affirmed the strengthening of government's hand by improving standards for teachers and students, raising salaries to again make teaching a competitive profession, establishing differing pay scales for teachers ("merit pay"), and creating innovative programs, such as "magnet schools," to enhance the attractiveness and the efficacy of the public school system.

But the public/private sector development that has attracted the greatest attention is joint industry/university efforts in research and development and scientist training to assist the expansion of local high-technology industries. Typically, these collaborative ventures include R & D and expansion of the student ranks as part of the same package. In California, North Carolina, and Arizona, such programs were developed when it was discovered that the available pool of workers did not match existing industries' projected needs, threatening the continuation of the states' economic growth. Mutual recognition of the problem by business and political leaders has made for alliances that in past years might have been considered suspect.

Arizona boasts a generally conservative political climate, a Republican legislature, a Democratic governor—Bruce Babbitt—and a burgeoning high-technology industrial base. Arizona projected an estimated need for 70,000 new engineers, technicians, administrators, assemblers, and service workers to staff its sunrise sector during the 1980s. A group of businessmen decided to approach the governor and ask for aid to meet this need. The committee was headed by G. M. Sollenberger, a conservative real estate broker and developer, and a member of the Phoenix Chamber of Commerce's board of directors for eight years. His latter duties had brought him into contact with representatives of the high-tech firms—Motorola, Honeywell, Intel—with bases in Maricopa County. In 1979 a vice president of Honeywell informed Sollenberger that the company was contemplating an expansion, perhaps in Phoenix, although other locations were under consideration. After discussing the relative merits and disadvantages of the project, the executive said, "Let me tell you our biggest worry. The problem facing our company and others is hiring engineers. It's a particularly acute problem here. The Arizona schools can't supply the number we want, so we've got to go outside and convince them to move to Arizona."

Nationally, it is difficult to document an actual shortage of engineers. But in specific states, the mismatch between open positions and available workers has been very severe, leading businesses that might have located in the state to set up shop elsewhere. The Phoenix Chamber of Commerce listened intently to the warnings coming from high-tech execs that business would assuredly relocate where there was a supply, not the other way around. In Arizona, Sollenberger was bluntly told, the good of Honeywell, the good of Motorola, and the good of the state depended on a strengthened engineering program at Arizona State University in Mesa, a Phoenix suburb. And that meant not only the improvement of undergraduate courses. An engineer must continue his schooling to advance in the field; without additional course work, technical personnel and researchers face obsolescence. A total overhaul of undergraduate and advanced courses at ASU was called for.

The advisory group established in the wake of this conversation comprised the presidents of several of the high-tech firms in the county and leaders of local, non-technology-based companies, but no politicians. Expecting to face the traditional antagonism between a Democratic administration and the desires of industry, the committee wanted to have a detailed case ready for presentation, in the likely event of automatic opposition. "We had a rehearsal of all the things we thought we had to convince Babbitt of," Sollenberger recalled in 1982. "But we didn't even get to make our speeches."

The private-sector representatives did not know Babbitt well. The scion of one of Arizona's three most prominent families ("The Babbitts *own* Flagstaff" is an oft-heard line), with a legal education at Harvard, the bastion of the Eastern establishment, and impeccable Great Society credentials, Babbitt had risen quickly to the governorship in 1978. Because of Babbitt's liberal background, the industry representatives were surprised, if not shocked, when they walked into the governor's office and he interrupted their opening remarks by telling them, "I just spent last week in Texas with Pat Haggerty, the co-founder of Texas Instruments, who's a friend. He told me about the need for a top engineering school to attract and hold high-technology businesses." After an hour and a half spent plotting strategies to convince the Republican legislature to cough up a portion of the $32 million it was estimated the program would require, the governor left the business representatives with one suggestion: "Think big. Don't think small."

None of the corporate representatives and Chamber of Commerce types remarked upon the singular irony of Babbitt's dictum: in past years, "think big" had been the directive that guided the social programs they had always despised. Now, they rejoiced to hear it applied to government aid to business. They did not realize that in Babbitt's mind there was no distinction between "economic" and "social" programs.

The cooperative strategy resulted in the founding of the Center for Excellence in Engineering at ASU, to which private industry had kicked in $9 million by 1982. The initial goal of the center is to produce home-grown engineers to feed Arizona's new industrial base. It is similar to Stanford University's Center for Integrated Systems, to which Hewlett-Packard, Xerox, and other companies have contributed

$12 million (with the state providing no funding whatsoever); the Robotics Institute at Carnegie-Mellon in Pittsburgh, which claims two dozen firms, including Westinghouse and Digital, supporting its research in cybernetics; and a program called MICRO, Microelectronics Innovation and Computer Research Opportunities, a joint endeavor of the State of California, the University of California system, and the state's electronics industry established under Jerry Brown. MICRO set up a $1 million fund that would match, dollar for dollar, industry contributions to basic research in microelectronics on any state university campus. A nine-person tripartite committee, with representatives from industry, academia, and government, devises policy for funding and research.

All the university/industry programs use the lure of advanced research, excellent facilities, and a generally supportive atmosphere to attract scientists and engineers, who thrive on continued access to education. In turn, the "techies" sustain the businesses of the information archipelago, which, as it expands, creates jobs for technicians, maintenance personnel, secretaries, and other service workers at a ratio that has been estimated at seven subsidiary positions for each advanced technical job. Sollenberger invoked the spirit of all these cooperative educational ventures when he told the National Conference on High Technology in Dallas in April 1982, "We have thus begun the difficult task of breaking down old images of business and education as wholly separate institutions, and building a new image of equal partners with a common goal of sustaining the economic health of Arizona."

A number of Washington's neoliberals, Paul Tsongas and Gary Hart prominent among them, have called for the passage of a "High-Tech Morrill Act" to facilitate these cooperative arrangements. The Morrill Act was the legislation that in 1862 gave to the states grants of land to establish public colleges to engage in agricultural research for the booming farming industry, eventually turning over 13 million acres to the states for the creation of sixty-nine institutions of higher learning, including Cornell and MIT. As proposed by Hart, the new act would grant federal funds to match the contributions of industry and state governments to colleges and universities instituting or enlarging programs in high-technology instruction or research.

Public/private sector cooperation may be the only alternative to permanently losing teachers, particularly math and science teachers, to business and industry. The math and science teacher population is dwindling and aging; in Minnesota, for example, the average age of a science teacher is forty years, up from thirty-four a decade ago. Equally critical to the crisis in math and science education is the fact that, as of 1981, half the new teachers employed to teach the two subjects in the nation's high schools were not certified. Partly as a result of the shortage and the apparent quality crunch, 50 percent of high school students take no science or math courses beyond the tenth grade.

Michael W. Kirst of Stanford University, in a report prepared for the California Commission on Industrial Innovation, labeled cooperative efforts the "key strategy" in bandaging this wound in the short run. Kirst recommended, and the commission adopted, a set of proposals involving both government and industry in nontraditional roles to bolster math and science education, including joint retraining projects to allow teachers already in the system to sharpen their skills and to certify in science and math those who teach other subjects; guaranteed summer jobs in industry for math and science teachers, and perhaps even time during the school year or regularly scheduled sabbaticals, to work in business or engage in research; and the use of private-industry employees to serve as part-time teachers in the schools.

A stumbling block to some of these joint ventures may be the opposition of the teachers' unions, which generally resist the use of noncertified personnel in the classroom. However, more than two decades ago the unions also stood against experimentation with teachers' aides, adults without teaching credentials serving as assistants in primary-school classrooms. Now, teachers' aides are fixtures in many districts, and in some jurisdictions have even been unionized themselves. And unions have embraced the adopt-a-school concept that is growing in popularity throughout the country, particularly in depressed urban areas. Under adopt-a-school, local companies are encouraged to support individual schools, lending employees for career counseling and tutoring, providing part-time work for students, even giving financial or in-kind support for extracurricular activities, and occasionally providing classroom teaching assistance. Chicago, Oakland, and Memphis are among the cities that have experimented successfully with adopt-a-school measures.

"As to whether there's something counterproductive in these cooperative arrangements, I guess it's a matter of philosophy," said Governor Hunt in response to a question about the potential danger of co-optation of the schools because of the joint ventures. "Some people see us fighting each other for what there is. If the corporations get more, we get less. But, first of all, I believe we can make the pie larger. Second, I believe we *can* help each other . . . particularly in education, which has to serve all these various purposes. So we've got to bring all these people in, who know what the purposes are, to help us plan it. Of course, we're not going to hand over the schools. The school boards are going to make the decisions. There are going to be recommendations out of business and industry that'll clearly be short-sighted and selfish and not in the best interest of the kids. . . . We're watching them as we're working with them."

In the final analysis, improvements in the education system and enlarging the ranks of the teaching force are government responsibilities, and both the funding and the innovation necessary to squeeze the most knowledge from the nickel must trickle down from the state and federal governments, to supplement the budgets of the locally funded school systems. In June 1982 Senator Hart introduced the American Defense Education Act, modeled, at least rhetorically, after President Eisenhower's National Defense Education Act, to provide incentives to local school systems to improve their programs in math, science, technology, and foreign languages. The Hart bill offers 2 percent of a state's average per-pupil expenditure to districts participating in the ADEA approach, at a cost to the federal government, if every school district in the country complied, of $4 billion. Declared Hart in his 1983 presidential campaign bromide, *A New Democracy,* "The cost of ignorance is far higher."

Another method of attracting teachers that has received attention from neoliberals is instituting salary differentials and merit pay. In the past, the teachers' unions have strongly disapproved of such proposals, insisting that all teachers be treated alike and paid only according to length of service and individual educational attainment; but even the National Education Association, in June 1983, gave cautious approval to a study of merit pay. "We have to get over this awful fear we have as educators and government officials that all teachers are the same," insisted North Carolina's secretary of education, Betty Owen, a former teacher herself. But, although the mere mention of the heresy of merit pay and salary differentials by liberals is a new occurrence, chances of it actually coming to pass are most likely well in the future, if at all. "The toughest thing to do is pure merit pay—every teacher evaluated based on how he or she is teaching, and paid accordingly," said Betty Owen's boss, Governor Hunt. "Eventually, if we can get measures that are fair to teachers, I think we'll have merit pay. But I don't see it coming right away."

But merit pay, while potentially part of a broad package for educational reform, is by itself a red herring. A few thousand dollars more a year will do little to attract to the teaching profession those for whom the average salary of $17,000 is simply too paltry. And merit pay requires a fair system of merit review, which is extremely difficult to achieve in the politically charged atmosphere of local public schools.

Another innovation successfully employed by the Hunt administration is a variation on the "magnet school" concept that was developed in the wake of the desegregation efforts of the 1960s–70s. With middle-class whites fleeing inner-city schools during the turmoil of those two decades, and with busing polarizing even those districts with no history of overt racial confrontation, educators needed a way to retain the middle class. Magnet schools, special schools designed to attract students because of their unique programs, were one of the most successful methods devised. Hunt established in 1981 the North Carolina School of Science and Mathematics, a magnet school and a model for the "high-tech high school" other states are considering creating. During its first two years of existence, Science and Math led the nation in the percentage of National Merit Award semifinalists among its student body.

The jewel of North Carolina's combined human-capital and industrial development policies is Research Triangle Park, and more particularly, the Microelectronics Center of North Carolina. Research Triangle, established in the late 1950s by Governor Luther Hodges, links the state's three major educational institutions—the University of North Carolina at Chapel Hill, North Carolina State in Raleigh, and Duke University in Durham—by giving them administrative jurisdiction over an industrial park modeled after the Stanford Research Institute. Over a twenty-year period Research Triangle grew, becoming the hub of an information archipelago that engulfed its three surrounding cities.

A fully converted "Atari Democrat" early in his first term, Jim Hunt envisioned a way to make Research Triangle even more attractive to business by improving its R & D capabilities, upon which high technology thrives. In 1981 he convinced the state legislature to appropriate $24 million to build the Microelectronics Center, an 80,000-square-foot facility housing one of the most advanced semiconductor R & D laboratories in the world. Industrial affiliates contribute funding to the center in order to have access to its facilities, faculty, and students. In addition to the three "triangle" institutions, two other schools—North Carolina A & T, and the University of North Carolina at Charlotte—administer the center. In its first three years it has attracted a spate of new operations into Research Triangle (including General Electric, Hewlett-Packard, and Texas Instruments) and has had the effect of increasing the number of engineering technicians needed in the area—a projected 643 a year through 1985—giving further impetus to Hunt's proposed job-training policies.

Effective employment of existing community college resources was one accomplishment of Jerry Brown's ambitious "Investment in People" program, the major initiative of his final term in office and a model for the national outline he is developing through his National Commission on Industrial Innovation. Designed by Fred Branfman, a former left-liberal antiwar activist, "Investment in People" consisted of four elements: improvement of public school math, science, and computer instruction; establishment of a public/private sector program in the state college system to produce more engineers; special training and retraining programs for welfare recipients and displaced workers; and the creation of a comprehensive system for employment-based training. Since the establishment of the California Worksite Education and Training Act in 1979, $35 million has been allocated to community colleges and to business firms for employment-based training, with more than 12,000 people placed in skilled jobs, at an average cost of $2,000 to $4,000 per trainee—$2,000 *less* than the cost of training an individual through California's federally funded and developed CETA Title VII program. Other accomplishments of "Investment in People" included the state board of education's inclusion of a three-year-math/two-year-science requirement in its 1982 model high school curriculum, the decisions by the regents of California State University and the University of California to raise entrance requirements in math and science, and the provision of nearly $10 million for staff improvement, teacher training, and curriculum development in computer and technology education. Governor Brown announced the formal "Investment in People" program in his January 1982 State of the State message. He requested $50 million. In California's tightest budget year since World War II, he received $25.7 million. "It amounts," said Fred Branfman, "to a redirection."

In a 1983 interview, Branfman assessed his transition from a Great Society–style education advocate to a human-capital theorist. "We on the left," said Branfman, "have been reactive, where we assumed that the corporations had the power and our job was simply to oppose them. Now, our job is to make it work. Ralph Nader–style liberalism is confrontational and reactive. It's 'Business does X, so from the outside we'll try to force a change,' instead of saying, 'How do we get business to do this?' Liberals have tended to fall back on the status quo; there was no premium on originality when we had a budget surplus. Now, there's no surplus, so the neoliberals have asked, how can we use existing funds in new ways?

"It's time," concluded Branfman, "to get more hardheaded. The Great Society rubric was to do things for *moral* reasons. It became a charity approach. I had to throw off the shackles of liberal thinking. A lot of what was done in the name of morality was immoral, because it didn't work. My answer now is that our society should give everybody the *right* to be trained. Not out of charity, but because it is an economic necessity."

CHAPTER 17

From Confrontation
to Cooperation

THE DOMINANT PRINCIPLES OF NEOLIBERALISM weave in and out of the ideas and programs neoliberal politicians and advisers have designed. The principle of appropriate technology motivates the attack on systems analysis, which is at the heart of the military reform movement; appropriate technology also leads to a clearer understanding of how decentralization can foster liberal goals, and it drives the neoliberals to consider the market as a force for reform. Investment, the second important neoliberal motif, underscores the role of the marketplace, and it also explains the emphasis on simplified taxes to assure capital investment in productivity and investment in human capital.

As has already been indicated, a major element of the neoliberals' human-capital policy is public/private sector partnership. It may seem surprising that liberals, who helped to hone confrontational politics in the 1960s–1970s, are now talking about cooperation, but this is yet another example of neoliberalism's influence on mainstream Democratic politics. The shift from confrontation to cooperation is the most dramatic element of the transition from liberalism to neoliberalism. No better personification of the change exists than Governor Richard Lamm of Colorado.

The irony was inescapable. Lamm had always been the Angry Young Man. It would never be easy to forget that decade-old image of the bespectacled college professor and state senator, a strand of hair slashed across his sweat-streaked forehead, finger up, mouth open, angrily denouncing the pro-growth forces that were befouling the Colorado environment. Yet here sat the state's legislators, many of them former colleagues of his, listening to Governor Richard Lamm deliver his eighth State of the State message. Its theme: cooperation.

Lamm was one of the half-dozen leaders of the 1972 political co-alition that prevented Denver from hosting the 1976 Winter Olympics. After a year-long battle, the ad hoc goup—a collection of environmental and antiwar activists, mostly, many of whom had migrated to Colorado during the Rocky Mountain renaissance of the late 1960s—forced the issue to a public referendum, in which the voters vocally declared "No!" to the games. State Senator Lamm—he also taught law at the University of Colorado, and had previously attracted attention as the chief sponsor of the state's new liberalized abortion statute—was the point man, one of the few elected officials to throw in his lot with the ragtag crew. Those who had served in the legislature with him would long remember Dick Lamm's passion as he vilified the developers and business moguls who would sully the Colorado landscape for their own selfish personal profit.

When Lamm was elected governor two years later (the same year Timothy Wirth was elected to Congress and Gary Hart to the U.S. Senate) he often took the opportunity to reinforce his confrontational style. As Michael Barone and Grant Ujifusa wrote in the respected *Almanac of American Politics,* "He managed to be abrasive without being effective." Two years into his tenure, Lamm's abrasiveness was rewarded with a state legislature firmly under Republican control.

As they recalled these images from their governor's past, on the evening of January 6, 1982, the state's assemblymen and senators certainly saw the irony, maybe even felt a bit shocked. For Richard Lamm was now a silver-maned statesman intoning the virtue of co-operation over confrontation. "I believe that one of the most heartening trends in Colorado is the development of the consensus approach to some of the most serious issues facing our state," said the governor, his words echoing through the chamber in the gold-domed Colorado statehouse. "I sense a new sort of cooperation between private and public sectors, a sense of shared values on fundamental issues, such as preserving our environment and investing for our future."

Lamm's speech was replete with the buzzwords of neoliberalism. He talked of "anticipating future trends," of "the newly developing high-technology industries," of government as "the catalyst." "The future," he asserted, "belongs to the innovators." He echoed Jerry Brown: "The management of information is becoming the central focus of the postindustrial economy."

Colorado was booming; Colorado Springs and Boulder and Fort Collins were exploding with information and service industries. The legislators did not require reminders of the importance of the new economy. But that was not the governor's point. Lamm's central thesis in his State of the State speech was that only through *cooperation* could the new forces of change be met. Japan's success, he said, was due to "the concept of consensus. Government, business, and labor all try to work together as allies, instead of as adversaries, as they too often do in our country." Colorado, he felt, should try to emulate the Japanese.

Lamm had become sensitized to the value and necessity of the cooperative approach through the work of his Front Range Project. The purpose of the project was to determine how 9,000 square miles of plains and foothills along a north-south corridor 80 miles long and 50 miles wide on the eastern slope of the Rocky Mountains, covering thirteen counties and including nineteen of the state's twenty largest cities, could accommodate more than a million new residents over a twenty-year period while maintaining and improving the quality of life. The task was formidable, given the number of actors—developers, environmentalists, local officials, state officials, businessmen—who would, of necessity, be involved in the drama. A comprehensive set of regulations seemed to be in order.

But research in other parts of the country showed development regulations to be ineffective. This was particularly true in Oregon, where regulations designed to keep people and businesses from settling in the state left Oregon ill prepared for a downturn in the state's timber industry that took hold in the mid-1970s.

The age of decline had set in. But the system of regulations of the 1960s and 1970s that was successful in controlling pollution and resource depletion was often economically counterproductive, blocking growth at a time when America was entering a serious recession. Moreover, these regulations cemented in place a deep-seated antagonism toward government by the private sector—business *and* labor.

So, simply for pragmatic reasons, Colorado had to find a method to involve all the parties—the state government, local governments, the business community, public interest organizations—in a cooperative effort aimed at promoting economic growth within environmental limitations. The only way to arrive at decisions was *consensus*. It would be Colorado's down-scale application of the Japanese style.

Much of it involved simply sitting the sectoral representatives together in closed sessions. "The Front Range Project had some incredi-

bly violent, cathartic kinds of experiences," recalled John Parr, director of the project, "where developers and environmentalists would be
in the same room talking about open space, going at each other tooth
and nail—'Well, if *you* guys hadn't screwed up in 1965 . . .' But because they all had the same future orientation, it kept holding them
in the room together."

The use of consensus planning was viewed in Colorado as the
logical—the only—response to the dilemma of growth in an era of
limits. This was the lesson Governor Lamm had learned, and the one
he relayed to his legislators in January 1982. "I believe that other
public/private initiatives can be developed," he said, "to ensure that
Colorado remains competitive in the changing economic climate the
whole nation will be facing in the future."

Lamm saw the connections. The postindustrial economy is a
global economy; it requires appropriate responses, one of which is
public and private investment in basic areas, such as human capital
and infrastructure. It also necessitates a sense of cooperation—the
final, all-embracing neoliberal theme.

The insistence that growth in an age of resource limitations requires a greater degree of cooperation between the sectors of the
American economy as well as between individuals is the strongest tenet of neoliberalism. The theme of cooperation arises whenever the
"new realities" and new ideas are discussed. The neoliberals couch
their advocacy of national industrial policies in terms of public/private
sector cooperation. Effective human-capital policies can only be devised with cooperation by government, business, and labor. The fascination with cooperative management systems, worker participation in
management, and worker ownership of industry derives not from an
ideological taste for socialism, but from the belief that giving workers
a stake in a business's bottom line creates a community of interest
whose members are all striving for the same goals—productivity,
progress, and profits. Finally, assertions that there is a national interest that transcends the interests of individual groups in American
society boldly characterize the new liberalism. Attacks on politicians
perceived as adhering to the presumed interest-group liberalism of the
1960s–70s—charges that former Vice President Walter Mondale, in
particular, has been forced to contend with—have been one of the
1984 presidential campaign's most salient features.

Some evidence indicates that the idea of cooperation, or community, or consensus, or the national interest—its guises are many, but its meaning the same—has seeped through to the nation's political and intellectual leadership from a deeply felt need in the citizenry at large. Pollster Daniel Yankelovich, in his 1981 book *New Rules,* concluded, "Survey data showing that Americans are growing less self-absorbed and better prepared to take a first step toward an ethic of commitment, though sparse, is fairly clear." But the urgency of the community motif expressed by the neoliberals seems to reinforce the notion that economic growth is the first principle of neoliberalism. The importance of community stems from the neoliberals' belief that the politics of antagonism and interest groups has been exhausted. *Only* by stepping beyond the myths of competition, the free market, and regulation to the politics of cooperation can the United States prosper internationally.

The model of cooperation is Japan. Lester Thurow touched upon Japan in *The Zero-Sum Society,* pointing approvingly to the country's Ministry of International Trade and Industry. MITI is Japan's planning agency. Through an elaborate information-gathering system, it identifies the growth industries in Japan, particularly those which will be competitive internationally, and using a variety of means—protection, exhortation, introduction of new technologies, encouragement of joint research ventures, tax incentives—it steers the nation's industries in those directions, while discouraging further development of industries deemed to be on the downslide.

But the book that really struck a nerve was *Japan as Number One: Lessons for America* by Ezra Vogel, a Harvard sociologist. Vogel addressed both the "shop floor" and national questions—that is, he detailed methods employed at individual plants to improve productivity, as well as MITI's policies to foster growth. In both cases he said that Japan's success was wholly dependent on the attitude of cooperation that permeates Japanese society. What's more, Vogel specifically raised the issues plaguing the neoliberals—declining productivity, decreasing international competitiveness, the rule not of law but of lawyers, the problems of the postindustrial society—and affirmed that Japan's cooperative approach had successfully dealt with them all.

The company's goals were the workers' goals, he pointed out, and consensus between management and labor, in all the diverse areas of a single factory, was an end in itself, a value esteemed above all others. Productivity-enhancing technology was not feared, because both lifetime employment and retraining were guaranteed. Children were taught cooperation from their first days in school, "however annoying they may find group pressures," whereas in the United States ". . . in the guise of pursuing freedoms we have supported egoism and self-interest and have damaged group or common interests." Japanese workers, noted Vogel, were concerned about the products they made, because responsibility for quality was vested in them, not in an omniscient quality-control manager. But in the U.S. factory "foremen stand guard to make sure workers do not slack off. Workers grumble at foremen, and foremen are cross with workers. In the Japanese factory, employees seem to work even without foremen watching."

Vogel advocated "selective" borrowing from Japan, including not only the imitation of its management techniques but the adoption of its political structure of a stronger central government and an elite corps to staff a renewed, efficient bureaucracy.

In his unabashed admiration for the Japanese way, Vogel ignored many of its blemishes—pollution, poor public housing, the fact that lifetime employment affects only a fraction of the work force, infrastructure decay—of which the Japanese themselves were well aware. On a broader scale, Vogel largely dismissed the American individualistic tradition, implying that the cooperative economy could be translated from there to here with few, if any, alterations—a dubious and naïve proposition.

Nevertheless, Ezra Vogel had opened the gates on the subject of cooperation. When Robert Reich, who would later achieve notoriety as the Democratic Party's most ardent advocate of an innovation-based industrial policy, arrived at Harvard in 1981, one of his first calls was to Vogel. The two set up a study group to design ways to instill Japanese-style cooperation in the United States. The attention paid to Vogel's book released a flood of other paeans to the Japanese method.

The term "cooperation," in the context of contemporary politics, is fuzzy, and the phrase "the Japanese way" even fuzzier. Nevertheless, the neoliberals' usage is quite clear. In a 1981 interview, Senator Bill Bradley said that in talks to business groups he would constantly be peppered with, "Why can't we be more like the Japanese? In Japan, almost 50 percent of the workers' income derives from productivity bonuses, and wages are relatively low—that gives everybody an incentive for the company to succeed." At labor union gatherings, the same initial question would be posed—"Why can't we be more like the Japanese?"—but union members would add, "In Japan, the difference between the highest-paid executive and the lowest worker is the smallest in the world."

"What do I draw from that?" asked Bradley. "It's *not* going to be Japan as a model. . . . The model we're going to find has to draw on *two* strains of American history: the strain toward individualism; and the other strain, which the Democratic Party has traditionally spoken for, and that's community, which I think can be translated in such a simple phrase as 'teamwork.' "

Having affirmed that cooperation is a necessity for growth in the postindustrial economy, the neoliberals take an additional leap and declare that only through cooperation can the context for risk-taking be created. "The idea that you're part of a community, and that every part of the community has to be involved in striving for economic growth is a very important concept," said Bill Bradley. "I think one of the means by which you strive is recognizing that the passer on the team is as important as the scorer. That's a kind of crude analogy, but *that's* what it is. You've got to recognize that the guy who runs those machines and maintains them is, in the long run, as critical to the overall performance of the economy as the introduction of the new machine. Assuming that you need the new machine, which I do."

Political support for a national cooperative strategy has been felt at the national level as a result of successful local experiences with sectoral collaboration. Governor Hugh Carey was faced with the dismal prospect of a bankrupt New York City almost immediately upon assuming office in 1975. To stave off default, Carey created the Municipal Assistance Corporation and named as chairman Felix Rohatyn, a senior partner in Lazard Frères, the international investment banking house. MAC's role was to coerce compromises between the major participants in the city's financial structure, mainly the unions, the banks, and New York City's government. MAC, Rohatyn wrote later, "was the linchpin between business, labor and government regarding those prickly issues of fairness and wealth." The municipal unions accepted a 20 percent work-force reduction and a temporary wage freeze; the banks holding the city's loans agreed to additional long-term, low-interest loans, which were guaranteed by the federal government; the state government provided credit assistance. In short, government coordination made possible public- and private-sector cooperation, which spurred investment and not only averted bankruptcy of the city but helped speed it toward an economic renaissance. From his experience with MAC, Rohatyn has drawn national implications, strongly recommending to Democratic Party leaders that they re-create the Depression-era Reconstruction Finance Corporation to act as a tripartite (business-labor-government) reindustrialization board for the entire nation.

In Lowell, Massachusetts, the heart of America's first industrial boom in textiles, and scene of the nation's first major industrial decline, sectoral collaboration helped the city enter the postindustrial economy. Native son Paul Tsongas, who'd witnessed the city's decay as a boy and vainly attempted to fend it off as a city council member, later as U.S. Senator developed the Lowell Plan with the city manager. "It was a blueprint for a collaboration between the public and private sectors," wrote Tsongas in *The Road from Here*. In his book he stated that federal loan programs, specifically the Great Society's Model Cities Program, had failed to reverse Lowell's decline because they ignored the need for private investment. Out of the Lowell Plan came the Lowell Development and Financial Corporation, an RFC-type mechanism that brought together the city government, the federal government, and eleven local banks in an attempt to induce Wang Laboratories to locate in Lowell. The high-technology firm was given assistance in the construction of its new headquarters. The Prince Macaroni Company, one of the last major remnants of old industrial Lowell, was also persuaded to stay with loans enabling it to build the nation's largest pasta plant. In each case, federal funds were granted contingent upon the firm's agreeing to provide matching investments. Prince and Wang helped to stabilize Lowell's economic and employment drift, which attracted other businesses to the city.

When thirty-seven-year-old Stanley Lundine was elected to the House of Representatives from New York's 39th District in 1976, he was the first Democrat to represent the upstate area in more than one hundred years. But as the three-term mayor of Jamestown, Lundine had successfully employed cooperative tactics to reverse the city's economic decline; his election to Congress—an unexpected landslide—was a reward for his creation of a new political dialogue. In 1971, two years into his mayoralty, a local manufacturer went bankrupt and another fled the city, sending Jamestown's unemployment rate skyward. Lundine helped to organize the Jamestown Area Labor Management Committee, a tripartite board charged with analyzing the town's economy and recommending methods to improve it. Years before the productivity problem became a national issue, it was recognized in New York State. Productivity improvement, the JALMC determined, was the key to Jamestown's vitality. But several sectoral agreements were necessary. Lundine detailed them in a handbook prepared by the Northeast-Midwest Institute entitled *Grass Roots Industrial Policy: Building on American Diversity in the '80s and '90s:*

> First, we agreed that productivity would be broadly defined and would not simply involve a speed-up of worker effort. Such objectives as reducing absenteeism, improving product quality and eliminating waste would be recognized as productivity advances.
>
> It was also understood that labor and management would work together on the development of programs and would share equitably in the results of any improvements. Without any up-front negotiation, it was agreed that the financial gains achieved as a result of the joint productivity efforts would be shared on a roughly equal basis between labor and the industry.

A tiny grant from the U.S. Economic Development Administration allowed for the creation of factory-level labor/management committees to oversee productivity agreements in the individual firms. By 1980 unemployment in Jamestown had been reduced by more than 50 percent. Lundine took this lesson to Congress, and has in his four terms been consistently in the lead in arguing for the cooperative route to productivity improvement and national economic salvation. "He is," noted *Politics in America,* a handbook of congressional information and statistics, "among the most single-minded legislators in the House." Lundine's initiatives have included a bill to establish a Federal Productivity Council inside the government, and another to require more details on productivity to be kept by the Bureau of Labor Statistics. Lundine was instrumental in adding a variation on the employee stock ownership plan to the 1979 Chrysler loan guarantee legislation, and shepherded through the 1978 Human Resources Development Act, which provided $10 million of federal funds for the organization of local labor/management coordinating committees.

In the three cases of New York City, Lowell, and Jamestown, the main characters all clearly recognized that private-sector investment—either in capital or human capital—was the key to economic success in their cities. Government served not as planner but as coordinator. MAC, LDFC, and JALMC were not central-planning bodies, but mediating structures that set up cooperative arrangements between the public and private sectors. In each case, too, the primary figure—banker Rohatyn, Senator Tsongas, and Congressman Lundine—emerged firmly convinced that a national cooperative strategy was not only possible but necessary. Each also affirmed that a balance must be struck between public and private investment, or, in Bill Bradley's words, between teamwork and individualism.

The neoliberals have placed themselves squarely in the center of a dilemma progressives have wrestled with for virtually the entire twentieth century: What is the proper balance between competition and cooperation? Traditional liberals have ignored the role risk and competition play in spurring the creation of new wealth; the neoliberals not only affirm the place of competition in our economy, but further assert that only by creating a cooperative context for the economy will people feel secure enough to take wealth-producing risks.

The issue dates back to the 1912 presidential race between Woodrow Wilson, a strict pro-competition Democrat, and former President Theodore Roosevelt, who argued strenuously for a cooperative society under the rubric of the "New Nationalism." (Incumbent President William Howard Taft was a distant third in the public's eye.)

To a large extent, neoliberalism of the 1980s hearkens back to TR's New Nationalism. In his acceptance address at the 1912 Progressive Party (known as the "Bull Moose" Party) convention, Roosevelt captured the internationalist tone of today's neoliberals:

> Concentration and cooperation in industry in order to secure efficiency are a world-wide movement. The United States cannot resist it. If we . . . do not allow cooperation, we shall be defeated in the world's markets. We cannot adopt an economic system less efficient than our great competitors. . . . Either we must modify our present obsolete laws regarding concentration and cooperation so as to conform with the world movement, or else fall behind in the race for the world's markets.

The comparison with economist Lester Thurow is dramatic. In *The Zero-Sum Society,* Thurow wrote:

> The futility and obsolescence of the antitrust laws can be seen from a number of vantage points. First, with the growth of international trade it is no longer possible to determine whether an effective monopoly exists by looking at local market shares. . . . In markets where international trade exists or could exist, national antitrust laws no longer make sense. If they do anything, they only serve to hinder U.S. competitors who must live by a code their foreign competitors can ignore.

Thurow's opinions on the archaic nature of American antitrust legislation have been endorsed, at least in part, by Bill Bradley ("I'm saying that maybe one of the ways we get people retrained and get companies to assume responsibility is that we don't look so hard on some greater concentration. . . ."), Gary Hart ("Banking and antitrust laws should be revised to allow the formation of U.S. export trading companies [to] allow small firms to pool their efforts to achieve profitable economies of scale. . . ."), and Paul Tsongas ("The antitrust laws were designed to prevent collusion and thereby prevent large companies from destroying competition. . . . But in their present form, they obstruct our capacity to survive in international markets.").

The New Nationalist notion of cooperation reappeared during the first stage of Franklin Roosevelt's New Deal, but in the late 1930s FDR abandoned it for a strict pro-competitive stance. Ever since, in American politics, policy has wavered between cooperation and competition. The neoliberals have offered the first truly original insight on this issue in forty years, stating that cooperation is necessary if entrepreneurial competition is to flourish and the United States is to survive in world markets.

In neoliberal dialogue, the theme of cooperation takes many forms. The most significant manifestation of it is the assertion that there is a national interest that transcends special interests in American society. The national-interest-versus-special-interest debate has been at the center of the Democrats' 1984 presidential nominating process, with Gary Hart, Reubin Askew, Ernest Hollings, and John Glenn all attacking front-runner Walter Mondale as the candidate of the special interests. It is another example of a neoliberal motif that has become a public issue. And one of the neoliberal programs likely to become the focus of public interest within the next several years is based on this cooperative theme: national service.

CHAPTER 18

National Service

FORTY-TWO-YEAR-OLD SAM BROWN'S BIOGRAPHY is a chronology of the student movement. He dropped out of Harvard Divinity School to help organize Eugene McCarthy's 1968 challenge to President Lyndon Johnson. A year later, he successfully stewarded the national Moratorium against the Vietnam War, an effort that culminated with 300,000 people converging on Washington on November 15 to protest the ongoing conflict. In 1974, he stepped out from the shadows of the organizer's craft and ran for office, defeating the incumbent Colorado state treasurer during the watershed election that brought Richard Lamm to the governor's chair and Gary Hart to the Senate. And, in 1977, Jimmy Carter took Brown to Washington to assume the burden of ACTION, the agency that coordinates the work of both the Peace Corps and VISTA. In 1984 Sam Brown contemplated a run for the Senate himself.

Fourteen years ago, Sam Brown was an ardent opponent of the war and the draft. Now, he speaks of the need for national service. Compulsory national service? "I think so, with military and nonmilitary options," said Brown in a 1982 interview. "But I think what's more important, and fits better with the ethos of America than compulsory service, is to build the ethic of service."

National service is one of the places the neoliberals are leading America. "When I graduated from college," recalled Sam Brown, "the question of whether you were going into the Peace Corps or whether you were going to do something different with your life was a big question for a lot of people. I would like to re-create that kind of question for people today, when they're seventeen or eighteen. It's a question that asks, What is it that gives you the broader experience to make the right decisions in life? That gives some shared experience, the sort the Rockefellers have to take part in too, because it's an *expected* thing to do? [Service] will do different things for different people. For some, it's a question of discipline, for some it's a question of education, for some it's a question of relationships with people unlike themselves, and seeing a little wider vision of the world. There are as many benefits to it as there are people who would potentially be part of it. It just seems like a terrific opportunity."

Brown came to Washington specifically because he saw national service and "a curious version of self-help" as two interlocking cutting-edge issues of the eighties. He had spurned Jimmy Carter's requests for support during the 1976 campaign, but Carter nevertheless approached him with an offer to join his administration. Brown accepted because he viewed ACTION as an opportunity where he could mold many of his sixties' ideals into workable form.

As an activist in Denver, Brown looked with alarm upon the deterioration of the public school system and the pernicious effect it was having on cherished American ideals. Unemployment had become a serious problem, and yet the institutions charged with imparting skills were no longer accomplishing this task. More ephemeral, but no less critical in his own mind, was the lack of a sense of community to encourage excellence and productivity and risk-taking; it is an ethic, he felt, that only the melting pot of public education can transmit. Sam Brown, like many of his fellow idealists from the restless sixties, wanted to find a way both to reinforce communitarian values and to teach skills to those who do not possess them. "The place where these two notions come together best," he said, "is national service."

To Brown's dismay, within a year Jimmy Carter had squandered the moral authority with which he entered national office. "I thought Carter should have said when he came in basically what Reagan said [four years later], but from a socially concerned standpoint—about voluntarism, about the great volunteer spirit of the country, and the history of it," mused Brown. "He might have called on all of us to be better than we are, to do better. At the beginning, he could have done this: Carter seemed sort of high-minded. . . . You can combine that call for living up to our best instincts with creating 'a government as good as its people.'

"I think a lot of America's potential remains untapped," Brown concluded. "There are a lot of things that could get done if people just directed their attention toward doing things *for* other people. Think if everybody's productivity went up just ten percent because they cared about the quality of what they're doing! I don't think you can have a society that doesn't both encourage and reward work, *and* make opportunities for it."

Brown's comments reflect the underlying value structure of neoliberalism and point to its roots in the 1960s. The idea of community as the bedrock from which spring justice and progress was fundamental in the counterculture of the 1960s. Neoliberals, and increasingly, mainstream Democrats, view community-based national service programs as the most effective way to create, or re-create, that missing sense of community in American life. It is closely linked to the same imperative that views worker participation in management, and even worker ownership of business, as an integral part of productivity gains; or that sees cooperation between business, labor, and management, or between industry and academy, as a necessary element in national progress.

But no matter how the question of national service is viewed, it is inextricably linked to the role and status of the military in American society. By 1980 the armed forces seemed to have passed from under the cloud of the sixties and seventies. Many of the most vocal proponents of national service, like Sam Brown, emerged from the antiwar tradition, and they include military service as a vital component of any national service plan. For some, this even means a recommendation that the draft be reinstituted. One of the most memorable features of James Fallows' *National Defense,* the influential military reform text, was the author's firm insistence on a return to conscription. "[The draft] should be enacted because, *whatever* the military policy, it will ensure that its consequences are borne by the same public that must give its assent to that policy, rather than being concentrated on the least visible, least influential few," asserted Fallows. As editor of the *Harvard Crimson* a decade before, Fallows had crusaded against the war and the draft, successfully evading both.

Gary Hart, who managed George McGovern's anti-war presidential campaign in 1972, has based his own run for the White House in part on opposition to the arms race and U.S. adventurism in Central America. Yet he too has come forward as an advocate of national service. ". . . I strongly lean toward universal service," Hart has said. "Compulsory national service may be the biggest issue of the eighties."

The discussion of national service is certainly not unrelated to the problems of the all-volunteer army. In 1980 more than half the army's enlistees were rated category IV, the lowest acceptable mental class. Despite marked enlistment increases recently, most experts expect the improving economy and the declining supply of eighteen-year-olds to pose serious manpower shortages for the army in the near future.

But the potential manpower shortage is only one of a host of reasons the question of national service has arisen in the eighties. Youth unemployment is also frequently cited. New York City Mayor Edward Koch, in announcing his support for a national youth service system in March 1983, excused his plan's probable $25–$30 billion price tag by noting the reduction in "the enormous cost of dependency and unemployment." (Acting on this principle, Koch announced a youth service program for New York City in January 1984. Eighteen-year-olds from poor backgrounds will have the opportunity to engage in a variety of public-service tasks, in return for a stipend of three-quarters of the minimum wage and other benefits.) Debate in the House over the establishment of an American Conservation Corps—passed in February 1983—made clear the Democratic leadership's view that the legislation is primarily a jobs bill for 100,000 unemployed teenagers. But beyond these reasons, the first phase of a study of a national service undertaken by the Ford Foundation, released in 1982, concluded: "A desire to establish a centrist national agenda that emphasizes the value of many of the social programs of the 1960s without replicating their structure [is] likely . . . to make national service a real issue" between 1983 and 1986.

The service debate promises to be confusing. The terms—"draft," "national service," "universal service"—signify different things, and proponents of one form or another have such widely disparate reasons for holding to their own pet notions that it can seem as if there is no coherent line of thought. Nevertheless, two simple and critical delineations stand out. There are those who maintain complete support for the military's All Volunteer Forces (AVF), opposing any form of service that is not strictly voluntary and not adequately compensated; and there are those who find the AVF unsatisfactory, a failed experiment. Some anti-AVF people criticize it purely on the grounds of military preparedness or efficiency; for the most part, this group supports conscription. But others find moral fault with the volunteer military, tying its creation and its consequences to a gradual breakdown in national values that occurred during the last two decades. Although far from all the members of this group would support reenactment of the draft, for the most part the neoliberals fall into this latter category.

Virtually all discussions of the draft-cum-national service cite the increase in the manpower pool available to the armed forces, and the consequent rise in the quality of recruits, that would result from the return to conscription or to a compulsory or quasi-compulsory national service plan. Nevertheless, support for it among neoliberals stems not so much from their worries over preparedness as it does from considerations of fairness and their belief that service would help to preserve a sense of national community.

Manpower was R. James Woolsey's top priority in the defense-policy segment of *The New Republic*'s 1982 "Democratic Agenda for the 80s." While Woolsey, a top adviser to presidential candidate John Glenn, avoided an explicit call for reinstituting the draft, his implied criticisms of the AVF and his language are revealing. The attempt to lure military recruits solely via economic incentives "has meant that the *burden* of combat . . . will fall on Watts, Appalachia, and South Boston, not on Groton and Santa Monica." The GI Bill should be reinstated, he maintained, in order to "rebuild the *partnership* between higher education and national security."

Banker Felix Rohatyn, a key Democratic economic adviser, has been even clearer in expressing his opinion of conscription. Writing in *The New York Times Magazine* in December 1982, Rohatyn stated, "The draft is not an economy measure but a philosophical one: National service cannot be limited to the children of the poor and minorities; it must include the children of the middle class and the well-to-do." And New York's Mayor Koch, who as a congressman from Greenwich Village was one of the earliest and most active opponents of America's involvement in Vietnam, invoked both "pragmatic" and "moralistic" reasons in raising the issue in early 1983. "An Army and Navy from which the upper and middle classes of America are largely missing is not representative of our nation, nor as effective as it could be," said Koch. Speaking at a fund raiser for the Boy Scouts of America, the mayor raised the spiritual value of service, implicitly placing it at the top of the list. Young people, he said, "are disaffected and lacking in purpose. Their outlook is narrow. Too often, they are out of touch with the spirit of altruism, which is a basic part of every human being."

The moral imperative behind the emerging national service debate is not new. Although hidden from view at least since the early seventies, it has a long tradition as an American theme. Harvard philosopher William James established the tone for the ongoing national discussion in his famous essay "The Moral Equivalent of War." Writing in 1910, as European militarism was building, soon to burst forth in the global cataclysm of World War I, and sensing that military conscription would be a divisive topic at home, James hoped to preempt the inevitable contention by promoting a pacifist alternative, an "Army enlisted against nature," a force to be sent "to the coal and iron mines, to freight trains, to fishing fleets in December, to dish-washing, clothes-washing, and window-washing, to road-building and tunnel-making, to foundries and stokeholes." The result would be greater "social cohesiveness." The campaign initiated by James was joined by such luminaries as President Charles Eliot of Harvard, Theodore Roosevelt, and former Secretary of State Elihu Root.

James's vision—and the model for virtually all subsequent suggestions for service programs—was realized with the creation of the New Deal's Civilian Conservation Corps. Over a nine-year period, the CCC employed 1.5 million men, all volunteers, to accomplish a myriad of tasks, including replanting 2 million acres of forest, building 37,000 bridges, and protecting 4 million acres of farmland from erosion.

Much of the current neoliberal talk about national service and the draft calls up the social stratification that resulted from the Vietnam draft, and the inequities that followed elimination of the draft. Eighty percent of the infantry's riflemen in Vietnam were draftees, and a draftee in the war had a 10 percent better chance of being killed or wounded than a volunteer. The student deferment assured that the burden of the war would fall on young people too poor to escape to college. The dismissal of the student deferment in 1968 opened the war's danger to the previously protected children of the vocal and powerful upper middle class, virtually guaranteeing that the Nixon-appointed commission, headed by former Defense Secretary Thomas Gates, would advocate the draft's death.

More significant, however, was the commission's ideological motivation. Driven primarily by conservative economists Milton Friedman and Martin Anderson (who later became President Reagan's first chief domestic policy adviser), the Gates Commission concluded that the draft is actually a tax that falls inequitably upon young people and thus violates certain tenets of conservative economic theory. Consistent with this interpretation was the analysis that a free-market approach to military manpower, using financial incentives to draw volunteers, would not only enhance the military's prestige but lessen training costs, and, incidentally, have little effect on the racial composition of the armed forces.

The Gates Commission was wrong on virtually every count. But dogmatic adherence to the marketplace model by a generation of military policymakers either beholden to the Friedman-Anderson economic theories or unwilling to challenge the perceived public reticence remaining from the sixties, has enabled the AVF to continue, if not exactly to flourish. It has also given the military reform movement some of its most potent ammunition in its ongoing war against the systems analysts. Larry Smith, Senator Gary Hart's former administrative assistant, and a military affairs expert, criticized AVF proponents as "classical liberals, by which I mean out of 1960s government, who use all of the methodology of Ph.D-dom and Rand-ism to justify what is essentially an ethical impulse, which is . . . that each individual ought freely to choose" whether or not to serve. The view is mistaken, asserts Smith; national service, he said in 1982, "is essentially a philosophical issue." Richard Danzig, co-author of the Ford Foundation study and a former deputy Assistant Secretary of Defense, who styles himself "on balance, a proponent of the AVF," nevertheless said that one of his reasons for undertaking the research was to provide a counterbalance to the limited, negative viewpoint that predominates in the Defense Department. "In the Pentagon," Danzig said, "one encounters thousands of analysts who can prove to you that anything which does exist could not exist, that the costs and analytic difficulties are very high. . . . In fact, I think these people often make very intelligent and acute points about many ideas that are around. But their strength is typically in disabusing people of notions . . . rather than a creative ability to take the occasional notion that's really good, and make it work."

The best-known member of the military reform movement to take national service options and attempt to make them work as policy is Charles Moskos, a professor at Northwestern University. Like Larry Smith, like James Woolsey, like James Fallows, Moskos is a harsh critic of the systems analysts—his conversation is riddled with attacks against "the Rand [Corporation]/DOD bureaucracy"—and he characterizes the emerging debate as a moral issue. "I think the current revival of national service is on the values side, rather than on the efficiency side," said Moskos in May 1982. His national service program, outlined in a series of position papers and in articles for publications like the *Wilson Quarterly* and *Foreign Affairs,* has garnered favorable responses from neoliberals, notably Bill Bradley, Gary Hart, Paul Tsongas, and Reubin Askew, as well as from centrists and conservatives like Ohio Senator John Glenn, who placed Moskos on his campaign's military-policy advisory group, and Georgia's Sam Nunn. "The starting point is not how are empty spaces to be filled," Moskos has argued in one of his papers, "but rather how substantial and representative numbers of American youth can serve their country."

Moskos' program would condition federal educational benefits, both grants and loans, on a period of service to the country, either in a military or (undefined) civilian capacity. He calls for the reinstitution of the G.I. Bill, and would establish a two-track personnel system for military volunteers, with options for career soldiers and citizen soldiers. Career soldiers, whose initial enlistment would be for a period of four years, would receive significant benefits in housing, medical care, technical training, and reenlistment bonuses; while not unlike the current AVF recruitment system, there would be a greater emphasis on reenlistments in this track, presumably correcting for the crisis in retention of noncommissioned officers.

The citizen soldier Moskos defines as "the functional equivalent of the draftee," a two-year soldier (or a five-year reservist) who joins, serves in combat arms or other labor-intensive positions, and receives lower pay. The citizen soldier's one perk is the reconstituted G.I. Bill, which in Moskos' scheme would end up paying the enlistee's college or graduate school costs. "A college or graduate education, or vocational training," wrote Moskos, ". . . would be the means to attract highly qualified soldiers who can learn quickly, serve effectively, and then be replaced by similarly qualified recruits." Lesser educational benefits—such as today's federally guaranteed student loans—would be granted to those young people who serve a brief period of time in unpaid or stipended civilian capacities. Those who do not serve would be ineligible for such programs.

Obviously, there are problems with the plan. As Moskos' program is designed, it would draw only those young people who must avail themselves of aid programs to pay for higher education, and so discriminates against middle- and lower-class kids in favor of the upper-middle class and the rich; what's more, students who live in states that have their own college-benefits programs are effectively out of the plan's reach. Proponents admit that the approach isn't all-encompassing, but they believe that by pulling in the great middle, it makes military service more palatable for all classes. "It promotes those elements of military manpower policies which would broaden the social class of the people who come in," claimed James Woolsey. "It would in-crease the cohesion of military units, and would have as many of the positive features of the draft of the fifties and early sixties—when the draft was working pretty well—as possible, without having to go back to a compulsory system." Woolsey also supports the civilian aspect of the proposal. "It ties together the notion of education and national service, which was only present in the G.I. Bill in earlier days. Indeed, it's been actively discouraged by government policy since then."

Objections remain, however. A 1982 background paper prepared for the DOD's Military Manpower Task Group faulted the notion that the Moskos plan—termed "benefits-conditional service" (BCS) because it would tie educational aid to voluntary service—would, in fact, instill a sense of duty and responsibility in the country's young people. "Rather than adopting a public spirit, participants may view BCS as a 'mickey mouse' requirement of a financial aid program," warned the report. "The danger, in short, is that BCS may trivialize public service."

Doesn't the neoliberals' advocacy of national service compromise their support for decentralization? The neoliberals don't see a contra-diction. Rather, they view decentralized authority as a fundamental element of the civilian component of any national service plan—that is, decisions about what constitutes service would necessarily be made at either the state or, preferably, the local level.

Some of the activities of ACTION provide the most immediate model for a nationally organized but locally administered service pro-gram. Although admittedly undertaken on a small scale, ACTION's Programs for Local Service (PLS) allowed local organizations to de-cide jobs and administer their plans within a clearly defined national context. In Seattle, for example, from 1973 to 1977, volunteers be-tween the ages of eighteen and twenty-five were paid 90 percent of the minimum wage for full-time work at a variety of organizations, each of which put up $150 for the privilege of choosing those appli-cants to whom it would extend employment offers. The volunteers were poorer than average, but also had a slightly higher educational attainment than the youth population as a whole. Seventy percent were unemployed at the time of volunteering, but 25 percent were re-ceiving academic credit for their PLS participation. Thus, Seattle's PLS served both as a jobs program and as a method of "rebuilding the partnership" between service and education.

A PLS-type program was begun in Syracuse in 1977 by Sam

Brown, who sought to revitalize ACTION and particularly the moribund VISTA, one of the Great Society's better-known programs. The Syracuse program was much more specifically aimed at unemployed young people. One out of every three volunteers was a high school dropout, and 57 percent were minority group members. Participants received $78 a week as salary and accrued a $33-per-month stipend, which could be applied to education and training. Half the three hundred sponsoring organizations were private, nonprofit institutions, 40 percent were local government agencies, and the rest were either neighborhood groups or projects initiated by the volunteers. Down the line, local officials praised the ACTION programs.

In Seattle, the state government took over the bulk of the funding as the federal agency's budget was increasingly squeezed. In Syracuse, the PLS was extended into outlying rural areas. "Simplicity was the major attribute of PLS," Sam Brown testified to a Senate subcommittee. "It was entirely local in scope, without bureaucratic 'experts' determining where and how a volunteer would work." To Brown, national service is a force for a "holistic economics": "We can no longer accept a volunteer program to fight poverty, a jobs program to combat unemployment and a health program to deal with medical problems, each separate from the other. We must begin to recognize the inherent interrelationship of these programs and stop compartmentalizing them for some imagined bureaucratic ease or preservation of territorial rights."

Brown's revitalization of ACTION was not universally hailed. An unabashed progressive, he sought to channel the agency's efforts, volunteers, and funding into social-action organizations whose challenges to the status quo and plainly leftward leanings irked conservatives. For this, Brown was the occasional subject of congressional disapproval. But the most salient criticism of Sam Brown's ACTION had nothing to do with politics; his agency was accused of overseeing not volunteer operations or a national service program, but thinly veiled jobs programs for the poor that had little or no viable service components.

"The fact is, it doesn't leave out the top rung of society if you do it right. There are reasons why [West Virginia Governor] Jay Rockefeller was a VISTA volunteer [in the sixties]," replied Brown. ". . . At the same time, it was important to me to break the stereotype of the Ivy League do-gooder, the let's-go-out-and-change-the-world type. The thing I'm proudest of in VISTA over the last four years is that, by the time I left, 60 percent of the volunteers were locally recruited, something like 40 percent were minority, and a substantial number, 12 to 15 percent, were older Americans.

"The question is," he concluded, "can people who come out of a community be motivated, for the munificent sum of eighty bucks a week, to help other people? And do people then learn skills, and if so, what skills do they learn? I think the answer is, given the opportunity and the leadership, you *can* create a cross-cultural, cross-racial, cross-class volunteer program, which will have all sorts of problems. It will not be easy by any stretch of the imagination."

Perhaps the best example of a service program is the California Conservation Corps, established by Governor Jerry Brown in 1976 and described by him as "an ecological militia with a high esprit de corps—a combination of kibbutz, a Jesuit seminary, and the Marine Corps." Its accomplishments have significantly raised hopes that a national program can be implemented.

Ironically, the CCC was originally conceived by Brown's predecessor, Ronald Reagan, as a jobs program for unemployed Vietnam veterans. Brown enlarged its focus, seeing his CCC as a model for a locally administered national service program. (The irony was further compounded when in 1981 President Reagan cut $4.2 billion of the CCC's federal funding.)

The California Conservation Corps, as its acronym implies, was structured after the original New Deal CCC. Approximately two thousand volunteers, male and female, based at twenty-five centers throughout the state, spend several million hours a year performing a variety of environmental tasks. In 1981 three million trees were planted by corps members in northern California. Fifty-two thousand CCC'ers were largely responsible for the construction of Yucaipa Regional Park in San Bernardino County. They rebuilt more than 140 miles of trails in Yosemite, Kings Canyon, and Sequoia national parks. But unlike the original CCC, emergency services highlight the corps' activities. Hundreds of thousands of hours are spent fighting forest fires. Under the direction of the U.S. Coast Guard, members of the CCC have helped to clean up oil spills off the California coast.

The California Conservation Corps achieved a public relations coup and provided perhaps the only bright spot during the state's 1981 infestation by the Mediterranean fruit fly, an attack that threatened to decimate California's $14 billion agriculture industry. Half of the CCC's total volunteers were dispatched to the Medfly battlefront during the two separate outbreaks to strip fruit from trees in Santa

Clara County, pulling down almost 3,000 tons of it. The corps' kitchen staff provided food not only for the CCC's own members but for National Guard personnel as well during the thirty-five-day ordeal that began in July 1981. While Governor Brown was lambasted in the state's press for his apparent indecisiveness in the matter (a factor that contributed heavily to his defeat in California's 1982 U.S. Senate race), throughout the crisis Californians—indeed, via the network news, *all* Americans—were treated to the sight of sweat-stained CCC volunteers gamely spending twenty hours a day in trees and sleeping on the ground without benefit of tents or cots. Referring to the CCC's national potential, *Los Angeles Herald Examiner* columnist Marianne Means wrote at the time of the crisis, "It is ironic that [Brown's] personal disaster turns on the same events which could bring the Civilian Conservation Corps closer to his ultimate goal for it."

Hopes for a truly national service program may rest with the presidential commission proposed by two neoliberals, California Congressman Leon Panetta and Massachusetts Senator Paul Tsongas. The commission, made up of twenty-five representatives from the fields of education, business, and labor, would research various alternative proposals and make recommendations to the President. More than a quarter of its spaces would be reserved for young people between the ages of seventeen and twenty-five. The commission's purpose, as its sponsors have declared in a variety of public forums, would be to focus the often-invoked "national debate" on the issue, to create a climate in favor of national service. "We need a strategy to raise consciousness about national service," Tsongas stressed in a 1979 talk before the Committee for the Study of National Service, telling the group, "The best part of my education wasn't four years at Dartmouth or three years at Yale. . . . My greatest learning experience was during two years in a small Ethiopian town . . . I was a Peace Corps teacher, but I hope my Ethiopian friends know how much they taught me." It is not surprising that many of those prominently associated with neoliberal politics were involved either with the Peace Corps (Tsongas, Connecticut Senator Christopher Dodd, New York City Council President Carol Bellamy) or VISTA (Arizona Governor Bruce Babbitt, West Virginia Governor Jay Rockefeller).

The Tsongas-Panetta bill has been stalled in Congress since 1980, but stands a good chance of passing in 1984.

With growing support from politicians and foundations, national service may yet emerge as a topic of debate—particularly in a Democratic administration. What the result will be is far from clear. "I'm not hopeful for it in the short run," said Sam Brown. "The unions say it's a form of sub-minimum-wage employment. Others say they're just going to be out raking leaves, anyway. Other people say we can't afford it, period. There are as many different complaints about it from as many different quarters as you can imagine. It's a social experiment of massive dimensions, and of course everybody's going to see all the little ways in which their own ox gets gored."

But the Ford Foundation's Richard Danzig, after enumerating in a 1982 interview many of those seemingly intractable obstacles, concluded the conversation with a tantalizing assessment. He cited a study of U.S. foreign development projects undertaken several years ago, actually an analysis of the analyses that went into the construction of major capital aid projects. The study concluded that if the proponents had foreseen all the difficulties before beginning their projects, they would not have approved them. But, once having started, and *then* encountering the problems, they resolved them in ways that *also* could not have been anticipated.

"That's a commentary on the limits of analysis, and I suppose it's encouraging," said Danzig. He paused a moment, then added, "Suppose I had said to you in 1905 that in this century there will be a time when virtually every American will have a driver's license and access to a vehicle, and will drive around at speeds of fifty-five miles per hour on roads here and there and everywhere; and what's more, I can predict that each year forty thousand people will die as a result of this?"

Danzig let the idea sink in for a bit, and concluded, "With the automobile, and now with the computer, you're talking about phenomena of technical change that cause social revolutions. The fact is, it *is* possible to consider social revolutions and achieve them."

CHAPTER 19

Industrial Policy

THE NEOLIBERALS, like the traditional liberals, hope to achieve nothing less than a social revolution. As industrial America gives way to the new postindustrial society, the only way to accomplish the traditional goals of liberalism, neoliberals maintain, is to shift to new methods of implementing them. Schumpeter is their favorite economist, not Keynes; they favor a politics of investment, not redistribution. They would move beyond big government to appropriate political technology and would replace special interests with the national interest. Finally, they prefer to avoid the liberal style of confrontation, choosing instead a context of cooperation within which economic growth can be achieved and its fruits equitably shared.

Neoliberalism's communitarian theme is most apparent in the neoliberals' support for industrial policy—the most controversial, least understood neoliberal program. Industrial policy has become the great political grab bag of the eighties. It is the Democrats' answer to supply-side economics—a pithy phrase with a thousand definitions that slides approvingly into the ear. The Democratic presidential candidates have flocked to the idea; traditional liberals like Walter Mondale have twisted its meaning to suit the needs of their perceived constituencies, but even so this affirms that the ideas which four years ago were just beginning to be called "neoliberal" have been rapidly adopted and co-opted by the Democratic mainstream. Industrial policy is the culmination of neoliberal themes, the manifestation of supply-side liberalism, a policy that promotes investment, cooperation and the use of market forces in order to make the United States internationally competitive.

Industrial policy is the program with which the neoliberals are most closely identified; it is a key to their social revolution. And its roots lie in an earlier social revolution, one that sputtered and stalled, but did not die. It was their experiences in the 1960s that eventually led today's neoliberal vanguard to toss out a political system based on confrontation and to attempt to implement one in which cooperation is a guiding value. This process is exemplified by Robert Reich.

Nineteen sixty-eight was the year of riots at the Chicago Democratic Convention, of Alexander Dubcek and the Prague Spring, of the murders of Martin Luther King and Bobby Kennedy, and the Days of Rage in Paris. That year a Grade-B, low-budget movie entitled *Wild in the Streets* asked what would happen when these anti-establishment war-protesting students finally *did* get the chance to run the show. The answer, supplied by a burnt-out rock-singing President, his Afro-coiffed drummer, and a fifteen-year-old whiz-kid graduate of the Yale Law School, was inane—compulsory retirement at thirty, mandatory LSD at thirty-five. But long after the film faded, the serious question remained: What happens when these kids . . . ?

One answer takes the form of a four-foot-eleven-inch former Rhodes Scholar and student leader named Robert B. Reich, Dartmouth Class of 1968, and a graduate of—hmm!—Yale Law, one of the seven students *Time* magazine put on the cover of its issue profiling "The Graduate—1968." The month *Wild in the Streets* premiered, *Time* reported of Reich, "He is in total rebellion against what he calls 'status-quoism.' " These days, Walter Mondale thinks he's the Lord Keynes of his generation. Fifteen years ago, Robert Reich declared, "We have to get over our fear of Communism or any other -isms." In June, 1982 presidential candidate Gary Hart personally invited him to discourse on policy at the Democratic Party's midterm convention.

A lecturer at Harvard's Kennedy School of Government, Reich has discarded both the anti-business arrogance of his left-liberal confreres and the anti-government nostrums of the Reagan Republicans. He has honed an argument for industrial policy, seeking to guide an entrepreneurial America into the 21st Century. His impact in the back rooms of politics has been sudden and tangible. His 1983 argument for industrial policy, *The Next American Frontier,* made him a political guru. His is "the second-most cited name by the neoliberals," according to Rutgers political scientist Ross Baker (Lester Thurow's is the first). Colorado Congressman Tim Wirth incorporated Reichian theory into the "Yellow Brick Road" economics paper he co-authored with Rep. Richard Gephardt for the House Democratic Caucus.

At its most basic level, industrial policy is, like supply-side economics, broadly concerned with increasing investment in the national economy to bolster productivity and improve America's international competitiveness. But whereas the conservatives have stressed macroeconomic affairs such as tax cuts and government spending, the neoliberal advocates of industrial policy claim that, in the eighties, it's microeconomics that matters: the issue is not so much the amount you invest, but *where* you invest it. When the supply-siders yell that this smacks of "central planning," Reich, a prolific phrase-maker, brands them "ideological neurotics."

"A neurotic," Reich said in September, 1982, "can't see the world as it is because of these paradigms that keep wandering around in his head. . . . No matter how much you explain and reveal that there was *never* a free market in this country, these people won't believe it. Government intervention sets the boundaries, decides what's going to be marketed, sets the rules of the game through procurement policies, tax credits, depreciation allowances, loans and loan guarantees, a thousand different schemes." The choice, he asserts, is not between the free market and planning: "The choice is between preservation and adjustment." If government already intervenes, let it intervene coherently, says Reich. If it's going to intervene coherently, let it intervene for adjustment.

The audacity of the intervention-and-adjustment argument garnered Reich his audience. At a time when Republicans were riding to victory on the crest of free-market philosophy, Bob Reich was publicly thumbing his nose and saying, *"Plan* for the future." In a period when organized labor, a traditional bastion of open markets and the Democrats' bedrock constituency, was crying for protection, he scolded, "Free trade." He is an attorney, yet he denounced lawyers and other "paper entrepreneurs" for the nation's productivity decline. He was a bureaucrat, having been a member of the Federal Trade Commission, yet by the time he reached prominence, two years after leaving Washington, he had an academic's credentials and the respect that accompanied them.

Reich's thesis is simple: "One must *adapt*—business institutions as well as political institutions. The economic reality of today has moved beyond the political and economic and business institutions we have." Adaptation is threatening to vested interests, and so Reich argues that it will only be possible if a cooperative context for economic change is created.

America's three greatest pastimes, Reich likes to remark, are baseball, lawsuits and politics: All are dominated by a sense of machismo, have clear winners and losers and are highly confrontational. "People throw up their hands and say, 'America is not Japan! Frontier! Cowboy!' and all that sort of stuff," he said in response to his own straw man. "Not only can it change, but we are changing in accepting the values of collaboration, cooperation, and interpersonal caring. We are getting away from the baseball-lawsuits-politics paradigm."

Reich maintains that the three most contentious issues currently embroiling U.S. economic policy—the strain between the free market and central planning, between smokestack industries and high technology, and between social justice and economic growth—are actually "false choices." The realities of the new global economy, the need for workers who can readily adapt to different systems in the human-capital-intensive economy, reveals that the proper path lies somewhere between these familiar opposites. "I don't think social justice is a charity that can be traded off against economic growth," asserted Reich, citing education and training as examples of programs erroneously deemed "social" by old liberals and conservatives alike. "I think it actually *undergirds* economic growth." This realization alone, he believes, will convince conservative businessmen to promote the so-called social programs, and push old-style liberals into swallowing their anti-business attitudes and recognize that commerce, too, has a place in the liberal society. Cooperation will reign. "Everything is not zero-sum," Reich said. "Everything is potentially positive sum."

"That," said former Federal Trade Commission director, and current commissioner, Michael Pertschuk, "is the most serious flaw in what Bob says." Pertschuk, who brought Reich into the FTC, issues from the Ralph Nader branch of the consumer movement, which has remained confrontational in its attitude toward business and regulation. "I find my own experience in government does not encourage me to place faith where Bob does, in the ability of those with power to share it with those who don't."

At the same time, Pertschuk, a friend of Reich's despite differing viewpoints, credits him with bringing an attitude of collaboration to the FTC. "But to make the jump from sitting down together and talking nicely, to negotiating to give up something, is a substantial leap of faith."

Reich asserts that the U.S. can achieve the cooperation that is characteristic of Japan. It is not the culture but the institutions in each country that allow for the collaborative attitude, he says. But there is that famous story about the differences between Japan and the U.S. that sets one wondering. The pilot of a Japanese commercial jetliner, distraught over personal misfortunes, decided to commit hari-kari by dumping his plane into Tokyo Bay on a landing approach, killing not only himself but all the passengers on board. The president of the airline personally visited the families of each of the dead passengers, bowing in contrition and asking their forgiveness. And not one lawsuit was filed. Could this ever be an American tale? Can cooperation of this sort flourish on *our* shores?

Still, Reich insists that a democratic industrial policy that favors adaptation, open markets, and investment is not only possible, but likely. Reich's belief in cooperation is infectious and uplifting, even if it is—as it may be—naïve. He shares these qualities with the others who have been identified with the new liberalism. They retain a faith in the system, and maintain that the system should, can, and will adapt to ensure a better future for all. Naïve or not, the sentiment, at least, is valuable, for it inspires individuals to work for change. "Unless you are by nature an extraordinary optimist, I don't believe you can really be a reformer," said Robert Reich. "I am a crazy optimist."

The neoliberals' version of industrial policy *is* optimistic. It is a leap of faith to believe that a plan for cooperation between government, business, and labor can promote competition, innovation, and adaptation rather than monopoly, stagnation, and protection. Past attempts at industrial planning have usually degenerated into systems of protection for favored and powerful industries and constituencies; this, in fact, was the legacy of Franklin Roosevelt's planners, whose centrally organized economy decayed into a "broker state" of vertical, public/private sector hierarchies in the 1960s and '70s. Instead of government agencies dedicated to promoting the public good, we have departments dedicated to preserving the status quo—a Department of Education that serves the education establishment or a Defense Department that is simply an arm of the aerospace contractors, for instance. The potential certainly exists for industrial policy to formalize and compound the existing problems of the broker state.

There is no way to judge what effect industrial policy will have, however, until there is agreement on what the term means. There are several different kinds of programs, some of which are protectionist, others pro-competitive, some targeted at older industries, others geared toward the entrepreneur. Some of the suggested methodology is benign: at the very least, the government should render coherent the myriad interventions, from tax preferences to protective tariffs, it already makes. Other schemes are more dynamic: the call for an independent commission, modeled after the Federal Reserve Board, that would target sectors of the economy for selective government investment and favored legislation. All the programs have in common the conviction that traditional, Keynesian manipulation of the macroeconomy will not suffice to guarantee and guide economic growth, and that microeconomic policies of some sort should be adopted.

Industrial policy first appeared as a serious policy alternative late in the Carter Administration. Investment banker Felix Rohatyn, who had successfully engineered New York City's rescue from the precipice of bankruptcy in 1975, had been urging a national policy similar to the state and local initiatives that had saved New York, which included negotiated concessions between the public employees' unions, the banks that held the city's outstanding loans, and the city government itself. Floundering around for a new economic policy that could save his faltering administration—which was being blamed for an unemployment rate of 7.6 percent, an inflation rate exceeding 10 percent, and interest rates approaching 20 percent—President Carter tentatively agreed to an experiment with industrial policy.

Initially, the administration's willingness to consider Rohatyn's idea was a response to Senator Edward Kennedy's challenge. One month before the 1980 Democratic Convention, Kennedy proposed the establishment of an "American Reindustrialization Corporation," which he characterized as a massive public/private sector "Marshall Plan" to revitalize the U.S. economy. The corporation's board, to be composed of representatives of business, labor, and government, would direct grants, loans, and loan guarantees to businesses, industries, and cities to stimulate new economic development and industrial revitalization. The President did not immediately respond, but having sensed that Kennedy's proposal had gained the senator some political capital, Carter adopted its outlines after his renomination. In August 1980, the President recommended the creation of an Economic Revitalization Board, composed of representatives from labor, business, and government, to promote the selective sectoral renovation of the American economy. To gain advantage with constituencies he feared would desert him, Carter named DuPont chairman Irving Shapiro and AFL-CIO president Lane Kirkland as the board's co-chairmen.

From the start, this supply-side liberalism had its detractors. Within the Carter Administration, Council of Economic Advisers chairman Charles Schultze was vehemently opposed to the President's adoption of the Rohatyn framework. Schultze, a Keynesian liberal, disputed government's "ability to do anything at precise targets." His most potent ammunition, which he used in congressional testimony as well as in interviews, was a Commerce Department list of the twenty industries which grew the fastest during the 1970s. Heading the list was poultry farming. "Who was going to pick that as a winner?" smirked Schultze. Industrial policy case closed. The Economic Revitalization Board went out of business with Carter, without having accomplished anything important.

But the idea of a coordinated investment strategy has refused to die, at least in the Democratic Party, and in fact it gained momentum with Jimmy Carter's defeat. Politically, industrial policy has proved to be an engaging alternative to the supply-side conservatism of the Reagan Administration, which, by emphasizing the *level* of investment through tax cuts rather than the *pattern* of investment through active or indirect channeling of capital, has hastened the decline of whole industrial sectors, particularly in the nation's industrial heartland, without appreciably increasing the amount of capital available for the country's sunrise industries.

Nevertheless, the Democratic Party is split over the question of industrial policy. Because the industries that have suffered the greatest—particularly automobiles and steel—are among the most heavily unionized, Democrats with strong labor ties want to use an investment policy for renovation of these industries. This is essentially Walter Mondale's position. Mondale ties his plan to degrees of protection from foreign competition for the favored industries. Others, sensing that cheap foreign labor makes these industries uncompetitive, advocate a policy that concentrates on promoting newer, primarily high-technology industries and specialty niches in older markets. Although even this characterization is too stark, for the most part this is the current liberal-neoliberal breach. (Many older liberals, of course, still maintain that Keynesian demand stimulation is the only policy the federal government can successfully administer.)

Much of the industrial policy talk centers on the letters "RFC"— the initials for Reconstruction Finance Corporation, the New Deal–

era agency Felix Rohatyn has proposed resurrecting. It is the best known of several suggestions for a national investment institution to manage American industrial policy.

The original Reconstruction Finance Corporation was a last-ditch effort by Herbert Hoover to help lift Depression-wracked America back to stability. Signed into law in January 1932, the RFC was originally designed to extend direct loans to only two industries—financial institutions and railroads. The Hoover Administration was turned out of office before the RFC could be effectively utilized, but the RFC flourished under the stewardship of Franklin Roosevelt, who by the time of World War II had given it a blank check to take *any* steps the President and the Federal Loan Administrator thought essential to the American war effort. Many of America's war industries—which became the basis for the spectacular growth of the economy in the postwar years—were financed by the RFC. After World War II the organization was placed under tighter control, and it was finally disbanded in 1954, amid accusations of mismanagement.

Felix Rohatyn's experience as chairman of New York City's Municipal Assistance Corporation convinced him that an independent body, sitting outside the sphere of government, business, and labor but including representatives from the three sectors, could aid in the revitalization of America's faltering industrial economy as successfully as MAC (which was chartered as a state agency) had saved New York City from brink of bankruptcy.

"The crisis had engulfed all the old actors," recalled Eugene Keilin, MAC's first executive director and later a senior vice president of Lazard Frères. "MAC came in, and had the power to convene the parties, to bring them together in a room. It couldn't say, 'You must do this and that.' It made deals, negotiated out among the parties, all of which were in the form of concessions each of them would have to make in order to keep the operation—New York—going."

What made MAC different from a run-of-the-mill mediator—and what makes it the model for Rohatyn's RFC—was that it had something to offer. "And what it had to offer," Keilin said, "was capital. It had the ability, which the city did not have, and which for legal and maybe political reasons the state did not have directly, to borrow money and use it, first, to avoid the city's bankruptcy, and then to keep the city's operations and services continuing, and finally to provide for new capital spending."

Felix Rohatyn's Reconstruction Finance Corporation is patterned after MAC. A coalition of government-industry-labor representatives, it would be a politically independent body, capitalized with $5 billion from the Treasury, and with the authority to raise $25 billion more through the issue of federally guaranteed bonds. It would thus become the tenth largest bank in the country, but it would have one special purpose: to bail out large cities in the Northeast and Midwest, and struggling major industries in these areas.

One serious criticism of Rohatyn's plan is that it is merely a bail-out mechanism, whose only purpose would be to prolong the agony of dying industries, at a greater long-term cost to the public than would be the case if their demise could proceed along a normal course. Rohatyn's response is that, first, certain industries, like steel, are necessary for national security reasons; second, the RFC's authority to purchase equity in corporations would be predicated on an equivalent infusion, of private money; and third, the private markets are not always the best determinant of the actual viability of a business.

But what has rankled conservatives and neoliberals about the Rohatyn plan is the RFC's insulation from politics. As now formulated, the RFC would be governed by a board of directors drawn from the public and private sectors, with the President having a great deal of flexibility in making the appointments. Staggered terms of four years' duration for the directors would, according to Keilin's draft of the RFC proposal, "seem appropriate so that the Board does not become intimately tied to any one Administration."

Such a system has drawn fire. Michael Kinsley, former editor of *The New Republic* and of *Harper's,* has called it "fascism." A top aide to former California Governor Jerry Brown, who actively supports a policy of "strategically planned investment," has publicly labeled it "technocratic planning beyond public accountability in any sense." George Eads, a member of Jimmy Carter's Council of Economic Advisers and now a Rand Corporation economist, has attacked the very notion that the RFC could be removed from politics. In an article in the *Wharton Magazine* entitled "Picking Winners and Killing Dogs," Eads maintained, "Any entity created by the Congress, given access to large amounts of government funds, and asked to deal with matters having great political importance could not be 'non-political.' "

But perhaps the most salient criticism of Rohatyn's RFC is that its concern for declining industries necessarily slights the growing areas of the economy. The RFC is thus *not* part of the neoliberals' economic game plan. It is too centralized, too prone to protectionist dominance, and too oriented toward older, larger industries. Nevertheless, it is the best-known example of an industrial policy mechanism, and the one organized labor is most comfortable with. Rohatyn, AFL-CIO President Lane Kirkland, and former DuPont Chairman Irving Shapiro (the latter two the co-chairmen of Jimmy Carter's short-lived Economic Revitalization Board) head the Center for National Policy's ad hoc Industrial Policy Study Group, which proposed in early 1984 that the Democratic Party officially adopt a labor-oriented RFC as part of its platform. Rohatyn's plan is the one from which all others must diverge.

Other people more directly associated with neoliberalism have proposed their own versions of a national investment institution to promote the economy's sunrise sector as well as to retool older industries. Because applications of productivity-enhancing technology to older industries will almost necessarily shrink their labor force, the neoliberals always tie this version of the industrial policy to a comprehensive human-capital program, through which workers will be retrained for jobs in newer industries.

Lester Thurow and former Illinois Senator Adlai Stevenson III have put forward their industrial policy plans, but the most detailed proposal of this nature emerged from Jerry Brown's office in the last year of his tenure. It was developed by his chief economist, Michael Kieschnick, now a senior fellow with the Gallatin Institute, and Nathan Gardels, the director of Brown's Pension Fund Investment Unit, who has remained with the former governor on his new National Commission on Industrial Innovation, a neoliberal think tank. They call their proposal an IFC, for Innovation Finance Corporation.

The IFC would be a public financial institution designed to absorb risk and increase the availability of long-term capital to targeted industries, primarily in high-tech. Two subsidiary corporations would direct capital to specific areas, much as the Federal National Mortgage Association ("Fanny Mae") operates today as one of the original RFC's permanent remnants. The Brown plan calls for the establishment of a Technology Development Bank and a Technology Development and Mortgage Assurance Corporation (nicknamed "Teddy Mac"). Teddy Mac and the TDB differ from each other in three substantive ways: While the bank could target investments, sometimes below market rates, Teddy Mac would provide for market-rate investment pools; further, the bank could make direct investments, while Teddy Mac's primary function would be to connect institutional investors, such as pension funds, with originators of loans, such as commercial banks and savings-and-loans. But most important, the bank would deal with large corporations and large-scale investment of $50 million or more; Teddy Mac, on the other hand, would direct funds specifically to small and medium-sized businesses by insuring risk and creating a secondary loan market.

Both agencies would be fulfilling an industrial policy formulated by the IFC, which would be made up of directors drawn from government, business, labor, and the scientific community, as well as representatives from regional or state subsidiary banks. The Technology Development Bank would thus be responsible for major development projects as well as bail-outs, but would focus more specifically on the technological retooling of those entities that are aided. Teddy Mac, with the regional banks operating as intermediaries, "would be oriented toward what we call development investing," explained Gardels in a 1982 interview. "Around here, that means something specific: it means small and medium-scale businesses, it means high-tech companies."

Despite the differences between their proposals, it is a mistake to see the Rohatyn and Brown development banks as mutually exclusive. The mechanisms of the RFC and the TDB are quite similar; it is the industrial *policy* they are to promote which differs. Rohatyn's plan fits better with Walter Mondale's political orientation, while the Brown proposal is consistent with the "Atari Democrats'."

There is, however, a growing consensus that a large national investment institution charged with formulating and carrying out an industrial policy may be too much, too soon. "To come in with a bill for an RFC, that's the fifth step," said Congressman Richard Gephardt in 1982. In the "Yellow Brick Road" economics paper for the House Democratic Caucus, Gephardt and Timothy Wirth recommended an intermediate jump, calling for the establishment of an Economic Cooperation Council, whose task would be to assemble data on international business trends, devise microeconomic strategies to enhance American competitiveness in world market, and serve as a forum for business, labor, and management to communicate and arrive at a consensus on shared goals. But this council would not actually allocate capital. "An RFC may be okay," said Gephardt, "but I think it's putting the cart before the horse. If you don't have a basic understanding and continual communication between the sectors that allows a consensus to be built that we want to starve these industries and nurture those, then the RFC will be a group without a consensus, a group without a mandate. And it won't work." New York Congressman Stanley Lundine has incorporated an Economic Cooperation Council into an omnibus industrial-policy bill. But Lundine's legislation also includes an RFC-type mechanism which Wirth, for one, opposes for its protectionist potential.

The New York Times gently criticized, but approved of, the Wirth-Gephardt proposal as a "MITI-Minus." The careful, indirectly interventionist Wirth-Gephardt approach to industrial policy is rapidly becoming the neoliberals' consensus position. Several proposals for a body to serve primarily as an information-gathering and -dissemination organization now exist. They range from the proposal that the President's Council of Economic Advisers be reorganized according to industrial "desks" (a suggestion that has been forwarded by Bill Bradley) to the recommendation that the Department of Commerce and the Office of the Special Trade Representative be merged into a cabinet-level Department of Trade. New York Senator Daniel Patrick Moynihan has introduced legislation amalgamating not only Commerce and the Trade Representative, but the trade functions of the departments of State, Transportation, Treasury, Labor, Agriculture, Defense, and Energy, as well as of the International Trade Commission, the International Development Agency, the Small Business Administration, the Export-Import Bank, and the Overseas Private Investment Corporation. President Reagan in April 1983 made a similar recommendation, but neoliberals fear that his Department of Trade would be a protectionist device.

Robert Reich's industrial policy proposal focuses on the collection and dissemination of microeconomic data. Reich propose a new institution, an "open industrial policy forum," in which all the decisions will be open to public scrutiny. "Instead of going through backroom deals and through their own private channels of communication to the largesse of the system, they would have to come and make their case as to what they needed, and why they needed it," says Reich. His new forum would be linked to the office of the Special Trade Representative, to ensure consideration of the international-market issues; it would have a senior support staff, like the Council of Economic Advisers, to act as a data-collection and industry-monitoring committee; it would be open to delegations from communities, and from all the groups affected by industrial adjustment. "There would be a regular debate," Reich states. "The heads of the auto industry in this country would be coming to talk, so would the labor unions. There would be government officials proposing various packages of subsidies." The details are hazy; the single most prevalent criticism of *The Next American Frontier* is that Reich's recommendations lack rigor.

This sounds like the activity surrounding the Chrysler bail-out of a few years ago. But the Chrysler situation, Reich maintains, was hopelessly confused by lack of reliable data, making Congress the captive of the competing groups asking for aid. More important, he adds, the issue was actually debated in the back rooms of the Treasury Department. "Sure, whether to give Chrysler a bail-out was debated in public, but *how* to give that bail-out wasn't a part of it. The relationship of Chrysler to its suppliers, employees, and the industrial midwest, questions about its relationship to Ford and GM, of the future of the auto industry, of the whole interlocking web, understanding how Chrysler was part of an industrial system—there was no opportunity to develop these themes. No place, no forum, no data. No real participants."

Reich stops short of advocating a massive development bank. Investment capital alone is not the problem, he insists. Rather, it is information on international market trends that is lacking. Also needed are explicit sectoral agreements through which industries can meet those trends, and not be upset by them. "The important point," said Reich in 1983, "is that we need a setting in which these things happen. It's data, argument, and negotiation. Wholesale negotiation."

Reich's proposal for a "new forum" and similar recommendations for a data-gathering and policy-planning body within the federal government are not really new. The last time industrial policy was a public issue was a national planning agency proposed by Hubert Humphrey in the early 1970s. Humphrey's agency was incorporated into legislation he co-authored with New York Republican Senator Jacob Javits, but was eliminated when Humphrey-Javits became the Humphrey-Hawkins full-employment bill. Humphrey envisioned a year-long public discussion of national industrial policy, with his planning agency serving only to assemble relevant data and devise projections, the ultimate authority to decide the policy remaining with Congress. The crucial element shared by the current recommendations and the Humphrey version is the belief that information is forcing; it is a recapitulation of the traditional liberal belief that assembling information, circulating it to the citizenry, and allowing the public to participate in the decision-making through its elected representatives will naturally lead to reform for the purpose of progress.

This traditional liberal notion is at the heart of the neoliberals' industrial policy recommendations. Instead of mandating through a politically independent, extragovernmental institution which industries will die and which will thrive, the neoliberals believe that the public and the market can and should make those decisions. Government can provide crucial information and, later, implement the plans.

To these ends, Ira Magaziner, an international business consultant and co-author with Robert Reich of *Minding America's Business,* a detailed and critically acclaimed argument for a national industrial policy, suggests that there is no one mechanism but rather a set of coincidental policies necessary to deal with four distinct business situations. Magaziner's approach was adopted by Gary Hart in *A New Democracy* and is perhaps the best example of what a comprehensive, neoliberal industrial policy would look like.

The first business situation the industrial policy must confront is the problem of older industries that are losing competitiveness to other countries due to wage disparities. Magaziner maintains that the only solution short of wholesale protection (which he agrees is economically counterproductive in the long run) is adjustment for the workers in the form of retraining and relocation assistance, and other human-capital programs. But there are also certain struggling "mature" industries—Lester Thurow refers to this segment as industries "hit by a string of bad luck"—which retain potential competitive viability and may be necessary to the economy for national security or other reasons. Here, Magaziner believes the government can play a carrot-and-stick role, offering investment capital, loans, and guarantees in return for a coherent revitalization strategy. This is not unlike the position Felix Rohatyn's RFC would play.

The third situation to be addressed is that of competition between developed countries in high-growth industries. The problem here is risk aversion and the inability of private markets, including the venture-capital market (whose payoff requirements are too short-term), to provide the necessary capital to finance new industrial development. The solution—as in the California plan for Teddy Mac—is the creation of a secondary loan market. Dick Gephardt has also proposed the creation of a secondary loan market for small, technology-based businesses. Finally, there is the question of future growth industries—biotechnology, fifth-generation computers, robotics—for which Magaziner recommends increased funding of R & D and government assistance to aid university/industry cooperative arrangements (for instance, Paul Tsongas' and Gary Hart's proposals for a "High-Technology Morrill Act").

The specific recommendations Magaziner and Reich make in *Minding America's Business* are quite modest. They resemble the proposals of other neoliberals and policy people. Nowhere is there a sign of the fearful "picking winners and losers" syndrome that is disparaged by detractors of industrial policy.

All the neoliberal proposals have this much, at least, in common: First, specific investment decisions are the province of the private sector; the government should respond to industry suggestions, not initiate its own. Second, while investment capability should be decentralized through the private sector, only the federal government is capable of gathering and analyzing the information necessary for the private sector to make rational investment decisions; or, as Robert Reich puts it, "Centralize resources but decentralize authority." Third, a large central bureaucracy should be avoided. And fourth, the goal is to stimulate the market, rather than the product. As in other areas, the neoliberals' industrial policy recommendations promote an active government role, but the neoliberals are more cautious than their liberal predecessors about the potentially deadening hand of bureaucracy.

The marriage of faith in the market with belief in planning is the most significant characteristic of neoliberal industrial policy. "[The neoliberals] are ahead of the thirties in that they understand that the market has a place," says historian Otis Graham of the University of North Carolina, whose several books on planning make him the preeminent historian of the subject. "The market has a sizable place in managing a modern economy under planning. *That's* the exciting development of the eighties."

PART FOUR

The Beginning of Neoliberalism...or the End of Liberalism?

THE CHALLENGE TO AMERICA, as the neoliberals see it, is one of accomplishment—accomplishments within constraints, but accomplishments nonetheless. Entrepreneurialism, as a political issue, is an
assertion of growth and individual freedom. The contention between
the free-traders and the protectionists in the Democratic Party, aside
from the economic arguments that can be mustered for either side, is
essentially a dispute between those who fear the future so much that
they want to guard our current status and those whose faith in progress
prompts them to presume that open trade and economic success are
not only compatible, but mutually beneficial. And what is high technology, ask the "Atari Democrats," if not the next frontier, the frontier that, in Frederick Jackson Turner's words, "is productive of individualism"? A belief in growth within limits, in individualism and
risk-taking within the context of the cooperative society, in horizons
grown ever broader through the development and application of new
technology—all of these are new manifestations of the American
progressive ideal.

Yet if neoliberalism, as a political tendency, is consistent and con-
tains promise, many of the neoliberal politicians seem bent on muting,
even detouring, that promise through deficiencies and contradictions
apparent in their style. Despite their disavowal of technocracy, the
leading neoliberals still come across as technocrats. For all their expressed fealty to a politics rooted in values, they nevertheless get
bogged down in details.

But that is not the only reason that neoliberalism is not as well understood as the neoliberals themselves. The neoliberals have been cautious about their differences with traditional liberals because they are afraid to challenge the vested interests that control their party. So instead, they disguise their dissension in a cloud of high-tech rhetoric. Because of this, they run dangerously close to repeating the tragedy of Jimmy Carter. Media critic Jeff Greenfield's description of what should have been Carter's finest moment—his acceptance speech after his renomination at the 1980 Democratic Convention—is trenchant. The President's address bears close resemblance to the public pronouncements of many of the neoliberals, and Greenfield's criticism of it resembles recent critiques of the neoliberal style.

> . . . Carter delved into the kind of language that had haunted him throughout his term of office: An engineer's language, flat, often complex ("with our new energy policy now in place . . . we will use American resources, American technology"; "our economic renewal program will . . . lower inflation, better productivity, revitalize American industry, [provide] energy security and jobs"; "industry will provide the convenience of futuristic computer technology and communications to serve millions of American homes and offices and factories"). It was the language of an industrial relations film strip for a high school, not a summons to a party in distress.

The neoliberals would do well to learn from Carter's failure and Reagan's triumph that the electorate, given a choice between the fox who knows fifty things and the hedgehog who knows one big thing, will invariably choose the latter. "There is a danger," warned *The New Yorker*'s Elizabeth Drew in March 1982, "that the Democrats will strain too hard for details now—they could find themselves splitting hairs and making laundry lists, at the expense of developing their themes and figuring out how to get them across." Unfortunately, in the two years since Drew contributed her analysis, the danger has been realized.

Because the neoliberals have not been sufficiently explicit about their new ideas, they and the mainstream Democrats who have adopted their programs and language have allowed President Reagan to co-opt much of what is fresh in their thinking. It was, after all, the President who developed plans for a cabinet-level Department of Trade, capitalizing on the rift between Democratic free-traders and protectionists to capture this one small aspect of the industrial policy debate. Despite the military reform movement, which disavows technocracy at every turn, the Democrats still managed to conduct their side of the MX debate using the phraseology of "throw weight" and "counterforce" and other such unapproachable jargon. By allowing the Republicans to set the terms of the arms control debate, and by keeping the public effectively removed from any sense of the discussion, the Democrats virtually consigned themselves to a loss. And they did lose, after several anti-MX Democratic congressmen—including neoliberal stalwarts Richard Gephardt and Albert Gore, Jr.— switched and voted in the affirmative. The Democrats have been unable to assail the Reagan Administration's bloated military budget, and the military reformers within the party, for all their detailed plans for substituting "smaller, cheaper," and more abundant systems for the large, unwieldy, and untested weapons desired by the Pentagon, have not been successful in translating the details of their doctrine into an easily understood philosophical position. Thus, the Republicans have been able to portray the opposition—which has fallen back on the nuclear freeze and the old "less is better" bromides—as antidefense.

The conclusion is inescapable: all the new ideas in the world will be to no avail without a context. A context for neoliberalism may be implicit in what its leading politicians and advisers do and say. Yet the neoliberals seem to fear the explicit revelation of their underlying ideology. Nowhere is this more apparent than in the presidential campaign of Gary Hart. After entering the race by positioning himself as the "candidate of ideas" and releasing a book, *A New Democracy,* highlighting many of these ideas, Hart has been reticent to test them on the circuit. He seems afraid of them, fearing that they might alienate the Democrats' traditional constituencies. "Some political professionals . . . suggest [Hart] has decided to play it safe in 1984," wrote Howell Raines of *The New York Times,* "rather than take the risk of innovation, namely that an idea might backfire and make the candidate seem a kook." Hart's book, added Haines, "shows some of the creative impulse that has rarely appeared in his speeches. Even so, his most interesting ideas on tax reform are laid off on bystanders as if they were hand grenades."

But the neoliberals' problems are not all related to deficiencies in their style and their fear of offending vested interests with too clear a call for a new politics. There are substantive difficulties inherent in neoliberalism's very foundation, separate from and much more serious than the political difficulties the neoliberals will have in selling their agenda to the public. Can the cooperative society be managed successfully without the domination of one sector? Specifically, can cooperation exist without the business interests taking over? Franklin Roosevelt's experiment with cooperative policies under the National Recovery Administration failed because the process of designing the NRA codes for each industry eventually fell into the hands of industry leaders. At its demise in 1935, the NRA had become an experiment in price-fixing and anticompetitive activity that effectively shut many smaller producers and distributors out of the market.

It is also conveniently overlooked that our government's unofficial policy since the close of World War II has been a continual romance with cooperation. What are we to call the relationship between the Pentagon and its major suppliers, if not public/private sector cooperation? Is not the Department of Education—Jimmy Carter's reward to the National Education Association for its endorsement and support in 1976—an example of government and labor collaboration? Our recent history with sectoral cooperation has not been happy, as private interests, whether labor or industry, have become the dominant partner in the marriage, often at the expense of the public interest. The cooperation between James Watt's Department of the Interior and the oil, mining, and timber industries, or worse yet, between Ann Gorsuch Burford's Environmental Protection Agency and industrial polluters, are only the latest examples of cooperation resulting in private gain that is contrary, not conducive, to the public welfare.

An industrial policy rooted in tripartite cooperation, either explicitly managed through an RFC-type institution or "devoutly to be wished" but not specifically legislated, is the mainstay of the new Democratic agenda. Few of the politicians or policy advisers who support the concept have given enough thought to its implications. Even the seemingly benign cooperative activities between private industry and universities within the information archipelago have dark overtones. At the Massachusetts Institute of Technology, the Whitehead Institute—a private, nonprofit foundation created by the millionaire head of a biomedical instruments firm—will have privileged access to research and facilities, share royalties on patents, and exert some control over faculty appointments in a joint program with the university. While there is no *inherent* conflict of interest, the potential certainly exists. But as MIT associate professor David F. Noble revealed, writing of the MIT-Whitehead arrangement in *The Nation,* the faculty sloughed off with blissful carelessness the possibilities for actual tension between the demands of commerce and the life of the mind. "Throughout the session [at which the vote was taken]," wrote Noble, "the faculty, few of whom knew—or cared—much about the details of the arrangement, seemed swayed less by the merits of the arguments than by a kind of jovial locker-room camaraderie, and a sense of the pioneering élan of which MIT is so proud."

Given the importance of basic and applied research conducted at universities and the effect it will have on the economic well-being of the United States in the information era, such nonchalance about university/industry joint ventures is shocking. Scientific knowledge, particularly in high technology and biotechnology, will govern America's ability to prosper as an economic unit. Even more than access to capital, access to scientific knowledge will determine the true winners and losers in society for years to come. The possibility certainly exists for such access to become controlled by large corporations. Whitehead is associated with Revlon; Hoechst A.G., a German-based multinational chemical firm, is involved with Massachusetts General Hospital; and other industry/university arrangements involve substantial commitments of funding from IBM, DuPont, Grumman, TRW, Hewlett-Packard. At the very least, the possibilities for conflict of interest will arouse mistrust on the public's part. When, in late June 1983, the American Medical Association denounced the media for fomenting a "wave of hysteria" over dioxin contamination and contended that they had "not found any documented human deaths directly attributable to dioxin poisoning," the conflict question arose in Congress. One of the formulators of the AMA statement taught part-time at the Washing University School of Medicine in St. Louis. Washington U. has a $24 million cooperative research agreement with Monsanto, a chemical manufacturer with political clout in Missouri. Monsanto made dioxin. The doctor denied any connection. Still . . .

Even in the emerging postindustrial society in which small business is the engine of growth, there is more than a slight chance that cooperation, cheered on by the neoliberals, will end up favoring the big guy. Carelessly managed cooperation could in the end create a form of business-directed socialism that would eat away at the very values the neoliberals seek to institutionalize. It would differ from the "state capitalism" of the left-leaning Economic Democrats only to the extent that control is vested in a different bureaucratic entity.

These warnings may be premature. The evidence so far indicates that the neoliberals have had the salutary effect of heightening the consciousness of our political leadership as well as of the public to a series of concerns that must remain front and center if we are to survive the current economic transition. Government activism, tax reform, and education have traveled in and out of public awareness over the years, but the current discussion of these issues owes a great deal to the efforts of the neoliberals.

Only a few short years ago Jimmy Carter called the American income tax system "a disgrace to the human race," but Carter slammed into a brick wall of opposition when he attempted to begin discussions about reforming it. Today, despite the interest groups gearing up to fight for the continuation of their favorite breaks, credits, and loopholes, the idea of a Fair Tax like the Bradley-Gephardt plan stands at the center of the tax reform debate.

Likewise, even though President Reagan has managed to preempt the debate over education policy by using the issue of merit pay to bury the question of whether the federal government is shirking its responsibilities to our schools, the connection between education and economic growth—the importance of investment in human capital— has been made, and will be much discussed in the foreseeable future. Despite the President's intransigence over federal funds for education and training, the new interpretation of the subject as an *economic* issue, rather than a *social* issue, will probably encourage public support for educational aid. There is a danger, of course, in viewing man entirely as *homo economicus,* which is why traditional liberal theory stresses so many noneconomic elements. We must all worry about how human-capital theorists will deal with the individual worker when that worker is no longer a factor in productivity growth. On the other hand, the virtue of emphasizing the economic importance of what were previously only thought of as social issues is that our social welfare programs will not automatically suffer the next time we are struck by a wave of anti-government hysteria.

The neoliberals' most important contribution to current political discourse is their establishment of a rational middle ground between the automatic reliance on government spending with which the Democratic Party has been associated and the equally instinctive rejection of government solutions now accepted as doctrine by the Republican Party.

Neoliberalism is being internalized by the Democratic Party. The party's June 1982 midterm convention in Philadelphia did not endorse a large-scale federal jobs program, in spite of more than 9 million unemployed. It did not re-propose national health insurance, even though medical costs were still soaring. It did not submit yet again a plan for a guaranteed annual income, although the American welfare system was still not operating efficiently. "Because the Democrats hardly mentioned the kind of proposals to expand government, which seemed to come automatically out of their mouths a few years ago," wrote Michael Barone, co-editor of the *Almanac of American Politics,* "the Philadelphia conference may some day be seen as a turning point for their party."

There is at least one problem that the neoliberals seem to be unwilling to deal with and which could bury the Democrats. It masquerades in the guise of "the special-interest problem," but its real name is Organized Labor.

Organized labor has been an important part of the Democratic coalition at least since the days of FDR and the New Deal. Labor has since become the most valuable member of the Democratic coalition, contributing the largest single bloc of funding to maintain the party. Democrats fear labor, and they will not buck its interest.

A clash seems inevitable, for virtually every single issue promoted by the neoliberals seems to run counter to the interests of organized labor as they are currently expressed. Even a seemingly benign platform plank like the soft energy path engenders labor hostility. The soft path is, by definition, composed of decentralized production and distribution facilities. Labor has long opposed these "cottage industries," because they are difficult to unionize. That's also true of the small high-technology industries of Silicon Valley and Boston's Route 128, hence labor's antipathy toward high-tech. And of course, no single issue currently divides the Democrats as seriously as the problem of free trade versus the protectionism that organized labor so dearly wants.

But there is more. The structure of the American union movement seems to be antithetical to the organization of postindustrial society. Labor's vitality has been dependent on large, national industries; collective bargaining has thrived on the ability of centralized unions to negotiate with centralized industries. An economy driven by entrepreneuralism may ruin this arrangement. Worse, an economy that requires constant adaptation to improve productivity and match the needs of the global market cannot admit of a labor movement whose very existence is predicated on a rigid system of rules. The labor movement was born during the industrial era and its unwillingness to reconfigure itself now that we have exited that era is diminishing its power. If, as the neoliberals state, the future depends not on the technostructure but on the entrepreneur, it is difficult to see how organized labor, as it now exists, fits into their political economy.

But the Democrats' problem runs much deeper than the intransigence of organized labor. There are other groups whose demands,
valid or not, override their concern for an equitable national program.
The "special-interest problem" involves Jews and America's Mideast
policy, blacks and social spending, feminists and equal pay—the list is
long, because the Democratic coalition is large.

And therein lies the essence of the Democratic dilemma. The
Democratic Party has been held hostage by its fifty-year-old coalition.
Coalition-building, by its very nature, implies compromises and trade-
offs to interest groups. While compromise is the substance of politics,
and communities of interest have always existed and will forever survive in a society that values individual freedom as much as ours, trading off has become the Democrats' mainstay, rather than the mechanism to achieve a greater good.

What does the Democratic Party stand for? What are its goals?
What does it believe? "Compassion" will not do as an answer; find a
Republican who does not believe in it. In fact, the existence of the
coalition has replaced any underlying philosophy. Contrast the Republican Party: one never hears of the "Republican coalition." The
Republican Party has a reason for existence which, although it admits
of variations on a left-right scale, acts as an umbrella to cover the diverse factions within. This idea—the less government the better—
binds the Republican Party as a unit. This the Democrats lack.

The neoliberals are attempting, in halting steps, to replace the
interest-group politics of traditional liberalism with a view of the national interest. Perhaps they can surmount the "special-interest problem" and reestablish the Democratic idea. It is not likely to happen in
the 1984 election. As Howell Raines of *The New York Times* has
noted, "In place of innovation, the main concern of the candidates
seems to be fear of offending the Democratic interest groups."

But even if the neoliberals triumph, there is reason to worry. Who
will look after the rights and needs of American workers, if not their
unions? The neoliberals' warmhearted view of business is naïve in the
face of the greed of corporate interests. And who will ensure that the
destitute ghetto dweller receives his fair share from a system from
which he's been effectively barred for generations? The National Education Association, as the country's second-largest trade union, has
been fair game for the neoliberal hunters of special interests for the
past several years. But the NEA's members, it is important to remember, earn an average of only $17,000. The *Washington Monthly* for
years has stressed the line, "The unions are killing our schools." But

the teachers' unions do not set policy or establish curricula. Nor have they gained for their members exorbitant salaries. The emphasis seems misplaced.

It's fine for politicians educated at Princeton, Yale Law, Harvard Law, Dartmouth, and Oxford to assert the national interest over special interests. But these politicians have the prestige of seats in Congress and guaranteed futures should they leave.

If one thing rings false in all the rhetoric of neoliberalism, it is that the "national interest" may be nothing more than the special interests of the liberal upper middle class.

Yet elements of neoliberalism are gaining acceptance. In the summer of 1983 both the National Education Association and the American Federation of Teachers cautiously endorsed study of the merit pay concept. Several major businesses were purchased by their employees beginning in 1981, and in 1982–83 that trickle looked to become a flood, breaking down labor's traditional opposition to worker ownership. And the tenets of neoliberalism—investment, appropriate technology, and the national interest—for all the conflicts, contradictions, and crises they will cause, are now an accepted part of American political discourse.

The Democratic Party, it is safe to say, is changing. Will the changes be permanent? Are they part of a neoliberal revolution? "When parties reach a dead end, they either develop a new program or they're replaced," Arthur Schlesinger, Jr., has said. "Or history shunts them aside and they linger on as insignificant cults."

That comment was about the post–Goldwater Republicans. As we know, the GOP learned the lesson.

Will the Democrats? Eventually, we will know.

Notes

For each chapter, major reference sources are grouped according to subject, books first, followed by newspaper and magazine articles, and finally by official documents and speeches.

PART ONE: REFLECTIONS

CHAPTER 1: THE DAY AFTER

Peter Steinfels, *The Neoconservatives* (New York: Simon & Schuster, 1973).

"American Politics on a Darkling Plain," by Arthur M. Schlesinger, Jr., *Wall Street Journal,* March 16, 1982.

"Automatic Political Responses," by Charles Peters, *New York Times,* May 3, 1981.

"Carterism Without.Carter," by Sidney Blumenthal, *Working Papers,* May/June 1981.

"Congress: Time for All Good Liberals to Cool It," by Martin Tolchin, *New York Times,* November 9, 1980.

"The Democratic Party After Ted Kennedy," by Arthur M. Schlesinger, Jr., *Wall Street Journal,* December 7, 1982.

"Democratic Party Games," by David Osborne, *Inquiry,* July 6 & 20, 1981.

"Democrats: An Aye for Business," by Steven V. Roberts, *New York Times,* March 1, 1981.

"Democrats in Search of Ideas," by Tom Wicker, *New York Times Magazine,* January 25, 1981.

"A Doubtful New Order," by Morton Kondracke, *The New Republic,* November 15, 1980.

"Ill at Ease with Questions on the Future of the Party," by Haynes Johnson, *Washington Post,* May 17, 1981.

"In Defense of Good Intentions," editorial, *The New Republic,* December 13, 1980.

"Liberalism's Brave Neo World: Two Views," by Michael Scully and Morton Kondracke, *Public Opinion,* April/May 1982.

"Party Is Trying to Chart Political Realities of the '80s," by Haynes Johnson, *Washington Post,* May 18, 1981.

"Reaganism with a Human Face," by Robert M. Kaus, *The New Republic,* November 25, 1981.

"The State of the Democratic Party," by Joe Klein, *Rolling Stone,* September 17, 1981.

Speech by Congresswoman Patsy Mink, annual convention of the Americans for Democratic Action, Washington, D.C., June 27, 1981.

CHAPTER 2: ROOSEVELT'S WORLD

Eric F. Goldman, *Rendezvous with Destiny* (New York: Knopf, 1952).

Godfrey Hodgson, *America in Our Time* (New York: Random House, 1976).

William K. Leuchtenberg, *Franklin D. Roosevelt and the New Deal* (New York: Harper & Row, 1962).

Arthur M. Schlesinger, Jr., *The Coming of the New Deal* (Boston: Houghton Mifflin, 1958).

Arthur M. Schlesinger, Jr., *The Politics of Upheaval* (Boston: Houghton Mifflin, 1960).

"FDR: A Practical Magician," by John Kenneth Galbraith, *American Heritage,* February/March 1983.

"From Calhoun to Sister Boom Boom: The Dubious Legacy of Interest-Group Politics," by Phillip Longman, *Washington Monthly,* June 1983.

CHAPTER 3: CARTER'S WORLD

Elizabeth Drew, *Portrait of an Election* (New York: Simon & Schuster, 1981).

Jeff Greenfield, *The Real Campaign* (New York: Summit Books, 1982).

Theodore White, *America in Search of Itself* (New York: Harper & Row, 1982).

"Carter Assails Opponents Who Seek to Block Drive," by Charles Mohr, *New York Times,* May 28, 1976.

"The Ignorant Press," by Charles Peters, and "The Winning Candidate," by John Evan Thomas, *Washington Monthly,* May 1976.

"The Passionless Presidency," by James Fallows, *The Atlantic,* May 1979.

"The Passionless Presidency II," by James Fallows, *The Atlantic,* June 1979.

"The Search for Carter," by Norman Mailer, *New York Times Magazine,* September 26, 1976.

"Third-Rate Romance, Low-Rent Rendezvous," by Hunter S. Thompson, *Rolling Stone,* June 3, 1976.

"What the Voters Want," by Daniel Yankelovich, *The New Republic,* October 23, 1976.

Chapter 4: The Neoliberal World

Paul Tsongas, *The Road from Here* (New York: Knopf, 1981).

"The Boston Magazine Interview with Paul Tsongas," interview by E. J. Kahn III, *Boston Magazine,* February 1981.

"Bunker Liberalism," interview with Paul Tsongas by Nicholas Lemann, *Washington Post,* 1980.

"A Day in the Life: Paul Tsongas," *Esquire,* December 1980.

"A Few Liberals Sober Up," by Fred Barnes, *American Spectator,* January 1982.

"The Other Senator from Massachusetts," by David Osborne, *Mother Jones,* July 1982.

"The Tsongas Liberalism," by Curt Suplee, *Washington Post,* September 23, 1981.

"Tsongas: It's Time for the Democrats to Keep Pace with Changing Times," by Jerry Hagstrom, *National Journal,* April 11, 1981.

PART TWO: REALITIES

Introduction

Robert D. Hamrin, *Managing Growth in the '80s* (New York: Praeger, 1980).

Thomas S. Kuhn, *The Structure of Scientific Revolution* (Chicago: University of Chicago Press, 1962).

Chapter 5: Growth in an Era of Limits

Jerry Brown and Dow Chemical

Dow vs. California: The Turning Point in the Envirobusiness Struggle, by Christopher J. Duerkson (Washington, D.C.: The Conservation Foundation, 1982).

"Brown in Pursuit of Big Business," by Dennis J. Opartny, *San Francisco Examiner,* September 5, 1976.

"Brown's Impact Ploy: The Super Hearing," by Gale Cook, *San Francisco Examiner,* December 9, 1976.

"California Weighs Industrial Growth for Alaskan Oil," by Joel Kotkin, *Washington Post,* December 7, 1975.

"Chemical Plant: Brown for It, Says Dad," by Nancy Skelton, *Sacramento Bee,* December 1, 1976.

"Comment: Environmentalists Put on the Defensive," *Daily Commercial News,* July 28, 1977.

"Dow," report by Bill Bucy for United Press International, December 8, 1976.

"Dow," report by Susan Sward for the Associated Press, January 20, 1977.

"The Dow Aftermath," by Anne Jackson, *Cry California,* Summer 1977.

"Dow Halted by California Regulatory Jungle," by Earl V. Anderson, *Chemical & Engineering News,* April 25, 1977.

"Environmental Backlash: The Battle Is Just Beginning," by Michael Storper, *Not Man Apart: Friends of the Earth,* Summer 1977.

"Industry vs. Ecology Showdown: The $500 Million Dow Plant," by Anne Jackson, *California Journal,* February 1977.

"Promising Measure for Cutting Red Tape," editorial, *Sacramento Union,* March 6, 1977.

"Regulatory Costs," editorial, *Los Angeles Herald Examiner,* June 12, 1977.

"The Playboy Interview: Jerry Brown," by Robert Scheer, *Playboy,* January 1976.

Growth and No-Growth

Martin K. Doudria, *Concerned About the Planet: The Reporter Magazine and American Liberalism, 1949–1968* (Westport, Conn.: Greenwood Press, 1977).

John Kenneth Galbraith, *The Affluent Society* (Boston: Houghton Mifflin, 1958).

Hamrin, *Managing Growth in the '80s.*

Donella H. Meadows, Dennis L. Meadows, Jorgen Randers, and William W. Behrens III, *The Limits to Growth* (New York: Universe Books, 1972).

Lester Thurow, *The Zero-Sum Society* (New York: Basic Books, 1980).

All statistics on budgets and entitlements from *The Statistical Abstract of the United States* (Washington, D.C.: Bureau of the Census).

"A Blueprint for Survival," *New York Times,* February 5, 1972.

"The Death of Liberalism," by Jack Newfield, *Playboy,* April 1971.

"The Future of Liberalism: The Challenge of Abundance," by Arthur M. Schlesinger, Jr., *The Reporter,* May 3, 1956.

"Growth and Survival," by H. V. Hoosan, *New York Times,* March 8, 1972.

"How I Got Radicalized: The Making of an Agitator for Zero," by John Fischer, *Harper's,* April 1970.

"The Luddites Were Not All Wrong," by Wade Green and Sona Golden, *New York Times Magazine,* November 21, 1971.

"Mankind Warned of Perils of Growth," *New York Times,* February 7, 1972.

"NASA (That's Right, NASA) Is a Good Thing," by Tom Bethell, *Washington Monthly,* November 1975.

"The New Agrarians," by Taylor Branch, *Washington Monthly,* September 1970.

"An Economic Strategy for the 1980s," draft platform by Senator Gary Hart. February 6, 1982.

CHAPTER 6: THE BUSINESS OF AMERICA

Charles Peters and the Washington Monthly

Charles Peters, *How Washington Really Works* (Reading, Mass.: Addison-Wesley, 1980).

"Department of Evaluation: Magazine Watches Government Closely," by Garrett Epps, *Washington Post,* February 25, 1979.

"Founder: Man with a Mission," by Reven Uihlein, *Advertising Age,* October 19, 1981.

"The Last Angry Men," by Richard Reeves, *Esquire,* March 1, 1978.

"A Neoliberal's Manifesto," by Charles Peters, *Washington Monthly,* May 1983.

"Planks in a Platform," by Charles Peters, *New York Times Book Review,* October 25, 1981.

"Softening Attitudes Toward Business," by Robert J. Samuelson, *Washington Post,* November 28, 1978.

"To Magazine Founder, This City Doesn't Function Very Well," by Barbara Gamarekian, *New York Times,* April 22, 1982.

David Birch and the Small Business Economy

"The Debate Over 'Who Generates Jobs?' " by William Schweke and Robert Friedman, *Entrepreneurial Economy,* February 1983.

"A False Religion," by Robert J. Samuelson, *National Journal,* November 20, 1982.

"The Small Business Share of Job Creation: Lessons Learned from the Use of a Longitudinal File," by David Birch and Susan MacCracken, MIT Program on Neighborhood and Regional Change, November 1982.

"Sources of Job Growth: A New Look at the Small Business Role," by Catherine Armington and Marjorie Odle, *Economic Development Commentary,* Fall 1982.

"Who Creates Jobs?" by David L. Birch, *Public Interest,* Fall 1981.

Statement of David L. Birch to the House Select Committee on Population, June 6, 1978.

Testimony of David L. Birch before Subcommittee on Regional and Community Development of the Senate Committee on Environment and Public Works (includes *The Job Generation Process*), April 10, 24, and 25, 1979.

Business and Entrepreneurship

Daniel Bell, *The Coming of Post-Industrial Society* (New York: Basic Books, 1973).

Galbraith, *The Affluent Society.*

Gary Hart, *A New Democracy: A Democratic Vision for the 1980s and Beyond* (New York: Quill, 1983).

Schlesinger, *The Coming of the New Deal.*

"A Democratic Economic Rift," by Edward Cowan, *New York Times,* May 30, 1983.

CHAPTER 7: "ATARI DEMOCRATS"

The High Technology Economy

Bell, *The Coming of Post-Industrial Society.*

Hamrin, *Managing Growth in the '80s.*

John Naisbitt, *Megatrends* (New York: Warner Books, 1982).

Lester Thurow, *Investment in Human Capital* (Belmont, Calif.: Wadsworth, 1970).

"California's Great Breeding Ground for Industry," by Gene Bylinsky, *Fortune,* June 1974.

"The Case for Technology Entrepreneurs," by Henry E. Riggs, *Stanford Engineer,* Spring/Summer 1980.

"Cities on the Rise: Research Triangle," *Christian Science Monitor,* June 15, 1982.

"High Tech and the Cities," on PBS's "The MacNeil–Lehrer Report," February 2, 1983.

"High-Tech Fever Grabs States, Cities," by Ken Banschick, *High Technology,* March/April 1982.

"Storm Clouds Over Silicon Valley," by Susan Benner, *Inc.,* September 1982.

"Traffic and Housing Woes Tarnish Coast's Suburban 'Utopia' of the '60s," by Robert Lindsey, *New York Times,* February 1, 1983.

"The Twilight of Smokestack America," by Peter T. Kilborn, *New York Times,* May 8, 1983.

Winning Technologies: A New Industrial Strategy for California and the Nation, report by the California Commission on Industrial Innovation, September 2, 1982.

Testimony of Governor Edmund G. Brown, Jr., before the Joint Economic Committee of Congress, February 24, 1982.

The California Economy

"California vs. the U.S.," by Richard Reeves, *Esquire,* February 1978.

"Governor Moonbeam Has Landed," by Mike Royko, reprinted in the *Los Angeles Times,* August 17, 1980.

"Should America Fence Off California?" by Mike Royko, reprinted in *Los Angeles Times,* April 23, 1979.

California's Technological Future: Emerging Economic Opportunities in the 1980s, report submitted by SRI International to the California Department of Economic and Business Development, March 1982.

"The Incipient California Industrial Policy," by Michael Kieschnick, California Department of Economic and Business Development, January 6, 1982.

An Industrial Strategy for California in the Eighties, draft report by the California Commission on Industrial Innovation, November 1981.

Investment in Economic Strength: An Update, a report to Governor Edmund G. Brown, Jr., October 1981.

The Economic Transition

"American Industry: What Ails It, How to Save It," by James Fallows, *The Atlantic,* September 1980.

"A Demographer in Demand, As Unlikely As It Seems," by John Herbers, *New York Times,* December 24, 1982.

"The New Economy," by Charles P. Alexander, *Time,* May 30, 1983.

"The Perfect Politician," by Diane Kiesel and Bill Hogan, *St. Louis Magazine,* November 1982.

"A Reporter at Large: The Democrats," by Elizabeth Drew, *The New Yorker,* March 22, 1982.

"Service Industries Gain in Job Totals," by Damon Stetson, *New York Times,* July 6, 1982.

"Two Areas Show Way to Success in High Technology Industry," by Fox Butterfield, *New York Times,* August 7, 1982.

Draft document for the Democratic Strategy Council by Congressmen Timothy Wirth and Richard Gephardt, October 17, 1981.

"An Economic Strategy for the 1980s," by Senator Gary Hart.

CHAPTER 8: THE GLOBAL UNIT

Bill Bradley

Bill Bradley, *Life on the Run* (New York: Quadrangle Books, 1976).

"Bradley in Washington," by Randall Rothenberg, *New Jersey Monthly,* March 1981.

Statistics on Trade and Economic Decline

Hamrin, *Managing Growth in the '80s.*

Hunter Lewis and Donald Allison, *The Real World War* (New York: Coward, McCann & Geoghegan, 1982).

Ira Magaziner and Robert Reich, *Minding America's Business* (New York: Harcourt Brace Jovanovich, 1983).

Globalism

Adam Smith, *Paper Money* (New York: Summit Books, 1981).

Robert Stobaugh and Daniel Yergin, eds., *Energy Future: A Report of the Energy Project at the Harvard Business School* (New York: Random House, 1979).

"Economics First," by Lester Thurow, *New York Times,* October 13, 1982.

"Making Industrial Policy," by Robert B. Reich, *Foreign Affairs,* Spring 1982.

"Thinking Ahead," by Daniel Bell, *Harvard Business Review,* May/June 1979.

"Why the World Can't Return to Bretton Woods," by Caroline Atkinson, *Washington Post,* May 22, 1983.

"Seeing the World with Open Eyes," remarks of Reubin Askew to the Houston Committee on Foreign Relations, November 11, 1982.

Protectionism

George Ball, *The Past Has Another Pattern* (New York: Norton, 1983).

"Congressional Anger on Free Trade Could Lead to Some Major Changes," by Robert W. Merry, *Wall Street Journal,* March 17, 1983.

"Deindustrializing America," by Sol C. Chaikin, *Foreign Affairs,* Spring 1982.

"A Domestic Quarrel: Two Views of the Local Content Proposal," by Randy Barber and Roger Vaughan, *Politics and Markets,* January 27, 1983.

"House Passes U.S. Auto Content Bill," by Robert D. Hershey, Jr., *New York Times,* December 16, 1982.

"In Congress, a Rising Tide Toward Protectionism," by Hedrick Smith, *New York Times,* December 14, 1982.

"Mondale Wants Imports to Contain U.S. Parts," by Irvin Molotsky, *New York Times,* May 5, 1983.

"Mondale's Tough Line," by James Reston, *New York Times,* October 13, 1982.

"Protectionist Stance Muted by Mondale," by Hobart Rowen, *Washington Post,* December 19, 1982.

PART III: RESPONSES

CHAPTER 9: BIG GOVERNMENT AND THE CULT OF EXPERTISM

Ball, *The Past Has Another Pattern.*
Bell, *The Coming of Post-Industrial Society.*
Goldman, *Rendezvous with Destiny.*
Robert Goldwin, ed., *Bureaucrats, Policy Analysts, and Statesmen* (Washington, D.C.: American Enterprise Institute, 1980).
Daniel Patrick Moynihan, *Maximum Feasible Misunderstanding* (New York: Free Press, 1963).

"The Business Role in the Great Society," by Jerald Terhorst, *The Reporter,* October 21, 1965.

"In Search of a New Public Philosophy," by Samuel H. Beer, in *The New American Political System,* edited by Anthony King (Washington, D.C.: American Enterprise Institute, 1979).

"The Politics of Peace," by Sam Brown, *Washington Monthly,* August 1970.

"The Uses and Abuses of Analysis in the Defense Environment: A Conversation with R. James Woolsey," American Enterprise Institute, 1980.

"What's Wrong with Policy Analysis?" by Michael Nelson, *Washington Monthly,* September 1979.

CHAPTER 10: MILITARY REFORM

Jeffrey Barlow, ed., *Reforming the Military* (Washington, D.C.: Heritage Foundation, 1981).
James Fallows, *National Defense* (New York: Random House, 1981).
Hart, *A New Democracy.*

"Army Is Reviving Use of Regiments," by Richard Halloran, *New York Times,* December 22, 1982.

"The Army's New Fighting Doctrine," by Deborah Shapley, *New York Times Magazine,* November 28, 1982.

"Congressional Military Reform Caucus Provokes Pentagon Ire," *Wall Street Journal,* April 13, 1982.

"A Democratic Agenda for the '80s," *The New Republic,* March 31, 1982.

"Hart on El Salvador: It's Their War," *Washington Post,* February 28, 1982.

"A New Kind of Reformer," by R. James Woolsey, *Washington Post,* March 13, 1981.

"$1,000,000,000 for Defense," on PBS's "Bill Moyers' Journal," June 5, 1980.

"The Uses and Abuses of Analysis in the Defense Environment: A Conversation with R. James Woolsey." American Enterprise Institute.

Address by Senator Gary Hart to the Council on Foreign Relations. June 11, 1981.

Robert Taft, Jr., *White Paper on Defense.* 1978 edition published in cooperation with Senator Gary Hart. Prepared with the assistance of William S. Lind.

CHAPTER 11: THE RISE OF APPROPRIATE TECHNOLOGY

Gary W. Hart, *Right from the Start* (New York: Quadrangle, 1973).

Paul Jacobs and Sol Landau, *The New Radicals* (New York: Random House, 1966).

James Ogilvy, *Many Dimensional Man: Decentralizing Self, Society, and the Sacred* (New York: Oxford University Press, 1977).

"Democrats: A New Path to Old Goals," by Gary Hart, *Washington Post,* September 23, 1980.

"Gary Hart: Heir Presumptive?" by Molly Ivins, *Politics Today,* January/February 1979.

"Sen. Hart Seeks to Blur Left-Right Stereotypes in His Re-election Bid," by David Ignatius, *Wall Street Journal,* August 20, 1980.

"Should This Man Be President?" by Robert M. Kaus, *Washington Monthly,* October 1981.

"Some Lessons for the Democrats," by Gary Hart, *Miami Herald,* January 11, 1981.

Address to Nebraska Jefferson-Jackson Day Dinner by Senator Gary Hart, April 11, 1981.

"Big Government: Real or Imaginary?" Address by Senator Gary Hart to the Western Electronic Manufacturers Association, April 20, 1976.

Chapter 12: Using the Market for Reform

Michael Barone, Grant Ujifusa, and Douglas Matthews, eds., *The Almanac of American Politics* (New York: E. P. Dutton, 1980).

Stobaugh and Yergin, eds., *Energy Future.*

Thurow, *The Zero-Sum Society.*

Daniel Yergin and Martin Hillenbrand, eds., *Global Insecurity* (Boston: Houghton Mifflin, 1982).

"Can Liberalism Survive Inflation?" by Alfred E. Kahn, *The Economist,* March 7, 1981.

"The Democratic Party After Ted Kennedy," by Arthur M. Schlesinger, Jr., *Wall Street Journal,* December 7, 1982.

"An Economic Agenda," by Bill Bradley, *New York Times,* June 24, 1982.

"Gores, Father and Son, A Tradition of Activism," by David Shribman, *New York Times,* June 2, 1983.

"Liberals Must Face the Facts: An Interview with Alfred E. Kahn, *Challenge,* November/December 1981.

"Overhaul: (1) Taxes, (2) Budget," by Bill Bradley, *New York Times,* June 23, 1982.

"Reaganism with a Human Face," by Robert M. Kaus, *The New Republic,* November 25, 1981.

"Reagan's Law," by Mark Green, *New York Times,* August 22, 1983.

Review of *Energy Future* by John Kenneth Galbraith in *New York Review of Books,* September 27, 1979.

"Vouchers, Emerging as a Theme, Provoke Debate," by Robert Pear, *New York Times,* February 8, 1983.

"Toward a Democratic Economy: An Alternative to Reagonomics," address by New York Governor Hugh L. Carey, January 1982.

Energy Policy

"Bradley Turns Rebel on Oil Price Controls," by Robert Cohen, *Newark Star Ledger,* March 22, 1981.

"Counting the Wounds," by Richard Corrigan, *National Journal,* October 8, 1977.

"Developing the Tools to Cope with the *Real* Energy Problem," letter to *New York Times* from Senator Bill Bradley, June 25, 1982.

"Energy Strategy: The Road Not Taken," by Amory B. Lovins, *Foreign Affairs,* Fall 1976.

"Ineptitude in Washington Compounds the Problem," *Business Week,* July 30, 1979.

"Jimmy Carter's Energy Crusade," by Richard Corrigan, J. Dicken Kirschten, and Robert J. Samuelson, *National Journal,* April 30, 1977.

"A Latter-Day David Out to Slay the Goliaths of Energy," by William J. Lanouette, *National Journal,* October 1, 1977.

"Soft Energy and Hard Times," by Phil Primack, *Working Papers,* July/August 1980.

"The Soft Energy Path," by Amory B. Lovins, *The Center Magazine,* September/October 1978.

On Job Retraining

Pat Choate, *Retooling the American Workforce: Toward a National Training Strategy* (Washington, D.C.: Northeast-Midwest Institute, 1982).

Roger J. Vaughan and June A. Sekera, *Investing in People* (Washington, D.C.: Corporation for Enterprise Development, 1982).

High Technology: Public Policies for the 1980s, by Pat Choate. A National Journal Issues Book, Washington, 1982.

"Human Resource Management," by Pat Choate, *Careers and the MBA,* 1983.

"Public Sector Role Still Crucial for Employment Policy," by Roger J. Vaughan, *Jobs Watch,* March/April 1982.

"Reform or Fall Behind," by Pat Choate, *VocEd,* October 1982.

"Worker Retraining," on PBS's "The MacNeil-Lehrer Report," February 4, 1983.

CHAPTER 13: THE ENTREPRENEURIAL ECONOMY

John Fred Bell, *A History of Economic Thought* (New York: Ronald Press, 1953).

George Gilder, *Wealth and Poverty* (New York: Basic Books, 1981).

Joseph A. Schumpeter, *Can Capitalism Survive?* Introduction by Robert Lekachman (New York: Harper & Row, 1978).

Joseph A. Schumpeter, *Capitalism, Socialism, and Democracy* (New York: Harper & Bros., 1942).

"America in the Eighties," by Felix G. Rohatyn, *The Economist,* September 19, 1981.

"The Birth of Silicon Statesmanship," by Andrew Pollack, *New York Times,* February 27, 1983.

"The Case for Technology Entrepreneurs," by Henry E. Riggs, *Stanford Engineer,* Spring/Summer 1980

"Entrepreneurial Economics," by Kevin Farrell, *Venture,* January 1983.

"Putting Yourself on the Line," by Charles Peters and the editors of the *Washington Monthly.*

"Reindustrialization: Aiming for the Right Targets," by Nathaniel J. Mass and Peter M. Senge, *Technology Review,* August/September 1981.

"Schumpeter and Keynes," by Peter F. Drucker, *Forbes,* May 23, 1983.

"Tension and Release," by Michael Kinsley, *The New Republic,* February 7, 1981.

"A Turning Point in American Liberalism," by George Gilder, *Wall Street Journal,* June 10, 1983.

"Why Other Harvards Aren't Discovering It," by Charles Peters, *Washington Monthly,* October 1976.

Address by Senator Bill Bradley to the graduating class of Yale University, May 24, 1980.

"Beyond Supply Side Economics: Tax Reforms for Economic Growth," by Roger J. Vaughan, Council of State Planning Agencies, October 1981.

"Economic Renewal: A Guide for the Perplexed," by Roger J. Vaughan, Council of State Planning Agencies, April 1981.

Investment in Economic Strength: An Update. Governor's Office, Sacramento, Calif., October 1981.

"Promoting American Invention in the 80's: How to Remain the World's Idea Capital," remarks by Congressman Timothy E. Wirth to the Rocky Mountain Inventors Conference, February 12, 1982.

State Activities to Encourage Technological Innovation: An Update, National Governors Association Task Force on Technological Innovation, February, 1982.

"What Kind of Industrial Policy?" Proceedings from the Symposium sponsored by the Democracy Project, January 1982.

CHAPTER 14: FROM REDISTRIBUTION TO INVESTMENT

Hart, *Right from the Start.*
Magaziner and Reich, *Minding America's Business.*
Thurow, *The Zero-Sum Society.*
"America in the Eighties," by Felix G. Rohatyn.
"Can Liberalism Survive Inflation?" by Alfred E. Kahn *The Economist.*

"Economic Jeopardy," by Bob Kuttner, *Mother Jones,* May 1982.

"Managing Our Way to Economic Decline," by William J. Abernathy and Robert H. Hayes, *Harvard Business Review,* July/August 1980.

"Pie Slicers Vs. Pie Enlargers," by Robert Reich, *Washington Monthly,* September 1980.

"Skirting the Fairness Issue," editorial, *Washington Post,* September 27, 1982.

"A Turning Point in the History of American Liberalism," by George Gilder. *Wall Street Journal,* June 10, 1983.

"Why Productivity Falls," by Lester C. Thurow, *Newsweek,* August 24, 1981.

"Denver Rotary," address by Governor Richard D. Lamm, Colorado, March 11, 1982.

Rebuilding the Road to Economic Opportunity: A Democratic Direction for the 1980s, Democratic Caucus, U.S. House of Representatives, September 1982.

"What Kind of Industrial Policy?" Symposium sponsored by the Democracy Project, January 1982.

CHAPTER 15: A TAX POLICY FOR INVESTMENT

Hart, *A New Democracy*
Thurow, *The Zero-Sum Society.*

"Consider the Saving Grace of a Consumption Tax," by Susan Lee, *Wall Street Journal,* 1983.

"Corporate Tax Upsets Reagan," by Francis X. Clines, *New York Times,* January 27, 1983.

"Flat-Rate Income Tax Debate May Spur Attacks on Some Tax Breaks," by Timothy B. Clark, *National Journal,* November 13, 1982.

"Flat-Rate Talk," by Robert S. McIntyre, *The New Republic,* July 19 and 26, 1982.

"Flat-Rate Taxation Gains Momentum Among Reformers," by John M. Berry, *Washington Post,* July 4, 1982.

"Impossible Rates, Unfair Advantages," by Joseph A. Pechman, *New York Times,* January 30, 1983.

"It's the Fairest Way to Tax the Public," by David F. Bradford, *New York Times,* January 30, 1983.

"The Mystery of the Free Lunch," by Michael Kinsley, *The New Republic,* May 23, 1981.

"Simpler Taxes," on PBS's "The MacNeil-Lehrer Report," July 12, 1982.

Alan J. Auerbach and Dale W. Jorgenson, "The First-Year Capital Recovery System," Harvard University 1979.

Address by Senator Bill Bradley, Democratic National Party Conference, Philadelphia, June 27, 1982.

Blueprints for Basic Tax Reform, U.S. Department of the Treasury, January 1977.

"Beyond Supply Side Economics: Tax Reforms for Economic Growth," by Roger J. Vaughan.

"Economic Renewal: A Guide for the Perplexed," by Roger J. Vaughan.

Rebuilding the Road to Economic Opportunity, House Democratic Caucus.

Statement of Robert S. McIntyre on President Reagan's tax proposals, Senate Finance Committee, May 18, 1981.

Statement on tax policy by Senator Bill Bradley to the Washington Press Club, May 27, 1982

"Toward a Democratic Economy: An Alternative to Reaganomics," address by New York Governor Hugh L. Carey, January 1982.

CHAPTER 16: EDUCATION: INVESTMENT IN HUMAN CAPITAL

Governor James Hunt, Jr., and North Carolina

"Challenge to Helms Builds in North Carolina," by Howell Raines, *New York Times,* September 22, 1982.

"Hunt Season," by Ferrel Guillory, *The New Republic,* July 4, 1983.

"North Carolina's Leaders Worried by Blemishes on the State's Image," by Wayne King, *New York Times,* February 22, 1978.

"Research Triangle," *Christian Science Monitor,* June 15, 1982.

"South Pressing for Wide Changes to Upgrade Education Standards," by Reginald Stuart, *New York Times,* March 20, 1983.

"Academia, Industry, and Government: The Organizational Frontier of Science Today," address by Governor James B. Hunt, Jr., to the annual meeting of the American Association for the Advancement of Science, Washington, D.C., January 4, 1982.

"State of the State Address," by Governor James B. Hunt, Jr., January 17, 1983.

On Education

"Boston Study Calls for Shifts in the Education of Workers," *New York Times,* April 26, 1982.

"The Case for Gifted Children," by Randall Rothenberg, *New Jersey Monthly,* September 1980.

"Democratic Group to Study Merit Pay for Teachers," by David Shribman, *New York Times,* June 10, 1983.

"Democratic Hopefuls Urge Funds for Schools," by Marjorie Hunter, *New York Times,* June 16, 1983.

"Education Emerges as Major Issue in 1984 Presidential Campaigning," by Phil Gailey, *New York Times,* June 9, 1983.

"In Age of Technology, the Three R's Are Not Enough," by Philip M. Boffey, *New York Times,* May 16, 1982.

"Looking Ahead to the Silicon Future," by Fred M. Hechinger, *New York Times,* December 1, 1981.

"Low Tech Teaching Blues," by Ellie McGrath, *Time,* December 27, 1982.

"Merit Pay Draws Criticism and Praise from Teachers," by Gene I. Maeroff, *New York Times,* July 2, 1983.

"More Schools Experiment on Improvements," by Andrew H. Malcolm, *New York Times,* April 14, 1983.

"Playing Politics with Math and Science," by Denis P. Doyle, *Washington Post,* March 20, 1983.

"President Presses School Merit Pay," by Francis X. Clines, *New York Times,* June 16, 1983.

"Shanker Says Union Could Back a Merit Pay Plan," by Judith Cummings, *New York Times,* July 5, 1983.

"Sputnik Recalled: Science and Math in Trouble Again," by Edward B. Fiske, *New York Times,* October 5, 1982.

"Teachers Meeting Debates Merit Pay," by Gene I. Maeroff, *New York Times,* July 4, 1983.

"U.S. Shortcomings Prompting Action," by Fred M. Hechinger, *New York Times,* November 8, 1982.

Address by G. M. Sollenberger to graduating class, Arizona State University, May 14, 1982.

Address to California School Boards Association by Governor Edmund G. Brown, Jr., December 10, 1981.

Improving Math, Science, and Technical Education, report prepared for the California Commission on Industrial Innovation by Michael W. Kirst, Stanford University, 1982.

The California Worksite Education and Training Act: Report to the Legislature. Governor's Office, Sacramento, Calif., January 1982.

Utilizing America's Technological Resources: New Challenges to the States. National Governors Association, February 1982.

CHAPTER 17: FROM CONFRONTATION TO COOPERATION

Governor Richard Lamm and Colorado

"Oregon: What's Left of Ecotopia?" by Peter Dreier, *Working Papers,* March/April 1978.

"Private–Public Sector Collaboration a Must," by Marshall Kaplan, *Rocky Mountain News,* May 4, 1982.

Front Range Futures: Final Report, Colorado Front Range Project, December 1981.

State of the State address by Governor Richard D. Lamm, January 6, 1982.

"The Geometry of Public Policy," address by Governor Richard D. Lamm, draft dated October 9, 1980.

On Cooperation

Herbert Croly, *The Promise of American Life* (New York: E. P. Dutton and Co., 1948).

Otis L. Graham, *An Encore for Reform: The Old Progressives and the New Deal* (New York: Oxford University Press, 1967).

Otis L. Graham, *Toward a Planned Society: From Roosevelt to Nixon* (New York: Oxford University Press, 1976).

Richard Hofstadter, ed., *Great Issues in American History: From Reconstruction to the Present Day* (New York: Random House, 1969).

Tsongas, *The Road from Here.*

Ezra Vogel, *Japan As Number One* (Cambridge, Mass.: Harvard University Press, 1979).

Daniel Yankelovich, *New Rules: Searching for Self-Fulfillment in a World Turned Upside Down* (New York: Random House, 1981).

"America in the Eighties," by Felix G. Rohatyn.

"The Cooperative Economy," by A. H. Raskin, *New York Times,* February 14, 1982.

"Drafting a Democratic Industrial Plan," by Sidney Blumenthal, *New York Times Magazine,* August 28, 1983.

"Government, Industry, and Academia Join Hands," by Thomas W. Lippman, *Washington Post,* December 27, 1981.

"Industry-Academic Ties: Profit Over Progress?" by Harold M. Schmeck, Jr., *New York Times,* February 1, 1983.

"Japan Struggling with Itself," by Steve Lohr, *New York Times,* June 13, 1982.

Grass Roots Industrial Policy: Building on American Diversity in the '80s and '90s (Washington, D.C.: Northeast-Midwest Institute, June 1982).

CHAPTER 18: NATIONAL SERVICE

Fallows, *National Defense.*

"An Albatross Named Universal Youth Service," letter to *The New York Times* by James V. Siena, October 16, 1981.

"The All Volunteer Force," by Charles Moskos, *Wilson Quarterly,* Spring 1979.

"B. T. Collins' Private War," by Betty Johannsen, *Sacramento,* June 1981.

"Brash B. T. Collins Handles the People for the Brown Camp," by Carrie Dolan, *Wall Street Journal,* July 19, 1982.

"House Votes Conservation Corps to Put 100,000 Youths to Work," by Robert Pear, *New York Times,* February 23, 1983.

"If Reagan Wants to Expand the Military, He May Also Have to Revive the Draft," by Michael R. Gordon, *National Journal,* August 22, 1981.

"In Command: B. T. Collins," by James B. Carroll, *California Journal,* March 1982.

"Koch Urges National Service at Age 18," by Michael Goodwin, *New York Times,* March 9, 1983.

"Making the All-Volunteer Force Work: A National Service Approach," by Charles C. Moskos, *Foreign Affairs,* Fall 1981.

"The Name's Brown—Sam Brown," by Derek Shearer, *Working Papers,* Spring 1976.

"Our State CCC Is the Only Hero of the Medfly Farce," by Marianne Means, *Los Angeles Herald Examiner,* July 23, 1981.

"Peace Corps Battling for Survival," *Newark Star Ledger,* April 25, 1982.

"The Politics of Peace," by Sam Brown, *Washington Monthly,* August 1970.

"The Revolution at VISTA," by Connie Paige, *Working Papers,* March/April 1978.

"Self-Help: An Old Idea Whose Time Has Come," by Sam Brown, *Public Welfare,* Winter 1981.

"Why We Need a Draft," by Eliot A. Cohen, *Commentary,* April 1982.

Address by Reubin Askew to the National Convention of the Delta Tau Delta Fraternity in St. Louis, Missouri, August 14, 1982.

California Conservation Corps: Annual Report. Report to the California legislature, 1981.

"Citizen Soldier and an AVF GI Bill," by Charles C. Moskos, Department of Sociology, Northwestern University, October 1982.

"Citizen Soldier and National Service," by Charles C. Moskos, paper prepared for the conference and Festschrift in honor of Morris Janowitz, University of Chicago, May 14–15, 1982.

"From Institution to Occupation: Trends in Military Organization," by Charles C. Moskos, paper prepared for delivery at the International Congress, Foundation Society and Armed Forces, The Hague, May 9–12, 1982.

National Service As an Alternative or Complement to the All Volunteer Force, Military Manpower Task Group, February 1982.

"National Youth Service and Federal Educational Benefits," by Charles C. Moskos, October 1982.

"Recruiting, Retention, and Quality in the All-Volunteer Force," by Robert L. Goldich, Congressional Research Service, June 8, 1981.

Remarks by Sam Brown to the National Youth Workers Conference. Bloomington, Ind., June 30, 1977.

Statement by Sam Brown on Youth Employment Legislation, Subcommittee on Employment, Poverty and Migratory Labor, Senate Committee on Human Resources, April 20, 1977.

Study of National Service: Phase I, report to the Ford Foundation by Richard Danzig, Peter Szanton, and James L. Lacy. March 1982.

"Youth Service and the Needs of the Cities," address by Sam Brown, 1978.

CHAPTER 19: INDUSTRIAL POLICY

Graham, *An Encore for Reform.*
Graham, *Toward a Planned Society.*
Hart, *A New Democracy.*
Magaziner and Reich, *Minding America's Business.*
William Ouchi, *Theory Z: How American Business Can Meet the Japanese Challenge* (New York: Addison-Wesley, 1982).
Robert Reich, *The Next American Frontier* (New York: Times Books, 1983).

"Aid Urged to Sunrise Industries: Nine Senators Favor New U.S. Bank for Risk Capital," *New York Times,* September 1, 1980.

"Alternatives to Reaganomics," by Felix G. Rohatyn, *New York Times Magazine,* December 5, 1982.

"The American Debate" sponsored by the Roosevelt Center for Policy Studies, broadcast by the Cable Satellite Public Affairs Network, November 7, 1982.

"American Industry: What Ails It, How to Save It," by James Fallows, *The Atlantic,* September 1980.

"An RFC for Today: A Capital Idea," by Randall Rothenberg, *Inc.,* January 1983.

"Can Creeping Socialism Cure Creaking Capitalism?" by Robert M. Kaus, *Harper's,* February 1983.

"Carter Economic Renewal Plan," *New York Times,* August 22, 1980.

"Carter's Vision of America," by Adam Clymer, *New York Times,* July 27, 1980.

"The Cynical Idealists of '68," *Time,* June 7, 1968.

"Death by a Thousand Cuts," by Lester C. Thurow, *New York Review of Books,* December 17, 1981.

"Debate Grows Over Adoption of National Industrial Policy," by Karen W. Arenson, *New York Times,* June 19, 1983.

"The Democrats and MITI-Minus," editorial, *New York Times,* Septemper 27, 1982.

"The Democrats' New Agenda," by Morton Kondracke, *The New Republic,* October 18, 1982.

"Diverse Factions of Democratic Party Seek Consensus on Economic Policy," by Edward Cowan, *New York Times,* October 24, 1982.

"Drafting a Democratic Industrial Plan," by Sidney Blumenthal, *New York Times Magazine,* August 28, 1983.

"Economic Jeopardy," by Bob Kuttner, *Mother Jones,* May 1982.

"The Erosion of American Industry," by Karen W. Arenson, *New York Times,* August 8, 1982.

"France's Atari Socialism," by Bob Kuttner, *The New Republic,* March 7, 1983.

"The Hoover Way to Help Sick Companies," by Ann Crittenden, *New York Times,* January 24, 1982.

"Japan vs. USA: The Hi-Tech Shoot-Out," on "NBC Reports," August 14, 1982.

"Kennedy Plan Aims to Revive Economy," *New York Times,* May 21, 1980.

"Mr. Industrial Policy," by Randall Rothenberg, *Esquire,* May 1983.

"On the Frontier of a New Economics," by Karen W. Arenson, *New York Times,* October 31, 1982.

"Picking Winners and Killing Dogs," by George Eads, *Wharton Magazine,* Fall 1981.

"Reindustrialization and Jobs: A Symposium," *Working Papers,* November/December 1980.

Review of Robert Reich's *The Next American Frontier* by Robert Lekachman, *New York Times Book Review,* April 24, 1983.

"A Supply-Side Economics of the Left," by George Gilder, *The Public Interest,* Summer 1983.

"Trade Department Plan Issued by Reagan," by Clyde H. Farnsworth, *New York Times,* June 2, 1983.

"The Twilight of Smokestack America," by Peter T. Kilborn, *New York Times,* May 8, 1983.

"White House Fact Sheet on Carter's Economic Program for 80's," *New York Times,* August 29, 1980.

"Why the U.S. Needs an Industrial Policy," by Robert B. Reich, *Harvard Business Review,* January/February 1982.

Federal Credit Programs: An Overview of Current Programs and Their Beginnings in the Reconstruction Finance Corporation, Office of Corporate Finance, U.S. Treasury Department, August 15, 1980.

Industrial Policy. Washington, D.C.: Council of State Planning Agencies, March 1981.

An Innovation Finance Strategy for the 1980s, Office of Governor Edmund G. Brown, Jr., 1982.

"Investment Banking," by Lester C. Thurow, Massachusetts Institute of Technology, January 1982.

"Memorandum Concerning an Agency to Assist a National Economic Recovery Program," unpublished article by Eugene J. Keilin, prepared for Lazard Frères & Co., September 23, 1980.

Rebuilding the Road to Economic Opportunity, House Democratic Caucus.

"The Two-Track Society," draft position paper by Amitai Etzioni, June 1, 1982.

"What Kind of Industrial Policy?" Symposium sponsored by the Democracy Project, January 13, 1982.

Winning Technologies: A New Industrial Strategy for California and the Nation, California Commission on Industrial Innovation, September 2, 1982.

PART IV: THE BEGINNING OF NEOLIBERALISM . . .
OR THE END OF LIBERALISM

Graham, *Toward a Planned Society.*
Greenfield, *The Real Campaign.*

"A.M.A.'s Dioxin Stance," by Robert Reinhold, *New York Times,* July 4, 1983.

"The Democratic Candidates: A Rush to Consensus," by Howell Raines, *New York Times,* April 28, 1983.

"The Democrats," by Elizabeth Drew, *The New Yorker,* March 22, 1982.

"Democrats in Congress Hunt for Policy Ideas to Counter Reagan's," by Dennis Farney, *Wall Street Journal,* April 1, 1982.

"New Trade Agency Outlined," by Clyde H. Farnsworth, *New York Times,* May 4, 1983.

"The Playboy Interview: Arthur Schlesinger," *Playboy,* May 1966.

"The Selling of the University," by David F. Noble, *The Nation,* February 6, 1982.

"Soft Energy and Hard Times," by Phil Primack.

"Study Says Weaknesses of Schools Pose an Economic Threat to U.S.," by Edward B. Fiske, *New York Times,* May 5, 1983.

"The Trouble with Unions," by Robert M. Kaus, *Harper's,* June 1983.

"What the Democrats Didn't Say," by Michael Barone, *Washington Post,* June 1982.

"Worker Ownership Slowly Comes of Age," *Politics and Markets,* June 23, 1983.

Index

80